FORWARD
TO THE
PAST

ANOTHER JOURNEY
IN ANCESTRY

RAE P. COLLINS

*The Wasey Arms: 'Fear Dishonour
Rather Than Death'*

ALAN SUTTON PUBLISHING LIMITED

To my husband Roy
without whose help, forbearance and support
this book
could never have been completed

First published in the United Kingdom in 1995
Alan Sutton Publishing Limited
Phoenix Mill · Far Thrupp · Stroud · Gloucestershire

British Library Cataloguing in Publication Data

Collins, Rae P.
Forward to the Past: Another Journey in Ancestry
I. Title II. Bantock, Anton
929.10941

ISBN 0–7509–0893–9

Typeset in 11/12 Erhardt.
Typesetting and origination by
Alan Sutton Publishing Limited.
Printed in Great Britain by
Ebenezer Baylis, Worcester.

Contents

Acknowledgements and Abbreviations   iv

PART I THE SEARCH

Parish Registers, Monumental Inscriptions, Wills, Deeds and Court Rolls   1
Origins, Heraldry and the Visitations   4
Permission to Use a Screwdriver and a Successful Long Shot   5
Printed Sources and PCC Wills   6
Church, School and University Records   8
The East India Company   10
Census Returns and Post-1857 Wills   12
Locating the Burial Place and the Berkshire Record Office   13
A Strange Coincidence   14
Investigating Discrepancies   16
The Source of a Legend   17
Family Collections, Newspapers and Other Sources   18
Chancery Records and Clues to Further Sources   19
Meeting the Descendants   21

PART II THE HOUSE OF WASEY

Chapter 1: Norfolk Roots   23
Chapter 2: The Physician   39
Chapter 3: The Soldier   56
Chapter 4: The Georgian Parson   75
Chapter 5: Two Clergymen and a Sailor   90
Chapter 6: The Twentieth-century Families   111
Pedigree Charts   125

PART III A DISTAFF LINE   129

Notes and References   144
Genealogical Sources and their Whereabouts   149
Bibliography   150

Index   151

Acknowledgements

My sincere thanks go to all those from whom I have gleaned information for this book. To St George's Hospital, Tooting, I extend thanks for access to the early Minute Books; and to the Curator, The Household Cavalry Museum, Windsor, Berkshire, for access to the Regimental Diary & Register. I am especially grateful to the late Miss Joan Wasey for permission to use photographs of family miniatures and other mementoes, and to Mrs Vera Wasey, Mr L.R.T. Wasey and the late Mrs Leigh-Pemberton for the use of family photographs, etc. I am also extremely grateful to Mr Anton Bantock for his fine drawings, and to my husband and son for their unstinting support.

Anton Bantock's drawing of the 'Wasey Candlesticks' is based on a photograph which appears in Sir George Clark's *A History of the Royal College of Physicians of London*, Vol. II.

A. Bantock's drawing of Joseph Wasey's farthing token is based on the original in Norwich Castle Museum (Norfolk Museums Service).

A. Bantock's drawings of 36 Gerard Street, Soho, and Leicester House, Leicester Square, are based on those in *The London Survey*.

A. Bantock's drawing of the reproduction of 'old' Rushton Hall from Dorman Bridge's *History of Northamptonshire*, Vol. II (page 68), 1791, is from Northamptonshire Record Office.

A. Bantock's drawing of Scottow Hall and Church is based on a photograph taken of a painting belonging to J.T. Durrant Shaw Esq., with his kind permission.

Reproduction of part of Rocque's Map of London, 1746, and the facsimile of the entry in the Sun Fire Register, Ms.11, 936/26, are from Guildhall Library, Corporation of London.

Reproduction of part of Potter's Plan of St Marylebone, *c*.1832, is from Westminster City Archives.

Reproduction of Estate Map (Pet.1095) from Norfolk Record Office, is by permission of Miss J. Kennedy, County Archivist.

'Swanbourne', a drawing by Elizabeth Fremantle from the Wynne Diaries, is by permission of Lady Cottesloe.

The illustration of HMS *Polyphemus* on the Rif Coast is from the *Illustrated London News*, 1848.

The drawings of Quatford Church and Quatford Ferry are from *Our Ancient Parishes* by Revd G.L. Wasey, 1859.

Abbreviations
Family Book, FB. Record Office/County Record Office, RO/CRO. Norfolk Record Office/Public Record Office, NRO/PRO. Norwich Consistory Court, NCC. Prerogative Court of Canterbury, PCC. Bishops/Archdeacons Transcripts, BTs/ATs. Monumental Inscription, MI. Parish Register, PR. Burke's *Landed Gentry; Peerage & Baronetage*; LG; PB. *Dictionary of National Biography*, DNB. Cokayne, George Edward (*Peerage* and/or *Baronetage*), GEC. *International Genealogical Index*, IGI. Society of Genealogists, SOG. Norfolk & Norwich Genealogical Society, NNGS.

PART I THE SEARCH

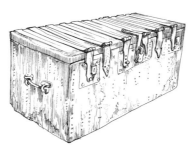

The Parish Chest, St Nicholas's Church, North Walsham

Lydia Wasey, my 4th great grandmother, fascinated me from the time I first knew of her. She married Daniel, the son of Rowland Clarke, a Norfolk clergyman, in 1734, and the name *Wasey* has remained as a Christian name in my mother's family ever since.

One of the most valuable legacies Lydia bestowed upon me was the opportunity to explore the past through her kinsfolk. The early Wasey family, from which both she and I descend, had no great claim to distinction, but the family's social status advanced with the success of Lydia's cousin, William, in the early eighteenth century. The families into which he and subsequent members married provided me with hours of happy wanderings into the pageant of Britain's history. They brought me into contact with characters who had previously appeared as flat as the pages on which their lives were recorded. First, though, had been the quest, mostly during holidays with my stoical husband, for the antecedents of Lydia and her Norfolk cousins.

PARISH REGISTERS, MONUMENTAL INSCRIPTIONS, WILLS, DEEDS AND COURT ROLLS

Research on the Wasey family began several years ago and ran parallel with the search for my Clarke forebears. The census returns had led me to North Walsham where three children of Daniel Clarke and Lydia (née Wasey) were baptised. By searching the BTs at the County Record Office (CRO) and transcripts kept at the Norfolk & Norwich Archaeological Society's library, it was soon found to be the home of Lydia Wasey's parents: their children were all christened there.

To confirm my findings, a visit was later made to view the parish registers, still kept at the church. During subsequent visits, access was granted to parish documents such as Rate Books, Churchwardens' and Overseers' Accounts – all contained in two huge chests – one secured with seven great locks and a lid so large it took three strong men to lift it.

While looking round the church during our first visit, we came across the inscription (with arms displayed) on the tomb of a 'Joseph Wasey' – one of many found during the search: 'Here lyeth the body of Joseph Wasey Gent he died Sept 12th 1701 aged 65 years.'

The church archivist showed us a book by Walter Rye, *Monumental Inscriptions of the Hundred of Tunstead*, in which were recorded this and other memorials, some no longer extant. Notes were made of two others, one for Robert Wasey who died in 1679 and another, giving birth and death dates and information on the arms of: '. . . William Wacey gent son of Joseph Wasey gent and of Mary . . . Arms: 1st impaled on a plain cross five roundels, 2nd a crosslet ermine between four ermine spots; the first for Wasey, the second for Durrant of Scottow.'

The Wasey arms had previously been noted from Rye's *Three Norfolk Armories* and it was from Rye's *Norfolk Families* that another interesting piece of information was gleaned: 'Wasey or Wacey is an old name in East Norfolk . . . Joseph Wasey of North Walsham and Richard Wasey of Tunstead disclaimed arms in 1664; . . . and [the name] may be corrupted from Wace.'

All Rye says of 'Wace', as do most other sources, is that it was a Norman name. I began to draw up hypothetical charts, using these various pieces of information, to work on:

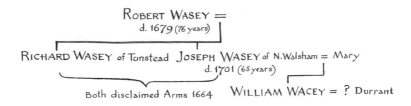

Gradually will indexes at the CRO were worked through (the Norfolk Archdeaconry; Norwich Archdeaconry; Norwich Consistory and the Peculiar Courts) and wills found to be relevant were photocopied. Relationships began to fall into place. The will, for instance, of Joseph Wasey, found buried in the church at North Walsham in 1701, showed him to be a grocer with only one surviving son, also named Joseph. It was encouraging to find the first witness was a John Wasey: my 5th great grandfather, Lydia's father, was John Wasey. On discovering *his* will, it was found that he too was a grocer, and *his* surviving son was Joseph (one of three so named, two having died as infants).

Of course none of the information used to build up the Wasey story was found in an orderly manner, falling neatly into place in sequence. It took years of searching, being gradually fitted together like a jigsaw, some of the pieces never being found. One missing piece is the positive identification of the first Richard Wasey's wife (also named Lydia). From a deed at NRO it was found that Richard had purchased property in 1660 from the executors of one John Andrews; they were selling to settle his debts and the residue of his estate was to descend to his daughter, Lydia. Since Richard is known to have married a Lydia in about 1660, it seems likely that it is Lydia Andrews whom he married. This supposition, however, was brought into doubt on finding that a Lydia Andrews witnessed Richard Wasey's will in 1675: although this could have been his wife's mother, i.e. John Andrews' widow.

Another slightly ill-fitting piece of the jigsaw is the want of positive evidence for the second marriage of Richard's widow, Lydia. Richard (known as 'of Tunstead') willed that the property purchased from John Andrews be sold at his death to provide for their younger children. The purchaser was a Norwich grocer, William Linstead, almost certainly Lydia's second husband.

Deeds dating from between 1680 and 1701 describe Mr Linstead formerly as 'grocer of the city of Norwich' and latterly as 'gent. of Stoak Ash, Suffolk'. His wife was Lydia and they are joint signatories to these documents, drawn up by the same solicitors as previously used by Richard Wasey. One makes provision for Lydia and her (unnamed) children to receive the yearly sum of £22 from the sale of Tunstead property worth £225, while the yearly sum of £26 was for William Linstead's own use and that of the children of them both.[1] One of the children from this second marriage would also seem to have been named Lydia because, significantly, Richard and Lydia Wasey's eldest son, Robert, referred in his will (1687) to 'sister Linstead' and their youngest son, John, referred in his will (1727) to 'my . . . sister in law Lydia Linstead'.[2]

Another difficult problem was distinguishing those bearing the same Christian name one from another. There were at one stage references to *nine* Joseph Waseys who, it transpired, were related to this family (some, albeit, short-lived), which made it necessary to number them. Those described as 'son of . . .' in a baptism or burial record could usually be placed without trouble. Those living to adulthood and leaving a will presented no problem. But what of the records stating merely: 'Joseph Wasey buried . . .'? Robert Wasey(1) began the sequence with a son, Joseph(1). He was beneficiary of two wills, lived to make one himself and was clearly described on his memorial. He *and* his brother Richard (the two who disclaimed arms in 1664) named a son Joseph. Both were beneficiaries of various wills and one appeared in several records, which made their place on the family tree quite firm. The others *were* identified eventually and the process was helped considerably by the use of manor court rolls which clearly set out relationships when property passed between members of the family. These were at the NRO, listed under Bishopric Estates.

Although, before 1733, the rolls are in Latin, admissions to property by virtue of a will are easily found, as the relevant section of the will (quoted in the rolls) is recorded in English. Also, during the Interregnum the rolls were in English and any exchange of property, whether admissions or surrenders, can be followed without trouble. The Robert Wasey, for instance, buried at North Walsham in 1679, was named in the court rolls when his father-in-law, Robert Wilton, died, the court having found that: '. . . Robert Wilton is dead . . . [into court] cometh . . . Sarah the wife of Robert Wasy . . . daughter of . . . Robert [Wilton] and bringeth . . . the last will of the saide Robert Wilton bearinge date the xxth day of October . . . 1652 . . .'.

In his will Mr Wilton named all the children of his daughter and her husband Robert Wasey – useful, since their baptisms have never been found. Some were also named in other wills and court rolls.

When admitted by inheritance to copyhold property, the beneficiary had to attend the court, bringing a copy of the will. The history of each parcel of property was given – from whom it was originally purchased or bequeathed, the date in which the transaction took place and a vague description, with its boundries. A tenant could also be admitted by purchase. If the death of a copyholder occurred, it would be announced at the next and two subsequent courts, giving an opportunity for claimants to come forward. If not taken up, the property reverted to the Manor.

Even prior to the Interregnum one can, with no knowledge of Latin, gain an idea of the transactions taking place since the rolls, except for the very early ones, are in book form, often annotated 'surrendered' or 'admitted' with the parties' names and sometimes the date, the whole (in Norfolk) well indexed.

ORIGINS, HERALDRY AND THE VISITATIONS

One of the three memorials recorded by Rye from North Walsham Church took on greater significance when I was casually looking through a volume of pedigrees, *Eynsford Families*.[3] Included were some miscellaneous notes on persons not placed in the pedigrees. One mentioned members of the Chapman family: 'Spencer Chapman m. Bridgit w. of William Wasey and daughter of William Durrant and died 1723 . . .'.

Had not (recorded Rye) 'William . . . son of Joseph Wasey and of Mary . . .' been buried at North Walsham in a tomb displaying Wasey arms impaled with Durrant of Scottow? On checking Scottow parish registers, sure enough, there, in 1688, was the marriage of William Wasey to Bridget Durrant. Her father's will referred to her as William Wasey's wife and, of course, William's own will (not found for several years) names his wife and their family.

Another useful browse through pedigree books occurred on finding, in the 1664 *Heralds Visitation of Norfolk*, one for the Woorts family of Trunch. Mary, the daughter of Robert and Susan Woorts, was shown as marrying '. . . Wasey'. When next at Norfolk RO I searched for Trunch material and found, among the Parish Deposits, Woorts documents showing their connection with the Wasey family. These were court roll copies (the originals for Trunch at that period were not at the RO) setting out the right of: 'Joseph Wasey gent one of ye sons of Mary Wasey deceased . . . late ye wife of Joseph Wasey of Northwalsham . . . Grocer . . . [he being] one of the coheirs of the said Mary . . . sister and heir of William Woorts gent deceased . . .'.

This, I was to learn years later, related to a lawsuit brought by Joseph Wasey(2) who became known as 'of Trunch' when he inherited his uncle's property there. His uncle's widow was later to marry Sir Isaac Preston and it was *his* brother, the Revd Charles Preston, whom Wasey sued.

By no means all information found for the name Wasey in the sources quoted, incidentally, was verified as relating to this family. Blomefield, for instance, makes reference to a Joseph Wasey as sheriff, but no evidence has been found to establish whether he was of this family. Neither have the origins of Robert Wasey, the first on this family tree, been discovered.

The name, although not common, was not rare in East Anglia even during the fifteenth century. Families bearing variants of the name prospered at Southrepps, Trimingham, Neatishead, Horning, Felmingham, Ellingham, Felthorpe, Cromer, Knapton, South Walsham and Scottow. Many bore the same familiar Christian names suggesting common ancestry.

At Great Hautbois one Robert Wasey, yeoman, married to Amy, mentions in his will, proved in 1640, a son Robert. This may well be the Robert, great grandfather of Lydia and her Wasey cousins, who settled with his family in North Walsham during the middle of the seventeenth century.

PERMISSION TO USE A SCREWDRIVER AND A SUCCESSFUL LONG SHOT

A memorial inscription which proved invaluable was unrecorded by Rye and could be only partly read without actually moving a pew. Having obtained permission, this we did at Tunstead Church where, on a slab beneath the choir stalls, with matrix which once had housed a small brass, were these words: 'Here lyeth the body of Robert ye son of Richard Wasey who died ye 13 Aprill 1687 aged 26 years.'

I knew from wills and court rolls that Richard Wasey (my 6th great grandfather) was a yeoman farmer of this little parish and that his eldest son was Robert, so this was a very useful find. Especially as the burial register described him as 'of Norwich', because listed in the NCC Will Index at Norwich RO is the will of Robert Wasey, proved in 1687. Described as a merchant of Norwich, he bequeaths property in North Walsham, refers to persons connected to the family and names his wife, Elizabeth.

This in turn led to the positive identification of the couple named Robert and Elizabeth Wasey whose children were found on the IGI being baptised in the 1680s at St Etheldred's, Norwich (now deconsecrated, with many inscriptions obscured). Monumental inscriptions previously culled from Blomefield's *Norfolk* Vol. IV then fitted into place: they recorded the resting place of these same children, at the same church, all confirmed by referring to the parish register. The inscription was also recorded there (without date) of 'Elizabeth widow of Robert Wasey'.

Many years ago, when first attempting to trace this family and with few opportunities to visit Norfolk's RO, I heard through our newly-formed Bristol & Avon Family History Society that a member, Alan Redstone, was compiling an index of early policy-holders with the Sun Fire Insurance Company, kept at Guildhall Library, London. He was sadly to die soon after, but his work is of enormous value to those searching in the counties he covered, one being Norfolk.

On receipt of my enquiry, he returned to me the reference numbers of two policy entries. One was for John Wasey of North Walsham, later confirmed as my 5th great grandfather; the other, dated 1728 (soon after John's death), was for 'Joseph Wasey grocer with Lydia & Susanna' of North Walsham. Since Lydia and Susanna were John's two surviving daughters, this valuable piece of information established that this brother, Joseph, was not one of those buried at North Walsham, but that he had lived at least until after 1728. This was later confirmed from John Wasey's will and from the court rolls.

At that period of the search there were two contenders for the burial-date recorded of a 'Joseph Wasey' in 1718: a choice existed between John's brother and his cousin, 'Joseph Wasey of Trunch'. It became obvious before long that it was for the latter; but the other was to take many years in revealing itself.

The Wasey family, then, had sprung from yeoman stock, farming and trading in the market town of North Walsham for nearly a century. They had had the good sense to marry heiresses and, over the decades, had acquired a considerable amount of property in the area. By the early 18th century the Wasey's menfolk were termed 'gentlemen', they bore arms and became one of the five North Walsham families to hold more than 90 acres of copyhold land in that parish alone.

It was after compiling their pedigree, from Robert Wasey's birth in 1603 to the 18th century, that, one day at Bristol University Library, I chanced upon a piece of information enabling me to further the history of the family considerably. I was consulting Venn's *Biographical History of Gonville & Caius College, Cambridge* for a Clarke forebear, when I happened upon an entry which stopped me in my tracks. No longer could I concentrate on the project in hand but felt compelled to hasten home and refer to my Wasey notes. The passage was: 'Wasey – William, son of William Wasey, attorney of Brumstead, Norfolk; born there . . . . Age 17 adm. pens. 1708. . . [more information] . . . Fellow of the College of Physicians . . . 1724 . . . President, 1750–1754 . . .'.

I recognized this William! He appeared on my Wasey chart: the son, baptised in 1691 at Brumstead, of John Wasey's first cousin, William. I was vaguely aware of the success of a branch of the family, references to which I had found from time to time in Norfolk and elsewhere. The North Walsham court rolls for instance referred to a 'Willus Wasey Medicina Doctor' whom I felt was probably connected to 'my' pedigree but, being otherwise occupied, I had not, until now, pursued this line of enquiry.

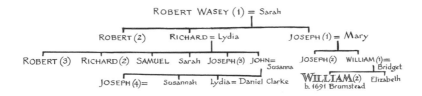

Armed with the information just discovered, however, I should be able to trace the progeny of such a distinguished personage as this William forward – providing he and each subsequent generation had produced at least one male heir. If so, it would be worthy of the forthcoming volume of *Norfolk Pedigrees* to be published by the Norfolk and Norwich Genealogical Society.[4]

PRINTED SOURCES AND PCC WILLS

On my next visit to Bristol Central Library I referred to *Munk's Roll* and the *DNB* given as references in Venn's *History*. Both gave interesting information on Dr Wasey but neither named his wife. Next, I referred to Venn's *Alumni Cantabrigienses* to see if sons had been sent to Caius or other Cambridge Colleges, and found: 'Wasey. William John Spearman. adm. pens at Clare, Jan. 9 1751. b. in London. Matric 1751'.

On looking up references to the name Wacey/Wasey in the index for the *Gentleman's Magazine* for that period, it yielded:

Vol. 22   Dr. Wasey continued President of Royal College of Physicians
" 27 1757. Dr. Wasey . . . his death
" 35 1765. Promotions in the 2nd Troop of Life Guards. Wm. Wasey exempt & Captain

Vol.81   1811. . . . the original Mickleton MSS (much augmented by the collections of Mr John Spearman, under sheriff of Durham, who died about 1705) are in the possession of Mrs.Wasey of Queen Anne St, West

"   87   1817. Obit. In Queen Anne Street, in his 84th year, Lt. Col. Wasey

Well, this Dr Wasey was the same person: he had died in 1757 (already found in Venn, *Munk's Roll* and the *DNB*) and the Lt.-Col. Wasey would seem to be the student, William John Spearman Wasey, admitted to Clare College in 1751. Assuming he was aged 18 when admitted, it made his birth year 1733: the year arrived at on deducting 84 years from the obituary date.

To further this hypothesis, assuming the captain in the Life Guards (later the lieutenant-colonel who died in 1817) was the son of Dr Wasey, the information indicated that Dr Wasey had married a Miss Spearman. And from the item about the Mickleton MSS, it seemed likely she would turn out to be a daughter or granddaughter of Mr John Spearman, one-time under-sheriff of Durham.

This jogged my memory. During early searches on the North Walsham family, I had come across a William John Spearman Wasey in the *Manor Court Rolls* being admitted to property there. I looked up my notes and, yes, the transaction was in 1757, the year of Dr Wasey's death. On obtaining a copy of this, I found it concerned the already discovered Joseph, Mary *and* William John Spearman Wasey, son of 'the late William Wasey MD'. There were many more entries concerning W.J.S. Wasey Esq., over the years.

WILLIAM WASEY (1)
|
DR WILLIAM WASEY (2)
|
Wᵐ. JOHN SPEARMAN WASEY

Continuing through other notes I had made of the name Wasey and variants, I found one culled from Whitmore's *Genealogical Guide* referring to Massue de Ruvigny's *The Plantagenet Roll of the Blood Royal*, no less. This great work, in four or more volumes, included the *Exeter Volume* indicated in the reference and there I found: 'Jemima Harriet Kindersley m. 24 Nov. 1853 to Rev. John Spearman Wasey, vicar of Compton Parva . . .'.

This was exciting, showing a descendant into the 19th century. But there still remained a 100-year gap with, perhaps, three more generations to find, before reaching this Victorian couple.

It was necessary now to discover the full name of Dr Wasey's wife. I asked an acquaintance to refer to *Boyd's Marriage Index* at the SOG but this proved negative. In the meantime, I consulted Venn's *Alumni Cantabrigienses* and Foster's *Alumni Oxonienses* to see what clues could be gleaned from Spearman students attending either university. Several referred to Rugby and other public schools, Foster's *Men at the Bar* and *LG*: Burke's *Landed Gentry*.

On looking through the index for this last work I found Spearman, for that era, was to be located in an early edition, entitled Burke's *Commoners*. Here, in Volume II, was the Spearman family of Co. Durham in which Margaret, the daughter of Gilbert Spearman, was shown married to William Wasey MD, of Gerard Street, Soho, Westminster. What is more, it records their son, William John Spearman Wasey, married to his cousin, Elizabeth Honoria (the daughter of Gilbert Spearman's son, George) – both great grandchildren of John Spearman, one-time under-sheriff of Durham, owner of the Mickleton Manuscripts.[5]

So far, so good. Now I needed to ascertain where William John S. Wasey and his wife had baptised *their* children. In the meantime, from the IGI, I learned that

Dr Wasey and Margaret Spearman had married at St Antholin's, in the City of London, recorded in the *Harleian* volumes of London parishes. And in Burke's *General Armory* William's Grant of Arms the previous year was found: 'Wasey (co. Norfolk and Westminster) granted 12 August 1729'.

A printed source later to become invaluable was found in London libraries such as Guildhall and Westminster. In several volumes, it is known collectively as *The London Survey* and contains a first-class description and history of the streets, squares and buildings, liberally embellished with illustrations. It also gives information on past inhabitants where known: many snippets of relevant information were gleaned from this most interesting work.

My next few London visits took me to the PRO in Chancery Lane where I searched the PCC will indexes hoping to find Dr Wasey's and perhaps more of the family's. To my delight there, in 1757, was the doctor's, naming his 'only son William John Spearman Wasey' and his daughter, Margaret. *Their* wills too were found, in 1794 and 1817. Also, there were those of the Revd Clement John Wasey and Revd George Wasey, sons of William John S. Wasey.

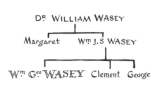

Margaret, in her will, referred to Eliza Honoria Margaret Wasey, 'daughter of my late nephew, William George Wasey'. He, to date, had not emerged from school, parish or other records searched, and, judging by the date of the will, he should turn out to be an elder, if not the eldest, son of William John S. Wasey since there was a grandchild involved.

It now occurred to me that, since these family members had had their wills proved in this prestigious court, perhaps I should find here the will (undiscovered in Norfolk) of Dr Wasey's father. I did. William Wasey's of Worstead was proved the year after his death, naming his son, William, daughter, Elizabeth, and wife, Bridget, all previously known to me.

Then an even more interesting thought struck me. Was the will of Joseph of Trunch here, quoted by my 5th great grandfather, John Wasey, in his Norfolk will? He said it was made in 1716 and I had to search on to 1719 for its probate date, but luck was mine again! It commenced: 'I Joseph Wasey of Trunch [and continued as found previously in John's will and the court rolls]: to . . . John Wasey my kinsman and Susan his wife [and]. . . his son Joseph . . .'. It went on to name the surviving children of his brother, William: 'William Wasey my nephew' (Dr Wasey, whom he made his executor), and niece, 'Elizabeth Wasey'. At last I had found the document which, with the court rolls, provided conclusive evidence that the family from which my mother's family had derived the name 'Wasey' as a Christian name, was definitely this one.

CHURCH, SCHOOL AND UNIVERSITY RECORDS

During my next London visit I spent an hour or so at Westminster RO where I learned that Gerard Street, Soho, was in the parish of St Anne's, Leicester Fields. And in the microfilmed register I discovered the baptisms of Dr and Margaret Wasey's two children: Margaret in 1731 and William John Spearman in 1733.

Now I returned to my notes taken from the *Alumni Oxonienses*:

Wasey, Clement John s. of William John Spearman Wasey of Westminster, arm., Oriel Coll., Matric . . . 1788 aged 18; B.A. . . . M.A. . . . rector of South Shoebury, Essex and of Ulcomb, Kent

Wasey, George s. of William John Spearman Wasey of Westminster, arm., Oriel Coll., matric . . . 1791 aged 18. Fellow All Souls College . . . B.A. . . . M.A. . . . B.D . . . Rector of Whitington, co. Glos., 1802 and of Ulcomb, Kent 1811 until his death . . . 1838. See Rugby School Reg.

Wasey, William George Leigh, 1st s. of George of Aldbury, Oxon. cler. . . . . Christ Church, matric. . . 1829 aged 18. B.A. . . .M.A. . .(as George William), vic. of Morville . . . and of Quatford, Salop, 1840 until his death. . . 1877

Wasey, John Spearman, 3rd s. of George of Swanbourne, Bucks., cler. Trinity Coll. matric . . . 1837 aged 20; B.A. . . . M.A. . . . of Priors Court, Berks. . . . vicar of Compton Parva, Berks., 1853.

The first two entries were clear enough and so was the fourth, bearing the name Spearman. It was evident that John Spearman Wasey (already found married to Jemima Harriet Kindersley in the *Plantagenet Roll*) was the son of George Wasey, who in turn was the son of William John Spearman Wasey of Westminster. The third entry, however, I had doubts about. Were there two George Waseys? It seemed unlikely to me that *one* could be of Whitington, Glos., of Ulcombe, Kent, of Swanbourne, Bucks. *and* of Aldbury, Oxon! More evidence, I decided, was needed.

The early published Registers of Rugby School, found in Bristol University Library, revealed the following:

Entrances in 1785
Wasey, Spearman, 4th s. of Col. William John Spearman Wasey, Queen Ann Street, Cavendish Square, London. Died at School . . . 1785 . . .
Wasey, George, 5th s. of the above Col. William John Spearman Wasey . . . b. about 1773. Oriel Coll., Oxford 1791. Fellow All Souls . . . B.A. . . . M.A. . . . B.D. . . . Rector of Ulcombe, Kent. d. 24 March, 1838

Entrances in 1832
Wasey, John Spearman, 3rd s. of the Rev. George Wasey of Wardington, Banbury; . . . Trinity . . . Oxford . . . B.A. . . . M.A. . . . Vic. of Compton, Berks. 1853–90. Of Priors Court, Newbury. d. 1900.

So now the Revd George Wasey was described as 'of Wardington' also!

During a visit to Kent that summer a call was made at Maidstone RO to inspect Ulcombe's parish registers, the living recorded as George Wasey's from

1811. He was seldom present, I found, signing the registers at infrequent intervals and employing curates over the years. No family baptisms, marriages or burials were performed there and his name did not appear in the Poll Books either.

Later, on going to the Bodleian Library, Oxford, I searched the register transcripts it then held for Albury/Aldbury[15] and found:

> Wasey, William George Leigh son of George & Anne Sophia b. May 26 1811
> Wasey, Willoughby Clement son of George & Anne Sophia b. Oct 12 1812

Also, in the parish register transcripts then held there for Wardington, Banbury,[15] was the marriage, in 1840, of: 'George Wingfield, clerk of Glatton, Hants. & Sophia Elizabeth Wasey of Wardington'.

Looking through the Archbishop of Canterbury's *Act Books* I found reference to the Revd George Wasey (of All Souls, Oxford, etc.) described as of Whitington, Glos., of Albury, Oxon., of Wytham, Berks. and also of Ulcombe, Kent! So he *was* one and the same person – and, to seal it all, the same information was found in Foster's *Ecclesiasticus*.

In the interim, I wrote to Bucks. RO asking if the marriage of the Revd George Wasey to Anne was recorded in 1810, the year prior to the eldest son's birth, at the small village of Swanbourne, one of the places to eliminate. It was not, but the archivist kindly sent baptismal details of three of their children, in which the Revd George Wasey is described as 'rector of Ulcombe, Kent'.

George Wasey had, it seems, officiated at the christenings – in 1816, 1817 and 1819 – but he was not, as it transpired, incumbent at Swanbourne or at Wardington. I later learned that, after relinquishing the livings of Whitington, Wytham and Albury, he had accepted his deceased brother's living, Ulcombe, and had simply resided, during different periods, at Swanbourne and Wardington. Other places of residence had been Gregynog, in Wales, and Brighton: fortunately these did not appear in the records, or there would have been even more cause for confusion!

THE EAST INDIA COMPANY

Before long I was to discover that a further royal line descended to the Wasey family, recorded in Ruvigny's *Plantagenet Roll* but not indexed. On page 508 were the descendants of Margaret Peirson and her husband, Gilbert Spearman – Dr Wasey's in-laws – and here, William George (the eldest son of Col. W.J.S. Wasey) was shown as having died at 'Palamcote in the East Indies'. This was the son named by his aunt, Margaret Wasey, in her PCC will found earlier.

The Kindersley pedigree, found in the same work, refers to Nathaniel Edward Kindersley of the HEICS; he is recorded as marrying Hannah, the widow of 'Captain William Wasey'. Was this, I wondered, 'William George', the colonel's son? So far, I had not ascertained the parish in which Col. W.J.S. Wasey had christened his children: they were not to be found in the St Marylebone area of Queen Anne Street, recorded as his home.

During a visit to the PRO Kew, Army Lists, Musters and various other records were searched for this Capt. William Wasey, without success. References were found only to William John S. Wasey during an earlier period, and so it began to look as though he might be found in the records of the East India Company.

After writing to the India Office Library and forwarding a small search fee, a most informative letter was received. With it was a photocopied page of *Monumental Inscriptions at Palamcottah* recording the burial of William George Wasey. It also gave his marriage date to Hannah, née Butterworth, widow of James Johnson, *and* the marriage date of Hannah, 'widow of William George Wasey' to Nathaniel E. Kindersley! Also supplied was the baptismal date of Wasey and Hannah's daughter, Eliza Honoria Margaret: the 'great niece' mentioned in Margaret Wasey's PCC will.

William junior had married Hannah in January 1785, four months before he died in the May. Their daughter was born in the October and the following year Hannah married, for the third time, Nathaniel Edward Kindersley. Hence the connection with that family and the subsequent naming of a son 'Kindersley' by the Revd George Wasey, thirty odd years before another of his sons married into the Kindersley family.

William George was not however in the East Indian Army or Navy but was a 'Writer' (clerk) and subsequently paymaster in the Hon. East India Company's Civil Service. 'Captain' was either a courtesy title, or one of many errors found in printed records.

Another fresh piece of information, gleaned this time from the Egerton Leigh pedigree in *Ruvigny*, was the identity of Anne Sophia, the Revd George Wasey's wife: 'daughter of Captain John Frodsham, R.N.'. She, as it turned out, was descended from a more recent royal personage than the two lines having Plantagenet ancestry already discovered. Anne was a descendant of the Princess Mary Tudor, younger sister of Henry VIII. I was beginning to feel myself in very distinguished company!

During my search I had found, in the 1858 edition of Crockford's *Clerical Directory*, a small piece of information not included in later editions and other references to the Revd John Spearman Wasey. This was that the patron of his living, Compton Parva, had been one J.T. Wasey Esquire. Who, I wondered, was this? Was it another uncle – another undiscovered son of Col. Wasey's?

Having been unsuccessful in finding the christenings of Col. Wasey's children in the vicinity of his West End address, Queen Anne Street, off Cavendish Square, I searched again the registers of St Anne's, Soho, where he and his sister Margaret had been christened about thirty years earlier. There it was that I found five of the colonel's children:

Anna Margaretta dau. of William John Spearman Wasey Esq., & Elizabeth Honoria his
    wife 1764

John	son of "	" 1765
Clement John	"	" 1769
Spearman	"	" 1771
George	"	" 1773

Here was a John but with no initial 'T' to follow and, in any case, on searching through the death register I found John had died a few months later.

Looking again through my old notes, I found among them some extracts taken from the 1873 *Return of Owners of Land*[6] listing everyone owning one acre or more in England and Wales. Having searched the index for every county, I had found and extracted:

	Address	*Acres*	*County*
Revd George L. Wasey	Bridgnorth	216	Salop
Revd George L. Wasey	Knollsands, Bridgnorth	110	Montgomery
Edward F. Noel K. Wasey	Maidenhead	27	Berks.
Miss Wasey	Priors Court, Chieveley, Berks.	1,260	Berks.
Revd John S. Wasey	Compton	6	Berks.

The information given in *Alumni Oxonienses* and the Rugby School Registers on John Spearman Wasey, it may be remembered, referred to him as 'of Priors Court, Berks.'! So there was evidently a connection here. Now, J.T. Wasey *and* Miss Wasey needed to fit into the pedigree! Had Col. W.J.S. Wasey, I wondered, christened another son, John T. Wasey, elsewhere? There *was* a four-year gap between the John who died a baby and the next child, Clement John. Another of my notes, made at Kensington Reference Library, London, now became relevant and made me determined to learn more of Priors Court. It was from *Who's Who in Berkshire*: 'Wasey, Willoughby Spearman. Captain, Royal Corps of Signals . . . born . . . 1899, Priors Court Farm, Chieveley, Berks., son of the late Edward J.S. Wasey Esq., . . .'

CENSUS RETURNS AND POST-1857 WILLS

Visits to London were becoming more frequent. I searched at Somerset House for post-1857 wills to learn of more recent relationships and looked up addresses in the census returns at the PRO.

In *1851*, before the arrival of the Revd John Spearman Wasey at Compton, I found, at Priors Court, John Thomas Wasey (born at Newbury), unmarried, aged 66 years: the mysterious J.T. Wasey Esq.! There were six servants and two visitors: Jane Stacpoole and Mary Wasey, both also born at Newbury.

At Priors Court Farm lived the farm bailiff and six servants, and at the Lodge were the gardener, laundress and groom.

At Knowle Sands, near Bridgnorth, Shropshire, was the vicar of Quatford: the Revd William George Leigh Wasey (born Albury, Oxford) married to Eliza Lenora (born India) and their two daughters, Sophia Honoria and Lenora Sabrina.

In *1861*, at Priors Court, Mary Wasey, aged 65, was now head of the household, and at Priors Court Farm was a farmer with his wife, children and eight servants.

At Compton Parva's vicarage, there now lived the Revd John Spearman Wasey (born Swanbourne), his wife, Hariet, and four children: Eliza M., Hariett J., Edward J.S., and Arthur F.

In *1871*, at Compton Vicarage, there lived still the Revd and Mrs J.S. Wasey, now with seven children at home: Eliza M., Harriett J., George K., Mary C., Willoughby F., Cyril L., and Lionel T., aged 9 months. Employed was a resident governess, nurse, wet-nurse, housemaid, under-nurse and cook.

Among the many Wasey wills to be found at Somerset House was that of Miss Mary Wasey late of Priors Court. She had died in 1880, her brother, John Thomas, and sister, Jane, having predeceased her. The bulk of her property, I found, was bequeathed to the Revd William George Leigh Wasey, entailed to his sons; in default of sons the next to inherit was Revd John Spearman Wasey; similarly, in default, Edward Frodsham Noel Kindersley Wasey. All three were the sons of the Revd George Wasey, but no relationship with Miss Wasey herself was hinted at.

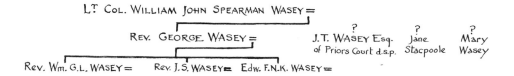

There were bequests to 'my Godson, Edward John Spearman Wasey' and to 'my late sister's Goddaughter, Harriet Jane Wasey': both children of the Revd John Spearman Wasey. Also there were bequests to the daughters of the Revd William George Leigh Wasey. Tantalizingly, throughout this missive, no relationships between the two families were given. But Miss Wasey did provide one clue. At the end of her twenty-page will, she declared: 'I desire to be buried at Shaw, near Newbury, where my family have been interred'.

LOCATING THE BURIAL PLACE AND THE BERKSHIRE RECORD OFFICE

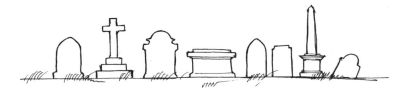

En route, during the next car-trip to London, a detour was made to Newbury and the whereabouts of Shaw Church found. Here, on wall plaques inside the church, were the following:

In a vault in the burial ground . . . of the church are . . . the remains of John Wasey & Anne his wife, the former of whom died June 6 1804 aet 52 years; the latter Mch 6 1820 aged 62 . . . . In the same vault are . . . the remains of Thomas Jones of Llanerfil . . . Montgomery (maternal uncle of Anne Wasey) who died 1793

. . . to the memory of James Frederick Wasey, son of John and Anne Wasey who while serving as Lieutenant . . . perished by shipwreck near the Bay of Dublin Nov 19 1807 aged 18

Sacred to the Memory of John Thomas Wasey of Priors Court in the county of Berks. Esq., born April 7th 1782. Died Oct. 8th 1852. For many years a Deputy Lieutenant & Magistrate for the County . . .

This find only served to baffle me more. Apart from John Wasey, the names did not fit. There was a Montgomery connection with the 'Norfolk' family but not until much later and I felt something was wrong. I could not, however, put my finger on it. For a family connection, this John Wasey of Newbury would have to be a son of Col. W.J.S. Wasey, because I knew he was the only son of Dr William Wasey, who was the only surviving son of William Wasey, attorney of Brumstead, who in turn was the only son (to have had children) of Joseph Wasey(1) of North Walsham.

John, the son of Col. Wasey, had been born in 1765 and died aged only five months. John Wasey of Newbury, according to the MI, had been born in 1752. I began to wonder whether Col. Wasey had sown his wild oats at 19 years of age and fathered a son, John – but surely he would not have borne the name Wasey?

Having checked the Manorial Documents Register at Quality House to see whether manorial archives for the Chieveley area were housed at Berkshire RO,[7] I felt a visit there was called for. Shaw's parish register revealed the burial records for those named on the monuments, and in Newbury's PR I found the baptisms of John and Anne Wasey's five children.

The Manor Court records proved to be earlier than required, but plentiful evidence from conveyancing documents, etc., showed the Berkshire Wasey family to have been affluent, holding a great deal of property in the area from the latter part of the 18th century until Mary Wasey's death in 1880. John Wasey, attorney of Newbury, and his surviving son, John Thomas Wasey, had become wealthy and influential, but there was nothing to suggest a connection with the 'Norfolk' family. Indeed there seems to have been an investigation in reverse at some time previously, there being an affidavit signed in 1862 by one Thos. Nalder:

> declaring John Thomas Wasey late of Priors Court . . .; Jane Wasey . . . widow of Hugh Stacpoole Esq . . .;and Mary Wasey now of Priors Court . . . spinster . . . to be the only surviving children of John Wasey of Newbury . . . Solicitor.[8]

Infuriatingly, the file which may have proved most useful, 'Documents relating to the name Wasey from 1710–1820',[9] proved to be 'fragile' (requiring restoration) and could not be seen.

A STRANGE COINCIDENCE

Since the Newbury family's pre-1858 wills were not to be found at Berkshire's RO, I felt a further visit to the PRO (for possible PCC wills) might prove fruitful. It did. Here was the record showing that J.T. Wasey had died intestate and Letters of Administration granted in 1852. Having learned from the church monument the death-date in 1804 of his father, John Wasey of Newbury, his will was soon found.[10] This proved to be a very interesting document but it only served to deepen the problem. Apart from bequests to his wife and children, there were the following:

> I give to my nephew Edward Bird of Aynhoe, Northampton . . . [and] I give to my cousin, Alexander *Pead* of Buckingham . . . the former on account of his being my nearest relation except my own family and the latter on account of his being my next nearest relation . . . .

So John Wasey of Newbury, apart from his own children, had no Wasey kin! He cannot, then, have been a son of Col. Wasey: he and two sons were living in 1804.

Interestingly, from the IGI for Bucks., it was found that a John Wasey of Stowe, victualler, had married a Mary *Pead* of Buckingham, at Haversham, on 6 November 1746. On contacting a record searcher, the baptisms at Haversham and Buckingham were consulted and several Stowes around the country checked, but no children of the marriage were recorded at any of these.

It seems likely, however, that this John Wasey of Stowe and his wife Mary *were* the parents of John of Newbury, and if there *should* prove to be a connection with the 'Norfolk' family in the male line, it would have to originate from a son of the elder brother of Joseph of North Walsham, namely my own 6th great grandfather, Richard Wasey of Tunstead, or earlier. But kinship from this distance would surely be lost from view, some four generations later.

Why then, I wondered, if no kinship existed, did Miss Mary Wasey bequeath to her namesakes the considerable estates acquired by her family during the 18th century? It was a mystery, and there the matter rested for some time: until, one day, reference was made to the *Victoria County History* for Berkshire. Here, in Volume IV, in the section dealing with Chieveley in Faircross Hundred, the following incredible story was to be found.

> . . .John Thomas Wasey was a bachelor with two sisters, and he seems to have been anxious to leave the large estates that he had acquired to someone who would perpetuate his name. He could find, however, no male relation . . .

It goes on to tell how, during a visit to Southsea, he met the Revd George Wasey and his young sons, playing on the beach. Having learned their name was also Wasey he became extremely interested. The families became friends and:

> . . . For long he sought unsuccessfully to prove them relations, and it was believed that he had intended making them his heirs, when he died intestate on 8th October 1852. His sisters Jane, wife of Col. Stackpool, and Mary, inherited their brother's estates . . .

The article concludes with the information that Mrs Stackpool died without surviving issue and that at her death Miss Mary Wasey left the Priors Court estates to their namesakes.

No wonder I had been unable to find a relationship! I now felt safe in assuming that if J.T. Wasey Esq., with his considerable resources, was unsuccessful in finding a connection, there was little point in my pursuing the matter further. Fact, I felt, in this case, was most certainly 'stranger than fiction'.

It was not quite the end of this strange story. Later, from the Wasey family, I learned the marriage details of John Thomas Wasey's parents. John Wasey (future attorney of Newbury) and Anne were wedded, as it happened, on 20 June 1781, at St Giles-in-the-Fields, London: a church some two or three hundred yards from Soho Square, the early married home of Col. W.J.S. Wasey. It was just off what is now Shaftesbury Avenue, in the lower part of which is situated the remains of St Anne's Church where Col. Wasey had christened his children during the previous decade. One of these was George, who became the father of the boys destined to attract the attention of John and Anne Wasey's son, J.T. Wasey Esq., of Priors Court, during a stroll on the beach at Southsea!

The more I researched into various families, the more I realized how much coincidence came into play: how many times the paths of our ancestors cross and how many times they *appear* to do so. This tale of the two Wasey families is, I feel, a cautionary tale. Nothing can be taken for granted, however likely. And no possibility, however unlikely, can we afford to ignore.

INVESTIGATING DISCREPANCIES

When endeavouring to learn more of the Leigh/Legh family from which Anne Sophia (wife of the Revd George Wasey) descended, it was not the surname which gave rise to confusion but the place-name of the family's origins.

This ancient family, settled in England before the Conquest, derived its name from High Legh in Cheshire and, being as prolific as it was distinguished, branches went out in all directions. Two remained at High Legh: those of the East Hall and those of the West Hall. A descendant of the latter family, Peter Leigh (who married Elizabeth, granddaughter of the 2nd Earl of Bridgwater) was rector of Lymm, Cheshire, about fifteen miles south-west of Manchester. The ancestor of another branch was Piers Legh who obtained, through his marriage in 1388, an estate at Lyme, also in Cheshire, about fifteen miles south-east of Manchester.

Pedigrees and histories of these families abound but their compilers, from Burke to Ormerod, frequently record the West Hall family as of Lymme, giving rise to some confusion. Investigations, however, showed Lymm, near High Legh, to be the parish relevant to the Revd Peter Leigh, ancestor of the present-day Wasey family.

More could have been learned, given time, during a holiday in Co. Durham, on the rather shadowy distaff family, the Peirsons, through which some of the family's royal blood passed. At Durham University Library are deposited the *Mickleton Manuscripts*, a brief inspection of which showed the existence of another claimant to the Spearman estates subsequently inherited by the Wasey family. But holidays cannot be sacrificed entirely to family history, however absorbing, and a line has to be drawn somewhere when deciding how far to delve into its ramifications!

Another discrepancy found in *Histories* and *Peerages* concerned the Hon. Mary Cokayne, wife of that same Robert Peirson (maternal grandparents of Dr William Wasey's wife). Surtees, for instance, in his *History of Co. Durham*, gives her variously as 'Mary, sister of Charles Lord Cullen' and as 'sister of Brien, 2nd Viscount Cullen'; Burke has her as daughter of the 1st Viscount Cullen; Cokayne gives only the heir, and the enormous, beautifully designed pedigree chart displayed on a wall at Delapre Abbey, once the home of the Northampton Record Office, shows Charles, 1st Viscount Cullen, as having, in addition to his son, Brien the 2nd Viscount, a daughter, Elizabeth (Elizabeth was the wife of Brien).

This particular puzzle was solved on making a visit to Northampton RO where plentiful archive material is housed on the Cokayne and allied families. Evidence was soon found to show that the Hon. Mary Cokayne was in fact the daughter of Charles, 1st Viscount Cullen and sister of Brien, the 2nd Viscount. There was for instance an agreement in 1667 between Brien, Lord Viscount Cullen and his sister Mary showing her to be still unmarried:

> . . . (Brien 2nd Vis. Cullen) acknowledges that his father Charles Lord Viscount Cullen did . . . setle upon . . . Mary Cockaine his daughter the summe of four thousand pounds for a

portion to remain in the hands of his sonne . . . Lord Cullen after his death until his daughter . . . Mary Cockaine shall attaine to . . . eighteen or be . . . married.[11]

In 1670 we find Mary married and an indenture is drawn up:

> . . . between the right Hon[ble] Bryan Lord Viscount Cullen . . . and Robert Pierson of fforcett . . . gent. and Mary his wife Sister of the said Brian Lord Viscount Cullen . . . .[12]

THE SOURCE OF A LEGEND

Once this type of error gets into print, it tends to become accepted as fact. Another example is found in information compiled by George C. Peachey on Dr William Wasey in his *History of St George's Hospital*. In the profile on Wasey he says:

> . . . Family tradition, of which no verification has been found, states that Dr. Wasey was Physician to George II, though his son's appointment at Court tends to support its probability . . . .

In fact there appears to be no substance to the belief that Wasey was appointed physician to George II. It almost certainly arises from the existence in the Wasey family of an ebony walking-stick bearing the royal coat of arms and the words: 'Presented to Dr. Wasey by H.M. George II'. As the Royal Archivist at the Round Tower, Windsor, suggests: 'he may have been called in to attend the King or one of his family on a particular occasion, without necessarily being appointed a Physician in Ordinary'. Certainly no record has been found of such an appointment.

Peachey seemed unaware that the duties of Silver-Stick-in-Waiting fell traditionally to the 1st Lieutenant Colonel of the Horse Guards and were not as a result of a Court appointment. If, as recorded by the family, these Silver-Stick duties were performed by the physician's son, it would be only when he, as 2nd Lieutenant Colonel, was deputizing for the 1st Lieutenant Colonel.[13]

During correspondence with the librarian at the Royal College of Physicians in my quest for information regarding Dr Wasey's involvement with George II, reference was made to S.D. Clippingdale's *Medical Court Roll* which lists medical men who have attended members of the royal family from the time of William the Conqueror. Wasey is listed thus:

> Wasey, William . . . Physician to St George's Hospital . . . said to have been Physician to George II (Z.,eeee)

My correspondent went on to say that the 'Z' at the end of the entry refers to *Munk's Roll* and 'eeee' refers to the *Biographical Catalogue of the Society of Friends* (1888). Since *Munk's Roll* had already been consulted, I looked in the *British Library Catalogue* under Society of Friends (Quakers) for the 1888 publication referred to.

The catalogue, I found, was at the Library, Friends' House, Euston Road, London, and on my writing there, the reply asserted that no reference to Dr William Wasey was given, either in the 1888 catalogue or in any of their standard sources. They suggested I return to my original source of information, since there must be a mistake. I subsequently made time to visit the library, with the same negative results.

Another letter therefore was written to the librarian at the Royal College of Physicians who reiterated that the reference given was indeed 'eeee'. But, it was suggested, perhaps there was an error in Clippingdale and the reference should have been 'eeeee' – which is none other than Peachey's *History of St George's Hospital*! *His* sources were *DNB*, *Munk's Roll*, Wasey's will and, yes, family information. So, we were back again to the silent evidence of the walking-stick!

No clue survives as to why or when this gift was made, except for a label on the reverse of a painting in the family's possession, said to be of Dr Wasey, bearing the words 'William Wasey M.D. . . . Honorary Physician to George II, 1722'. This was, of course, when the future King George II was still Prince of Wales. If presented then, the inscription on the stick must have been placed there at a later date, when the prince became king.

Incidentally, a visit made to St George's Hospital to view the Minute Books revealed Peachey's *History* to be so comprehensive that little additional information was gleaned. Oddly, Sir George Clark's *History of the Royal College of Physicians* makes no mention of Wasey (although he was president from 1750 to 1754) except to devote a page to an illustration of the 'Wasey Candlesticks'.

FAMILY COLLECTIONS, NEWSPAPERS AND OTHER SOURCES

Some of the most rewarding finds have been made when browsing through the indexes of family collections deposited at county ROs. One such was a document found at Norwich RO in the *Walpole of Walterton Collection* (I knew that both Lord Walpole and the Wasey family had owned property in the same area). This was an indenture made in 1720 between Dr Wasey, his sister Elizabeth, their stepfather, Spencer Chapman, and one Robert Britiffe of Norwich Esq.:

> . . . being a person nominated and appointed Trustee for and on behalf of the Right Hon. Robert Walpole of Houghton, Norfolk Esq., one of His Majesty's most Honorable Privy Councillors . . . .

This proved very revealing, throwing light on a period about which little had hitherto been known. Another relevant find, this time from the *Norfolk Record Society Catalogue* at NRO, was a deed between W.J.S. Wasey, his wife, a cousin and 'the Rt. Honorable Harbord Lord Suffield . . .'. Drawn up in 1787, it was a 'Release of the ffreehold part of an (Wasey) Estate at ffelmingham and North Walsham' incorporating an attractive plan. More relevant deeds and another estate plan were found among the *Petre family archives*, many of which helped to complement the findings for that era.

Newspapers proved rewarding, especially on finding, among early editions, items relating to characters one has come to 'know'. A cutting from *The Times*, found much later in the search in the Waseys' *Family Book*, enabled me to locate the story again in the *Illustrated London News*. It told of exploits at sea by a Wasey descendant, with a sketch of the ships concerned. Not even the National Maritime Museum at Greenwich had been able to provide illustrations.

Another rewarding find was at Bristol Central Library. Looking through the enormous *British Library Catalogue* under the name Wasey, I discovered that two members of the family had gone into print. One 18th-century cleric had published a poem, and a 19th-century vicar, a local history and well-acclaimed sermon.

CHANCERY RECORDS AND CLUES TO FURTHER SOURCES

The public records which provided the most interesting insight into this family, however, were those found among *Chancery Proceedings* at the PRO, an important factor being that even the early ones are in English.

It was Margaret Wasey's will (1794) that made me wonder whether these might prove useful. Margaret made several bequests of her 'Court Annuities' and, knowing that she and her brother were well placed after their father's death, I wondered whether they might have been involved in property disputes and the like.

First, I searched a section of the index during the appropriate era for the Entry Books of Decrees and Orders under the reference C33. The index books are compiled yearly, divided into the quarters and indexed (roughly) alphabetically under the name of the plaintiff only. The name Wasey leapt out at me: Wasey v. Herne and, further on, Wasey v. Howard. Having noted the page numbers and ascertained the order references, I indented for them and in due course two huge books (parts 1 and 2) appeared for each reference.

The first was certainly a Margaret Wasey suing a Norfolk man; the second was definitely recognizable, the plaintiff being William John Spearman Wasey and his wife. Neither, however, told me much about the actual suits; they were orders of the court which, in these particular instances, were rather uninformative.

More perusing of the indexes revealed Wasey v. Heath. Surely not another suit, thought I? It proved to be Margaret Wasey, named as sister of W.J.S. Wasey. Yet another, Wasey v. Brograve, revealed the plaintiffs again to be W.J.S. Wasey and his wife. They were all brought within a thirty-year period and I noticed the same attorneys' names were cropping up.

On subsequent visits I searched the indexes for the proceedings (under the reference C12 for this era). They proved much more rewarding: the actual bills of complaint, which were very informative. Reading these enormous documents, however, was extremely time-consuming and, being unused to them, I found that to take abstracts made interpretation of their content more difficult. So, to keep the whole in context, I transcribed great chunks or had them photocopied for more careful study later. In all, I was to find fifteen suits brought by members of this family, covering 150 years and five generations.

The suit brought by Margaret Wasey against Paston Herne Esq., lord of several manors in Norfolk, dealt with loans made to him, first, by one Elizabeth Coulson of Thorpe-next-Norwich, then, when they remained unpaid, by Dr Wasey, who consented to the mortgage debts being assigned to him.

Curious about the Herne family, I referred, when next in Norwich, to *Herne* in the name index at the RO and Local Studies Library. Here was evidence that Paston Herne and his father had themselves been involved in lengthy litigation, resulting no doubt in their resources being drained and the necessity to borrow. It is one of those odd coincidences that Dr Wasey's father (William Wasey(1)) had, six years before he died and also because of lengthy litigation, borrowed from that same Mistress Coulson of Thorpe-next-Norwich. When Wasey's nine-year-old son (the future Dr Wasey) grew up, the debt was assigned to Sir Robert Walpole (as learned from the deed found in the Walpole Collection).

It was not long, however, before Dr Wasey was in a position to repay the debt and it may have been as a result of his own experience that when he became prosperous he was sympathetic to Herne's position, taking over his debts and allowing them to increase considerably. After Dr Wasey's death, of course, his son and daughter had the task of recovering the loans.

To return to the proceedings in general, having seen what could be found in each case and digested their content, it was necessary to return to Class 33 in order to find the outcome. This was not always clear, however: the case may have been withdrawn or settled out of court. On the other hand, there may well be several entries over a long period relating to just one suit, since they often took years to resolve. Because suits are usually indexed only under the plaintiff's name, the picture tends to be rather one-sided, as it would be only by chance or by prior knowledge that a case in which someone appears as defendant is found.[14]

The suits named family connections and gave addresses previously unknown, thus providing a link to further sources such as rate books, land tax assessments and maps. Wasey v. Howard was interesting in that the defendant (a Lichfield man) proved to be a friend, not only of Wasey's in-laws, but also of Dr Samuel Johnson: ascertained by enquiries to Staffordshire RO whose staff were very helpful, sending extracts from *Johnsonian Gleanings*.

The suit brought by W.J.S. Wasey against Brograve was a long and involved one, providing a great deal of information on the family's doings and, in turn, led to more research in other directions. There were details about Wasey's eldest son, such as his date of birth (unknown until then) and his death in Palamcottah, which would have been of great value had I not already learned it from East India records. Interesting too was the fact that Wasey claimed his legal advisor and his own two sons were 'confederating against' him in the course he was taking. And, even more important, I learned that Wasey finally obtained an Act of Parliament to force his opponent's hand.

On requesting information from the Clerk of the Records at the House of Lords, copies of the petition, order, judge's report, entry in the Committee Book and the act were supplied for a very reasonable cost.

Having found listed on one occasion Wasey v. Pearman I guessed this would prove to be Spearman; it provided evidence of a family dispute, undetected until then. The most important, however, were the early suits: Wasey v. Ward, v. Baispoole, v. Preston, and v. Themylthorpe. Brought at the beginning of the eighteenth century, they sometimes referred to events which had taken place the previous century. I found them often easier to interpret, with less repetition and legal jargon. They gave a much greater insight into the early family than would otherwise have been possible. It was fortunate too that, for some, the bills, answers and replications were filed together, giving a more complete picture without the necessity of further searching through indexes.

From one of these, brought by Anne Wasey – who turned out to be sister-in-law to John Wasey, my 5th great grandfather – I was at last to learn what had happened to John's other brothers. Robert, the eldest, it may be remembered, was buried in Tunstead Church aged 26 years in 1687.

Anne is described as widow and executrix to 'Joseph Wasey . . . who was brother and administrator to Richard Wasey deceased . . .' (both nephews of) 'Robert Wasey the younger of North Walsham' (who died in 1670). In addition to these and other relationships, the date of her husband's will is given. It revealed too that since Anne's husband, Joseph(3), had become the next beneficiary of their uncle's will, then their other brother, Samuel, must have predeceased him.

From this suit it was learned that Joseph(3) had gone, at 16 years of age, to fight for king and country and that on his return he became a weaver by trade. At his death, Anne appears to have been left in poor circumstances and was granted the right to prosecute 'in forma paup[er]is' which, as Jowitt's *Dictionary of English Law* explains, was available to any poor person who could swear that he/she owned property worth no more than £5 except wearing apparel and the subject-matter of the intended action (this was not repealed until 1883). Anne, assigned an attorney and the means to bring her action without payment of court fees, won her case. This, in turn, encouraged her husband's kinsfolk, Dr Wasey and Elizabeth Postle, to try and recover the legacies which should have been received from this same uncle (Robert Wasey(2)) by Joseph Wasey of Trunch and Mrs Postle's husband and which, ultimately, would have benefited them.

Apart from relationships, all sorts of other interesting information was learned from these records. There was a peep, for instance, into an ancestor's seventeenth-century home, telling of '. . . her Closett, Cabinett and Trunks' and a servant's opinion of her: '. . . [she was] of a free and generous disposition . . .'. Another records an ancestor's reaction, when roused: '[they] did so provoke and irritate [me] . . .', and the exasperation of another: '[he] gave me a very flighty answer . . .'. They are authentic details and utterings: gems encapsulated in those dusty parchments for nearly three hundred years. They transport one back as no other archive does, in the absence of letters or diaries. Most, however, are lengthy; all are repetitious and always refer to people in the third person, some yielding more information than others. But they are well worth the finding.

MEETING THE DESCENDANTS

Although I have not succeeded in working the senior Wasey line, i.e. the descendants of Richard Wasey(1), further forward than the 18th century, tracing this younger branch has given me great satisfaction. One of the most rewarding aspects of the search, worked *forward*, latterly, rather than back, was meeting the present generations. Having worked my way through the records described, I was now able to identify members of the present older generation and, feeling the pedigree I was compiling should, if possible, include their offspring, I decided to make contact.

We were kindly received and subsequently given every facility to further what had by now become a desire to 'write up' and record the family's history. My main concern, initially, was to learn whether there were male heirs. Sadly there was none from this century's senior line, but, after more enquiries, I found a cadet branch had produced a son. Mention was made of another branch, virtually unknown now to the rest of the family. Had this line, I wondered, produced sons? Eventually I was rewarded by locating what transpired to be the senior male descendant of Joseph Wasey(1) of North Walsham and became instrumental in introducing this 'lost' cousin to the family.

Although few family archives survive, a wonderful old tome known as the *Family Book* provides endless snippets of biographical detail about eighteenth- and nineteenth-century members I had come to 'know' and I feel privileged to have had access to it on numerous occasions. It records, incidentally, correspondence in 1857 from the Wasey Sterry family regarding a possible connection,[16] on which I have been able to shed some light.

A wealth of memorabilia was made available to us for photographing: from the beautiful little drawings and watercolours inserted into the *Family Book*, to the family miniatures, Grant of Arms and royal walking-stick. All of which, with information gleaned from the sources described, have, I hope, enabled me to bring the story of the family more sharply into focus.

No doubt, given time, more information could be found lurking in various archives around the country. However, of what use would it be to subsequent generations if, instead of recording it, bits and pieces continued to be gathered up and stacked in the files which are beginning to take over my home? Having appointed myself to this task, I feel it is time to bring the search to a close, hoping that others will find the saga which has unfolded as fascinating as I have found it fulfilling.

North-east Norfolk

PART II THE HOUSE OF WASEY

Chapter One: Norfolk Roots

As the sun began to sink across the wide open skies of East Anglia, Robert Wasey trudged back to his roomy farmhouse in the little market-town of North Walsham in north-east Norfolk. Up since daybreak, he looked forward, as he fed and watered his horses, to the meal prepared on the spit before the large open fire. The light had faded before supper was over and candles or rushlights were used for the last hour or two. Robert then looked to his accounts or read aloud from the Bible, while his wife and daughters worked their needles, before climbing the stairs to bed.

Born in the year of Queen Elizabeth's death, Robert's youth had been spent in a period of poor trade, bad harvests and severe plagues; he thrived, however, to marry, in about 1630, Sarah, the sole surviving daughter of a prosperous North Walsham farmer.

During the discontent of Charles I's reign, most of Norfolk's yeomanry and gentry turned from the royal cause to that of Cromwell, and there were few local disturbances during the Civil War of the 1640s when Robert's family was growing up. His children were probably educated at the renowned Paston school established in the town and in due course Joseph, the youngest son, was evidently apprenticed to a grocer, since he was later to engage in that trade. The two eldest, Robert(2) and Richard, became, like himself, yeoman farmers.

Their land, freehold and copyhold, will have produced cereals as well as hay for winter feed and, besides beef cattle, there would have been a milking-cow to provide dairy products. Sheep were no doubt kept, wool being Norfolk's staple product, as well as poultry for the table and to ensure a good supply of eggs, while a litter of pigs would be housed in the yard near the stables.

It was during Cromwell's reign that Sarah's father, Robert Wilton, died, his will being proved, not in the church court, but 'by oath at London before the Judges'. In 1656, she inherited[1] and his property in Knapton, Bacton, Witton and Swanton Abbott, as well as North Walsham, came to the Wasey family[2].

RETURN OF THE MONARCHY

With the return of the monarchy in 1660, even the erstwhile supporters of Cromwell must have rejoiced after eleven years of Puritan repressions. Old customs and traditions such as the May Day, harvest and Christmas festivities were restored and life became relaxed and enjoyable once more. Rates and taxes were still payable, however. In April that year Robert Wasey was appointed churchwarden and was involved in setting the local parish rate[3]: he can be found paying 4s 3d, while his son Richard paid 2s 9d on property at Eastgate and 5d at Hollgate.

The following year they appeared on the Subsidy Rolls, paying what amounted to a wealth tax. Robert paid £1 10s and Richard, at nearby Tunstead, £1.[4] He and his wife Lydia started a family that year, presenting Robert with his first grandson, Robert(3).

Another tax was 'chimney money' paid on the hearths in each house; Robert paid for four, denoting quite a comfortable lifestyle.[5] The house was probably of flint, consisting perhaps of two good rooms on the ground floor and sleeping chambers above, served by the main chimney descending through the centre. There would be projecting rooms, too, used as scullery, dairy and brewhouse, with chambers over for servants; and grouped around the yard outside were the stables, barns and cowsheds.

The furnishings would include a heavy oak table, chairs for the master and visitors, and forms and joint-stools for extra seating. Chests, trunks and court-cupboards provided storage, while status possessions such as a carpet, looking-glass and the silverware, mentioned later in their bachelor son's will, added brightness.

There were only about thirty other houses in the town at that date with four or more hearths, including the three mansions owned by the gentry. Most of the other 120 or so taxable dwellings had only one hearth, as did about another 80 not liable for tax.[6] Robert's youngest son, Joseph, paid on a substantial five-hearthed house in the town, while his middle son, Richard, paid the two shillings on each of his three hearths at Tunstead.

In April 1660 this son, Richard, had been party to a contract with the executors of one John Andrews who claimed that proceeds from the sale of the deceased's lands and houses were insufficient to pay his debts. As a result they sold, to Richard Wasey, more of the deceased's property in Tunstead and Beeston St Lawrence which otherwise would have descended to Andrews' daughter, Lydia: possibly the Lydia whom Richard married.[7]

During this period the Wasey sons bore arms. Perhaps during the 'troubles' they had actively supported Cromwell's regime and were awarded the right to a coat of arms in recognition. Or it may have been a case of their having simply adopted arms to which they had no right, as did many another up-and-coming family. Later, with the restoration of the monarchy and probably at the Heralds' Visitation, they were required to disclaim them.[8] Officialdom, however, was disregarded and the family continued to bear arms.

DEATH NO STRANGER

Having brought up five of their family to adulthood, Sarah lived to see three of them marry and present her with grandchildren before she died in 1666. Robert lived well past his three score years and ten but was to experience, during those latter years, the sorrow of having his two eldest sons die before him. Robert(2) his namesake, who had benefited substantially from the will of his grandfather Wilton, died in 1670. Although still in his thirties he was already a man of considerable property, leaving legacies to the, then, youngest son of each of his two brothers, Richard and Joseph, and to the son of his sister, Sarah, now married to Samuel Postle of Brumstead.

Bequests to the needy were made: £10 'to the poore people of the towne of Northwalsham' and £5 to 'the poore of ye towne of Bacton'.[9] His sister, Mary, still then a spinster, was made executrix and residuary legatee of his real estate, said to be worth (later, in a law suit) £150 per annum, plus a personal estate 'consisting of ready money, plate, jewells, rings, household goods & implements of

The Market Cross, North Walsham

husbandry, cattle, corn & other stock etc. etc.' amounting to 'one thousand five hundred pounds or thereabouts'.[10]

Seven years later Robert senior was destined to follow the funeral cortège of his next son, Richard, when he died leaving a young family of six children. Providing for them, Richard left his widow, Lydia, 'my household stuffe, brasse, pewter, linnen, woollen, plate, beds, bedding and utensils of household . . .' together with an annuity for four years of £10 towards the maintenance of his children. He made his father executor, directing that after his wife's death his North Walsham property should go to his eldest son, Robert(3), while the Tunstead and Beeston property should be sold and the proceeds equally divided among his other children, to be paid, on their reaching 21 years, 'at or in the porch of the parish church of Tunstead'.[11]

Robert Wasey senior had little time to carry out his son's wishes, for, at the end of the following year, he himself died. He was buried beneath a black marble slab in the church of St Nicholas: 'Here Lyeth interred the body of Robert Wasey who departed this life 11th day December 1679 aged 76 years'.

In his will[12] Robert named all the children of his deceased son, Richard, specifying that their legacies, 'ffourscore pounds of good and lawful money' for the younger children and £200 for the eldest, should be paid when they reached 22 years, in North Walsham Church porch.

After leaving £10 to the poor of North Walsham and absolving his son-in-law, Samuel Postle, from the £100 debt to him in bonds, he made bequests to both daughters, Sarah Postle and Mary, directing that they share his belongings at their old home, Brunstead-next-Happisburgh. His lands and property there, with the residue of his 'Lands Grounds & Incloses . . . in Northwalsham' together with his 'moveable Goods Corne Cattell Chattells ready moneys & Utensills', he left to his youngest and only surviving son, Joseph.

THE GROCER

Joseph Wasey(1) was a grocer and mercer by trade. Grocers originally dealt in large quantities of imported commodities, the name being derived from merchants who imported goods in gross. Mercers, strictly, were those dealing in

Joseph Wasey's Token

silks and other costly materials, although the name came to be used by drapers generally, a trade often coupled with that of a grocer. These in fact were the two leading trades in the guild hierarchy, coming before even those of the gold- and silversmiths.

When Joseph married, it was to Mary, the daughter of Robert and Susan Woorts of Trunch and Bacton,[13] a family whose pedigree is traced back to 1482 and recorded in the 1664 Heralds' Visitation – probably the occasion calling for the Wasey brothers to disclaim their use of arms. During the troubled times of the Civil War and Interregnum small change had been in very short supply, a situation which continued for some time: so much so that Joseph Wasey, prospering in his business, found it necessary to issue his own farthing tokens.[14] On one side were the Mercers' Arms and the words 'Ioseph Wasey'; on the other, 'Nor Walsham' and his initials, 'I W'.

In addition to retail trading, he was almost certainly what would now be termed a wholesaler, dealing in commodities such as sugar, dried fruit and tobacco as well as ginger, cloves and other spices then used so liberally. Such items too as writing and wrapping paper were much in demand, as were candles, red lead, sealing wax, brushes, pewter, china and even glass.

When Joseph's elder brother, Richard, had died in 1678 making their father, Robert(1) his executor, he (Richard) willed his Tunstead and Beeston property be sold for the benefit of his younger children as they came of age. Since Robert(1) himself died in 1679, it fell to Joseph, as *his* executor, to arrange its sale. This was carried out in 1680, the property going, for £500, to William Linstead, a Norwich grocer, who is thought to have become the second husband of Richard Wasey's widow, Lydia.[15]

This being so, Richard's children will have been brought up in Norwich and it is no surprise therefore to find young Robert(3) there, setting up as a merchant, marrying a young woman called Elizabeth and having a family. Their children, a son, Robert, and two daughters, were christened at St Etheldred's and, alas, were buried there as infants.[16]

St Etheldred's stands towards the end of King Street, that historic thoroughfare where many a merchant's ancient, timbered and flint-clad house still stands. Part of its way runs parallel with the river, the main route, via Yarmouth, to other large British and European ports.

Norwich was then at the height of its prosperity and said to be beautiful, like 'a city in an orchard'. The diarist, Evelyn, described it as 'one of the largest and certainly after London, one of the noblest in England for it's venerable Cathedral, number of stately churches, cleanesse of streets, and buildings of flints so exquisitely headed and squared . . .'.

THE MARRIAGE AND DEATH OF THEIR SISTER MARY

It was during this period, on 3 June 1684, that Mary, the spinster sister of Robert, Richard and Joseph Wasey, fulfilled her promise to marry Edmund Themylthorpe Esq., tying the knot at Horstead, across the River Bure from Coltishall. Mr

Themylthorpe, a well-to-do attorney, had a house and considerable estate at Worstead, in addition to a house in Norwich where the couple chiefly lived. Mary's nephew, Robert Wasey(3), when setting up as a Norwich merchant, came to a business arrangement with this uncle, borrowing the sum of £70 to be repaid with interest.

Mary continued to employ Elizabeth Blackhead, her trusted servant of many years, who described Mary as being 'of a free and generous disposition', allowing her to entertain friends when they came to visit and talking over her private affairs with her. Indeed, Elizabeth claimed that several times she heard Mary, her mistress, tell Mr Themylthorpe that she believed she should never have married him if she (Elizabeth) had not persuaded her to it![17]

The newly-weds were not long together, however; a year later Mary, who must have been well into her forties, died, perhaps in childbirth. Mr Themylthorpe provided a handsome memorial with heraldic shield for her tomb when he buried her at St. Nicholas' church, North Walsham, on 4 July 1685.[18]

More deaths were to follow, those of the young Wasey males being particularly sad, bringing the family almost to extinction. Richard's eldest, Robert(3), the young Norwich merchant, died only four years after receiving the first half of his grandfather's legacy, and two years after receipt of the other £100. In his will he directed his North Walsham property be sold to provide for his wife and for 'maintayning of my daughter with good and sufficient meat drink cloathing . . . and alsoe allow her good educacon'.[19] Should they not survive, his brothers and sisters were to inherit, 'my sister Lynstead only excepted'. He also directed that Mr Edmund Themylthorpe be paid the 'seaventy pounds that I owe him with

Robert (3)'s Tomb, Tunstead

interest'. His body was brought back to Tunstead and buried in the chancel of its ancient church where the choir stalls now stand. Ten months later, at the end of the old year,[20] in February, Joseph(1) and Mary lost their eldest son, also named Robert(4), aged 25 years. Tragically these two cousins, taken in their prime, saw history repeat itself, their uncle, Robert(2), having also died a young man.

CAUSE TO REJOICE

The children of both Joseph and his brother Richard had been born during the early years of Charles II's restoration and grew up in an era of gaiety not to mention profligacy, much tempered by the chasteness of puritan Norfolk. As they grew to adulthood, however, fear and suspicion prevailed with the threat of Catholicism returning. Subsequently, with the death of the king, it became a distinct probability when his Romanist brother, James II, came to the throne, making it obvious that he intended to force, by one means or another, the 'old religion' on an unwilling nation.

Demonstrations against the king's arbitrary measures welled up throughout the land, not least in Norfolk, and there were ugly scenes in Norwich itself. Eventually, in 1688, a fearful but determined nation invited the king's daughter, the Princess Mary, and her husband the Prince of Orange to take the throne, and there was rejoicing from the Protestants of the land.

At their North Walsham home Joseph and Mary Wasey had cause to rejoice too when one of their two surviving sons, William, married Bridget, the youngest daughter of Margaret and William Durrant Esq., an armigerous family seated at nearby Scottow. The marriage took place in the fine flint church there on 23 October 1688,[21] just two weeks before William of Orange landed on the south coast. Subsequent generations remained closely associated with the Durrants and allied families, in particular Bridget's sister, Margaret, who married Robert Blake Esq.[22]

With William and Mary on the throne, stability and prosperity returned to England once more. William Wasey too prospered as an attorney which, at that

Scottow Hall and Church

time, involved conveyancing and the management of property: collecting rents and dues, deducting taxes and sums for maintenance and also the lending of money on interest, all of which subsequently became the province of estate agents, banks and building societies.

At 20, William Wasey was already a man of substance having lately purchased property for £522 in various nearby manors. He decided now, upon his marriage, to purchase a house and what must have been a considerable estate in Worstead called Topcliffe's from a Mr Edward Cooke of London. Cook, we learn from a lawsuit brought several years later,[23] had been approached, in 1686, by one Miles Baispoole of Worstead who wished to borrow £1,000. He assured Mr Cook that the property put forward as collateral 'was of ye yearly value of one hundred pounds and free from all incumbrances . . .', whereupon Mr Cooke granted the loan with much of the property, including Topcliffe's, as security.

When Baispoole failed to repay the loan, Edward Cooke, as learned from Wasey's testimony, 'did enter upon ye . . . premises and . . . found . . . Miles Baispoole had deceived him in ye value of ye lands and ye quantity thereof . . .', there being some 18 acres short of what was claimed at the time of the loan. Mr Cooke, 'finding himself thus deceived and abused . . . and likely to lose six or seven hundred pounds by ye . . . mortgage . . . applied himself to Miles Baispoole for satisfaction . . . and threatened to proceed against him . . .'. Baispoole agreed to pay £200 towards the debt but only £35 was in fact paid, and as time went on Baispoole made 'claims and pretences' to the premises.

In due course, however, when Mr Cooke finally felt satisfied that Baispoole had settled the claims 'he, living at a distance from ye . . . premises, did endeavour to sell . . . and for a considerable time could not meet with any purchaser that would give any more than six hundred pounds . . .'. It was at this point that William Wasey, about to marry and obviously keen to possess such a desirable estate, 'hearing the same was upon sale and wanting a house for his owne habitacon and believing that all ye claimes . . . by Miles Baispoole was quieted', agreed to purchase for the sum of £700.

The Baispoole family, however, continued to give trouble, claiming the premises were subject to mortgages, etc., to which Wasey countered '. . . they well know ye said mortgage money was paid and satisfied . . . above twenty years since'. Over the years other claims were made, such as an entitlement to a rent charge which, as Wasey was to assert, 'they well know if there be any such, ye same was fraudulent and [he added] . . . to keep [me] further in ye darke they refuse to [disclose] what such rent charge . . . is . . .'.

All of which explains why William and Bridget made their home for most of their married life at Brunstead (or Brumstead), five miles away, where the family still held property. Their five children were baptised there, only two of whom survived: a son, William(2), and a daughter, Elizabeth. It explains, too, why William found it necessary to borrow a sum of money from one Elizabeth Coulson of Thorpe-next-Norwich:[24] fighting the Baispoole family through the courts was an expensive business.

RETIREMENT AND MORE LEGAL ACTION

Joseph Wasey(1) was now nearing sixty and his other son, Joseph(2), was managing, for the most part, their grocery and estate business interests. They

were evidently accustomed to lending money on interest (the normal method of
investment in the days before banks and building societies) but these arrangements
sometimes went wrong. In June 1688 one George Ward of Brooke in south-east
Norfolk, 'having occasion for a summe of five hundred pounds applied himself to . . .
Joseph Wasey the elder to borrow the same', offering land and property as security.

All seemed well enough at first, despite the fact that Mr Ward's property was
already mortgaged to three parties and he needed the loan to pay them off. He
'made a voluntary affidavit before a Master of Chancery extraordinary . . . that
there were no more incumbrances of any kind . . .', whereupon the loan was made
and 'Joseph Wasey the elder [was] to have had and received the interest . . . and
the principall upon the same . . .'.

But, says Wasey's evidence in a lawsuit brought in 1693,[25] 'George Ward . . .
refused to pay . . . in his lifetime . . .'. His widow and son subsequently also failed
to pay, claiming there were incumbrances but, said Wasey, they 'refuse to discover
[state] what premorgages . . . [there are] . . . and for what summes . . . which
actinges and doeings . . . are contrary to . . . justice . . .'.

In 1699 there was cause for another lawsuit. Joseph(2), who liked to conduct
business affairs over a friendly drink, had been duped by a distantly-related cleric
he employed to serve the cure of Tunstead, a living acquired by sequestration for
an unpaid debt as a result of yet another action[26] brought successfully at the
Norfolk Assizes.

William Wasey, his brother, meanwhile, had come to the end of his patience
with the Baispoole family over the Topcliffe property; for years they had '. . .
sette up . . . titles [to] weary [him] out with tedious and vexatious suits . . .'.
Finally, in 1700, William took his case to Chancery with the expectation that
Miles Baispoole 'shall be charged and clogged in Equity'.

Baispoole had, claimed William, through deceit and contrivance, conveyed the
property (subsequently purchased by himself) to Mr Cooke as freehold, while
over the years he made continual pretences to incumbrances of one sort or
another. The Baispoole family, asserted Wasey, should 'surrender ye same' and he
requested that they may, 'by Injuncon . . . be stayed of further proceedings . . .',
for he had 'expected quietly to have [and] enjoy . . . ye . . . premises'. Instead, he
was threatened he should 'never live in quiet' unless he give them 'a considerable
summe of money . . .'.

THE SADDEST CHRISTMAS

At the end of August 1700, Mary, the wife of Joseph Wasey senior, died. On
2 September, at St Nicholas' Church, Joseph had her buried, not in a shroud of
wool, but in one of linen, considering her worthy of the 'fine' of £2 10s incurred
for so doing.[27] The church accounts record that year: 'We certifie that Mary wife
of Mr Joseph Wasey, and Anne wife of Wm. King were both buried in Linning
this year and all other p[er]sons in woollen'.

More sorrow came three months later when Joseph's married son, William,
was suddenly stricken ill. As he had not made a will, one was drawn up hurriedly
on Christmas Eve, the night before he died, and dictated to relatives as they
gathered about him[28]: 'I William Wasey of Worstead give . . . unto Bridgett my
loveing wife all . . . my Messuages lands [etc.] . . . in Brunstead Stalham Ingham

Lessingham Worstead Westwicke and Sooly . . . untill such time as William Wasey my sonne shall attaine to his age of one and twenty . . . [when he should inherit, providing he paid] unto Elizabeth Wasey my Daughter . . . one thousand pounds . . . att or in the Porch of the Parish Church of Brunstead . . .'.

The property in Scottow and elsewhere, in which 'Bridgett my wife have a disposing power',[29] was also bequeathed to their son after her death. To Bridget he left all his stock 'within doores as without' and to the poor of each of the parishes of Brunstead, Worstead and North Walsham he gave forty shillings.

He died the next day, aged 32, bringing the saddest Christmas possible to the grieving family. Three days later he was buried in St Nicholas' Church, North Walsham, where, on a black marble slab bearing the Wasey arms impaled with Durrant, the following inscription was made: 'Here lyeth the body of William Wacey, gent son of Joseph Wasey & of Mary. He was born 11 Nov. 1668 & died 25 Dec. 1700'.

Nine months later, almost exactly a year after his wife's death, Joseph Wasey senior left this world for the next. Only a son, two grandchildren and his nephews were left bearing the name Wasey to follow his hearse to the grave where his tomb, with arms displayed, remains extant near the chancel of St Nicholas' Church. Unconcerned apparently for his soul or propriety, Joseph made no bequest to the poor in his will. He left all his property in 'North Walsham, Swanton Abbott, East Ruston, Worstead & Smalburgh' together with his 'mortgages & securityes for money bills bonds & all other my debts & P'sonall estate' to his only surviving son, Joseph(2), making him executor. The will was made in June that year[30] and his first witness was his nephew, John Wasey.

Joseph Wasey (1)'s Tomb, North Walsham

TWO 'GENTLEMEN' GROCERS

When Joseph the elder died in 1701, his son was 38 years old and his nephew about 26. These two Wasey cousins, Joseph(2) and John, continued to live out their lives in or near North Walsham: the only male members of the family to do so. Joseph's brother, William, recently deceased, left a son, William(2), who would soon be going to school in Norwich, eventually to become a London physician. John's eldest brother, Robert, the Norwich merchant, had died in 1687 without surviving sons; his next brother, Richard, also of Norwich, had died in 1681 and more is learned of his closest brother, Joseph(3), from his widow's testimony, later, in a lawsuit.[10] He, she says, at about sixteen years of age 'went into the service of King William and continued in the wars and remained beyond seas under the service of [him] and the late Queen Anne above twelve years'. No mention is made of children.

Joseph Wasey(2), as an only surviving son, inherited his father's estates and grocery business (employing his cousin, Robert Postle, for many years). He was also bequeathed property in Trunch by his maternal uncle, William Woorts, who died without issue.[31] His income therefore derived from these sources and latterly he was designated 'gentleman'.

John Wasey, also a grocer, was married, soon after his uncle's death, to Susanna, the daughter of Stephen and Susannah Bunn. Mr Bunn was churchwarden at St Nicholas', where John and Susanna took their vows, and here they returned regularly throughout the years of Queen Anne's reign to christen their large family. But, as with the queen herself, they were cruelly required, almost as frequently, to bring back their little ones for burial.

THE AFFAIR OF THE 'LOST' RECEIPT

Bad blood continued between Joseph Wasey(2) and the Revd Charles Preston. There had been a kinship with this gentleman since Elizabeth, the widow of Joseph's deceased uncle, William Woorts of Trunch, married this clergyman's brother, Sir Isaac Preston.[32] The affair began when Wasey, who was not unused to taking legal action when necessary, won a lawsuit for unpaid debts of £40 from a Revd Wrentmore with the sequestration of his Tunstead living until the debts were paid. Wasey subsequently appointed the Revd Preston to serve the cure of Tunstead for a fee of £8 and, during that time, sold and delivered to him goods and merchandise to the value of £24 11s. When the bill remained unpaid, Wasey sued.

In his evidence against Preston,[26] Joseph claimed that one day, while talking business at Preston's house, Preston had promised to pay the outstanding amount of £16 11s 'and did then desire [me] to sign him a discharge for ye same [saying] he would immediately fetch ye money to pay . . .'. And so Joseph 'signed ye . . . receipt and intended to keep ye same in [his] hands until he [Preston] should fetch down ye money . . .'.

But, claimed Joseph, 'continuing in discourse [we] fell to drinking together . . . and ye said receipt lying by your Orator [Wasey] . . . Charles Preston did in a consealed manner take away ye same . . . which [I] soon after missed and did enquire for . . . but . . . Preston denied that he had ye same so that [I] thought [it] had been casually lost'.

Wasey went on to say and 'expressly charge it to be true that . . . Preston did not pay ye summe', or any part of it, and so he brought Preston to trial at the Norfolk Assizes whereupon, to Wasey's astonishment, 'Charles Preston did produce ye said receipt'. Taken unawares and 'not expecting such dealings from . . . Preston', Wasey 'had not . . . witnesses ready to prove ye money was not paid . . .' and 'was nonsuited in ye . . . Cause'. These 'practices' of Preston and Jacob his son 'did so provoke and irritate' Wasey that he admitted he 'might [have] use[d] some passionate expressions against them for ye said ffoule practice'.

Consequently Charles Preston threatened to sue Joseph for slander. Lamenting that Preston 'did intend to run [me] to great charges', Joseph countered that he, likewise, had several causes for actions against the Preston family – for slander and scandalous words spoken against him.

The position was becoming so out of hand that to 'appease such mutual Actions', Joseph claimed that he and Preston, with the mediation of friends, came to an agreement on 29 September 1699 setting out that Preston should pay the outstanding sum of £16 11s, acquitting and discharging Wasey from 'all Actions or causes for slander'. Joseph, likewise, absolved the Preston family and agreed that upon receipt of the sum concerned 'which was to be paid in some few days' he would give Preston a general discharge: which agreement, Joseph said, was mutually signed by the parties 'and left in ye hands of Sir Edmund Doyly Bart'.

But, said Wasey, they 'have neglected to perform ye . . . Agreement and do expressly refuse . . . in as much as . . . Edmund Doyley who could prove [it] . . . is since dead',[33] whereby, complained Joseph, he had not only lost the benefit of Sir Edmund's testimony, but also 'ye . . . Agreement . . . cannot be found'. At this, Joseph claimed, the Preston family took 'advantage of ye . . . misfortune to threaten to Sue . . . giving out in speeches that ye . . . receipt signed by [me] as aforesaid will cutt [me] of all [my] demands . . .'. He therefore appealed to the High Court of Chancery for a 'Writ of Injunction to stop proceedings at common law . . .'.

CHARLES PRESTON'S DEFENCE

In his defence, Charles Preston claimed that on 13 June 1699 he had gone to Wasey's dwelling house in North Walsham and reckoned with him regarding the outstanding debts. Although he previously claimed Wasey had not paid him for serving Tunstead Church, he now agreed Wasey had allowed him £8 2s 6d for this service.

Regarding the shop debt, he claimed that 'some time after . . . to wit on . . . the 29th day of August' he went with his son, Jacob, to Wasey's house, five miles from his own, 'and carried money with [him] with intent to pay. . .'. But, said he, Wasey 'not being then at home', Wasey having at the same time gone to *his* house, he 'forthwith returned home' where he found Wasey, who had been asked by his wife Mary 'to tarry till they returned home again'.

Then, claimed Mr Preston, he paid the outstanding amount 'at ye very same day and place . . .', Wasey first making allowance for the sum of £8 10s, being a debt due from the Revd Benjamin Wrentmore[34] to Preston 'for boarding horse meat and other things'. Wasey had, apparently, on winning his case against Wrentmore, undertaken to pay this at Wrentmore's request, on being granted, not only the sequestered living of Tunstead, but 'also another Living . . . of greater value to wit at Swafield . . .' with its profits.

Preston stuck to his claim that he had paid and received a receipt from Wasey. Mary, his wife, of course, supported him, as did their son, Jacob, who added that his father, 'minding . . . to pay ye Complainant his debt and to be quit of him sent [him, Jacob] . . . to Kipping Fair above twenty miles off his dwelling house . . . to receive some monies due to . . . Charles Preston from ye inhabitants and parishioners of Little Massingham where . . . Charles . . . hath a Living'.

He went, he said, and met several of these people at the fair, receiving about £20 which he brought home to his father. Jacob claimed his father then paid Wasey, who 'carried away with him . . . the said eight pounds . . . [he, Jacob] tarrying in his company till he went away . . .'.

It was not the first time Charles Preston had been tardy in paying his debts to Wasey. This time, however, unable to prove the receipt was obtained by chicanery, Wasey failed to pursue the action and, in 1703, the order was given that the 'Plaintiff's Bill do stand dismissed out of this Court for want of prosecucon' – with costs of £17 15s 8d, a large sum in those days.

PARISH AFFAIRS

The Wasey cousins were active in parish affairs during the early years of the new century. Joseph was churchwarden in 1702, and both were overseers at various times. In 1705 the records reveal[35]:

Item: the s^d Joseph Wasey standeth charged by one bill of assessment dated 25th day of August 1705 wth the Collection of £48 13s 9¾ [and] Moneys distributed by the s^d Joseph Wasey the 14 weekes Ended the 30th day of Sept. 1705 [some of which were]:–

Pd for Indentures for Riches child	3s	8d
pd for Hen^tt Helsdon quarters rent	7s	6d
pd for shirts for [?]Wicks children	3s	7d
pd for a shroud for Will. . .	2s	8d
pd Mr. Tompson for John Woodhouses rent	40s	0d
pd to myself ye debt due to me att Easter 1705	5s	2¾
pd Mr. Pell [the doctor] for curing Batchellors leg	40s	0d
pd Mr. Pell for Curing of Batchellors boy	28s	0d

Overseers were appointed yearly and at North Walsham each fulfilled his duties in a three-monthly period. John took duty the following year: 'Money distributed by John Wasey in 13 weeks ended September 22 1706'. And the fiscal year concluded with: 'The accomptants stand charged by 4 rates wth the collection of £175 18s 2¼'.

In 1708 John and Susanna had another son and, for the third time, the name Joseph was chosen; he was destined, despite frequent epidemics and lack of medical knowledge, to survive. Before long they had another daughter, naming her after her mother. Although she lived to delight them for two years, in 1712 she died, three weeks after they buried little Anna, aged 6. Their next daughter arrived at the end of the year, the second to be named Lydia; she survived to become the writer's 4th great grandmother.

In 1714 the county elections took place in Norfolk, with Thomas de Grey, Sir

Jacob Astley, Erasmus Earle and Sir Ralph Hare as candidates. John Wasey apparently owned insufficient freehold property to be eligible for a vote, but his cousin, Joseph, polled for Hare and Earle, the Tory candidates.[36]

John and Susannah were to have only one more surviving child: a girl, named after her mother. With the bearing, in 1717, of her tenth child, Susannah's life, as well as the child's, was forfeited and they were buried together on 2 June in North Walsham's so familiar churchyard.

Joseph Wasey(2) became ill at about this time, perhaps from the stress of the long, drawn-out and unsuccessful litigation. During the course of yet another lawsuit, two old friends were deponents: Robert Wade of Scottow, gentleman, and Edward Fuller, a friend of about forty years' standing. Both declared Wasey to be of good circumstances and reputation. Joseph, these friends and Mr Edmund Themylthorpe, his deceased aunt Mary's widower, were, it seems, all on good terms. Regularly on market days they met at North Walsham to enjoy a drink together, Mr Themylthorpe coming habitually from his house at Worstead where he, more often than not, spent part of each week 'except such time as [he] was at London about his business'.[37]

On such good terms were they, that Joseph failed to press Themylthorpe for the second half of the legacy due to him from the will of his deceased uncle, Robert(2). He had received, at 21, the first £100, but as his aunt had become Mistress Themylthorpe and died within the year, the other half of the legacy was never paid. Since Joseph was not apparently pressed for money and he valued Mr Themylthorpe's friendship, there the matter appears to have rested, until, in 1714, Mr Themylthorpe died – without paying the various legacies charged to his deceased wife's estate.

This was when John Wasey's sister-in-law, Anne, left in poor circumstances at her husband's death, took advantage of the 'legal aid' of the day which granted, gratis, an attorney and council to act for her. This enabled her to sue for the legacy bequeathed by that same uncle to her husband's brother, Richard Wasey(2), at whose death and as heir and executor, her husband, Joseph(3), had become entitled.[38]

Anne claimed that her husband several times requested the legacy of Mr Themylthorpe and had eventually, in 1714, employed, as attorney, a Mr Clive to write to him. Mr Themylthorpe replied: 'Mr. Clive, I have been ill a great while or else should not be so long in paying [the] . . . just debts, and when restored to health will give a further and satisfactory answer . . .'.[10]

But, according to Anne, Joseph her husband 'being soon after the receipt of this letter much afflicted with sickness did not . . . receive the . . . legacy' and Mr Themylthorpe, still declining in his health, 'did not in his life time pay it off'. Her husband had subsequently requested the legacy of Themylthorpe's son, Charles, who 'did not object to the justness of such his demand but only desired time to look over his papers'.

Anne maintained that since her husband's death she had several times asked Mr Themylthorpe to pay her the £200, only to receive the reply that she or her late husband 'ought sooner to have claimed the . . . legacy . . . and that this being a stale demand they are not obliged to pay . . .'. Anne, however, won her case and was awarded, with interest and costs, £469 6s, a fortune for her.[39]

THE DEMISE OF JOSEPH WASEY(2)

In about the year 1716, Joseph Wasey(2) left North Walsham to take up residence in his house at nearby Trunch. Within a short time, however, his health deteriorating, Joseph was made a guest at the Worstead home of Mr Spencer Chapman, the second husband of his brother William's widow. One day Mr Themylthorpe's son, Charles, visited them with two friends, Thomas Berney Esq., of Lynn, and Edmund Lock, and the question of the legacies arose – probably as a consequence of Anne Wasey's successful lawsuit.[37]

During the discussion, Mr Lock asked Joseph, who was known now as 'of Trunch', why he had not received his uncle's legacy. Joseph answered that he had often requested it of Mr Themylthorpe senior, but the reply was always that there were insufficient assets from his uncle's estate. Mr Lock went on to question whether, if there were sufficient assets, he would not have got his legacy long before. The matter, however, was never settled and within a year Joseph, who remained at the home of Mr Chapman throughout his illness, died, at the age of fifty-four.

Joseph's will made bequests first to his cousins, John Wasey and family, and to his niece, Elizabeth Wasey, who, as stepdaughter to Mr Chapman, still lived with him at Worstead; but the bulk of his fortune was bequeathed to his nephew, William Wasey(2). After leaving £20 to the poor of North Walsham, he appointed 'the Revd. Mr. Thomas Jefferey the present Vicar of Northwalsham . . . to preach a Sermon at my ffuneral', giving him five guineas for his trouble, and adding that 'if he be dead then I appoint the Revd. Mr. John Jeffery Rector of Trunch . . . to preach the same'.[40]

The bequest to John was the messuage 'wherein . . . John Wasey now dwelleth . . . in Northwalsham . . .' plus another messuage (probably The Three Mariners) with its appurtenances, then occupied by a Mr Wenn. Also, to be held until John's son, Joseph(4), reached the age of 21, were four closes of land comprising about 16 acres.

John had probably lived in the first of these properties since his marriage. It will be remembered that Joseph's father, Joseph Wasey(1), had become trustee to the children of his elder brother Richard. Perhaps when it came to availing his youngest nephew with his share, at 21, he had been rather slow to carry out this directive. It would explain why, five months after his uncle's death in 1701, John was able to marry, the hypothesis being that John's cousin, Joseph(2), had made a house available to him in lieu. Perhaps this was why at *his* death it finally became John's.

PROSPERITY

After the death of his wife and cousin, John no doubt threw all his energies into the running of the business. Before the days of glass-fronted shops, wooden shutters opened outwards on fine days, to form a display counter. In bad weather customers adjusted their eyes to the gloom afforded by the small, deeply recessed windows, to view wares stacked on shelves around the room, while bolts of fine worsteds and other materials were displayed along the counter. From the Overseers' Accounts we find cloth was supplied for the inmates of the town's poorhouse: 'Mr Wasey for cloth, fear nothing [a stout coating material] and other things 9s 11½'.[41]

Arrangements had to be made for the transport of stock – bales of cloth, buttons, braid, ribbons and thread from London merchants, as well as imported goods, such as tobacco, sugar, spices, dried fruit, linseed oil and Dutch cheeses, shipped up the coast to Yarmouth. There were the workmen and apprentices to instruct and control, and the wares of travelling salesmen to inspect. Long hours of bookwork, using quill pens, were required, often by candle or rushlight. Parish duties were undertaken, which were obligatory and time consuming, although they afforded companionship in organizing the town's affairs. Roger Primrose and Henry Francis were two other grocers in the town, and Micah Ransome, a miller, was another contemporary.

One wonders if John had similar problems to those of Mr Ransome, who was an elder of the Quaker sect, one of a conscientious and hard-working body of people. The story goes that once, when work at the mill was underway, the men were being irritatingly slow over it, and so Micah, while they were at dinner, rubbed thyme over the work. When they returned, they complained 'someone has muddled with our work, it stinks of thyme'; to which Micah replied, he 'thought it did stink, very much of time'. The men apparently took offence and left, much to Micah's satisfaction, who thereupon employed quicker workmen![42]

In 1721 John Wasey decided to insure his business stock, taking out a policy with the Sun Fire Insurance Company: 'John Wasey of North Walsham . . . Norfolk Grocer for his goods & Merchandize in his Dwelling House only . . .'.[43] The following year he made his will.[44] Perhaps he realized that, like so many of his kinsmen, he would not make old bones; if so, he was proved right. Five years later, in 1727, he died, leaving three teenage children. In his will, he referred first to the bequest of his '. . . kinsman, Joseph Wasey late of Trunch' in which he 'devised to me all yt Messuage wherein I . . . do now dwell', etc., which, at his own death, was to be shared by his children. He left legacies of £250 to each of his daughters at 21, providing they make to his son Joseph(4) such release as 'he shall be advised necessary . . . of their Title . . . in ye . . . premises'. In addition his son was bequeathed 'my two Butchers Stalls situate . . . in ye Butchery in North Walsham'. The messuage 'known by ye name of ye Three Mariners'[45] went to his daughters, while the residue was devised to his executrix 'my loving Sister in Law, Lydia Linstead',[46] requesting she invest the sums specified for his children until they reached 21 years, giving her £100 'for & towards her trouble & Care in Managing ye trust . . .'.

THE FOURTH GENERATION

In the year following John's death, his three surviving children can be found insuring their joint property with the Sun Fire Insurance Company.[47] Of this, the fourth generation, Joseph(4) married Mary, the daughter of John Greene, gentleman, of North Walsham, whose property she inherited in 1733.[48] This was probably the J. Greene who was witness to John Wasey's will and steward of the Manor Court. They appear to have moved to Worstead, where, over the years, they baptised two sons, William(4) and Joseph(5), and four daughters, Alice, Mary, Ellen and Elizabeth.

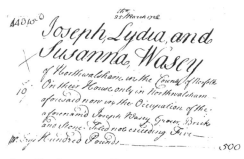

Sun Fire Insurance Entry

In 1734, when John's daughter, Lydia, reached the age of 21, she too married. She took for her husband Daniel, the son of the Revd Rowland Clarke, rector at nearby Skeyton and Brampton, and it was in the little thatched church at Brampton that they plighted their troth.[49] Four years later Lydia's father-in-law officiated at the wedding of her sister Susanna when she married Joseph Saul. Both sisters endeavoured to perpetuate the name Wasey in their respective families and it is due to the persistence of Daniel and Lydia that it survives in their family to this day.

Under the provisions of his father's will, Joseph(4) was now obliged to make over to his sisters a sum of money in return for the family home and business. This necessitated its sale, which took place in 1734 to John Rendall, one of four sitting tenants.[50]

Four years later Daniel and Lydia Clarke sold most of the property known as the Three Mariners.[51] In the transaction Daniel is described as 'Mercer of Northwalsham', suggesting that perhaps he too for a while had entered the Wasey family business. By 1745, however, the couple had removed to Cley-next-the-Sea, and North Walsham ceased to be a permanent home to members of the Wasey family for the first time in nearly a hundred years.[52]

The Porch of St Nicholas Church, North Walsham

Chapter Two: The Physician

William Wasey(2), the other male member of the fourth generation, was to become the patriarch of the family which settled in Westminster and later still in Berkshire. He was only 9 and his sister, Elizabeth, 6 years old when their father died on Christmas Day, 1700. Within a year all four of their grandparents too were dead and their mother had married again to Mr Spencer Chapman, a well-to-do brewer of Worstead. Here in this little town, famed around the world for the cloth it produced, the passing of King William III was observed and Queen Anne's coronation celebrated, before William was sent away to Norwich Grammar School at the age of about 11 years.

The school building, which stands in the Upper Close, hard by the lovely old cathedral, had seen many pupils come and go since its foundation in the 14th century. Now, as the 18th century unfolded, William watched the dignified houses being built in the Lower Close, leading down to the river, where he and his school chums rowed in summer and skated in winter. During those years William came to know the old walled city well, seeing quite a lot of his maternal aunt, Elizabeth, married to Joseph Greenaway, a Norwich grocer. Their son, also named William, was a friend with whom he remained on close terms for the rest of his life.

News from home in 1706 told of the arrival of a half-sister named after their mother, Bridget. She, alas, lived for only eight months and just over a year later their mother too died. Possibly William, at 16, was allowed to accompany his stepfather and the funeral cortège to North Walsham where Bridget was buried with her first husband. The adversity experienced by William appeared to strengthen his character and, being the only surviving son, he was to benefit materially as heir or co-heir to several estates as a consequence.

In 1708 William was admitted, aged 17, to Caius College, Cambridge, and in 1712 he gained his BA degree. His was probably the 6-year Parker Scholarship,[1] for those going in for medical studies, which ran until 1715. When this was completed, he stayed to secure his MA degree before transferring, on 1 October 1716, to Europe's leading medical university, Leydon, in Holland.

When, two years later, William's uncle, Joseph Wasey of Trunch, died, making him his heir and executor, it was necessary to return to England where he proved the will the following year.[2] It fell to William to ensure that bequests made to his kinsmen, John Wasey and family, at North Walsham were complied with, and that his sister Elizabeth received the sum of £500 in the porch of North Walsham Church. He himself became possessed of land and property in 'Smallburgh, Northwalsham, Swanton Abbott, East Ruston, Happisburgh, Brunstead, Trunch, Knapton, Gymingham, Mondesly, Sco Ruston and Worstead', as well as the 'goods Cattle and Chattles' not already disposed of.

By September 1719 William was termed 'doctor of physic' in an indenture in which he sells to his maternal uncle, Thomas, freehold property in Scottow bequeathed him by his grandfather, William Durrant.[3]

Soon after, he and a cousin's widow, Elizabeth Postle, decided to sue Mr Edmund Themylthorpe's son, Charles, for the legacies which should have been received from the will of Robert Wasey(2) many years before: in Elizabeth's case, by her husband; and in William's, by his uncle, Joseph Wasey of Trunch. Anne Wasey, after all, had succeeded in winning her case.[4] The legacy would help considerably towards the still-outstanding mortgage-debt incurred by William's father to Mistress Coulson of Norwich, and so lawyers were instructed to make out their case.[5]

Wasey did not return to Leydon but began, presumably, to gain practical experience under the tutelage of established physicians. He had the advantage of his education at Caius, famed for its teaching in 'physic', as well as his Leydon training, and it was a measure of his progress that he had sufficiently impressed philanthropist, Mr Henry Hoare, with his abilities, to be soon accepted as physician to a proposed new hospital in Westminster.

A HOSPITAL AT WESTMINSTER

Henry Hoare, a rich merchant banker, and three other like-minded friends had met at St Dunstan's Coffee House in Fleet Street early in 1716 to discuss the need for a hospital in Westminster. Of the whole population of England and Wales, roughly 13 per cent was crowded into London, Westminster and the surrounding area, where the only two existing general hospitals, which survived from the monastic foundations, were St Bartholomew's at Smithfield and St Thomas', across the river in Southwark.

Although Westminster was traditionally the abode of the royal family and the nobility, they had, in recent years, moved further north and west, leaving their mansions in the fields around the Abbey and Royal Palace to be divided up as dwellings for numerous poor families. It was extremely unhealthy: low lying and subject to flooding from the Thames. The marshy waters merged alike with well water and with sewage from the countless privies of the mean huddled tenements, causing frequent outbreaks of such maladies as typhoid, malaria and the common flux.

The area was isolated too – inaccessible from London, except by boat, or by entering a narrow gate into King Street, through a long, dark, dirty passage, part of the old crumbling palace complex, and then out again by yet another gate. It was certainly in stark contrast to the bracing air of Norfolk's countryside known to William Wasey.

To Mr Hoare and his friends it was clear that something must be done to help the teeming poor of the area when sick. Since parish relief was often ineffectual and those falling into debt were clapped into prison, many were driven to begging on the streets. Mr Hoare made the first subscription of £10 and others followed suit according to their pockets. Appeals were made for goods such as bedding, clothes, furniture and kitchenware, while voluntary assistance was sought from apothecaries, physicians and surgeons.

Dr Alexander Stuart, also a one-time Leydon student, promised to become physician to the new hospital. They acquired a matron, and early in 1720 a house was rented in Petty France. An inscription in gold letters displayed: 'Infirmary for the Sick and Needy' and the first hospital in London to be supported entirely by voluntary contributions was founded.

On 4 May that year Dr Wasey was appointed second physician and, a week later, their first patient was admitted: John Kelly, suffering from 'Evill in the joints and Scurvy'. In less than a month Kelly had improved sufficiently to be discharged. Members of the Royal Household became enthusiastic subscribers: the King, the Prince of Wales and his wife, Caroline of Ansbach, their daughters and the royal governess.

THE CASE OF THE UNPAID LEGACIES

Later that year a commission was 'issued out of . . . His Majestys High Court of Chancery' before four worthies at 'The Sign of The Rampant Horse in Norwich' regarding the suit brought by William Wasey and Elizabeth Postle against Charles Themylthorpe.[5] One witness was Mrs Postle's son, Robert, aged 22, whose status was 'gentleman of Ingham'. He described the visit he made a few months before, to Worstead, when he asked Mr. Themylthorpe for the legacy never paid to his father and now due to his mother. But, said he, 'Mr. Themylthorpe gave a very flighty answer, saying he knew nothing of the matter . . .'.

Subsequently Robert 'did by the direction of his mother, deliver a letter . . . to the . . . dwellinghouse of . . . Mrs. Themylthorpe'. A servant carried it to her mistress, who 'came. . . into the hall and opened [it] saying she did not know who this Mrs. Postle was [and that she] knew little of the matter but if Mrs. Postle would come to her house in Norwich she would talk further with her about it'.

The Square, Worstead

William's sister, Elizabeth Wasey, recalled, when questioned, the incident at their stepfather's house when their uncle, Joseph of Trunch, had asked Mr Themylthorpe for the £100 legacy still due to him. Other witnesses told of Themylthorpe's father (Edmund) having been possessed of several estates 'in the right of . . . Mary [née Wasey] his wife'; one was her servant, Elizabeth Blackhead.

After a week's adjournment, Blackhead gave further evidence, saying she 'believes . . . Mr Themylthorpe after his intermarriage with the said Mary received the rents and profits of [the] real estate . . . given her by . . . her brother . . .' (Robert Wasey(2)).

In another statement, however, she retracted, saying she 'doth not know or even heard that her . . . mistress had any personal estate except household goods and apparel and about twenty pounds in gold', claiming that during the time she lived with her mistress she '. . . never heard or knew any person . . . [who] came to pay her . . . interest money due upon mortgage bond or other security . . .', although she was 'frequently entrusted . . . with the keys of her Closett, Cabinett and Trunks'.

Blackhead's reneging was probably as a result of realizing the prudence of backing the Themylthorpe brother and sisters whom she had known 'from their infancies' (and to whom she had probably been nurse) rather than the beneficiaries of her one-time mistress, dead now for 35 years. Evidence was brought to show that the fortune of Mary Themylthorpe (née Wasey) had been 'considerably advanced' as residuary legatee of her brother's will, out of which legacies amounted to only £525, from a personal estate of £2,500 and real estate worth £150 per annum.

It was shown that Edmund Themylthorpe's heirs, having proved the will and possessed themselves of his estate, were well able to pay all his debts and legacies 'with a great overplus'. The plaintiffs asserted they had several times requested the legacies: in William's case, 'soon after [his] return from beyond sea [Leydon] but they refuse to pay . . . pretending they have not assets sufficient . . .'.

Eventually the court ordered that as there *were* sufficient assets, the defendants should pay what was due: the legacies, with interest at £5 per cent per annum, and costs.

The Themylthorpe family, however, sued for a re-hearing,[4] arguing their dissatisfaction because of the length of time that had elapsed 'being above thirty four years, the legacies ought to be presumed satisfied . . .'. They claimed they had had to borrow in order to pay Anne Wasey as a result of her suit two years earlier and they exhibited a schedule of outgoings incurred at their father's death, including such items as:

paid the Overseer of St. Johns Parish and for sweeping the streets due Xmas 1714	00 02 05
paid the Watch and the City Waites	00 05 00
paid Mr. Calver half a years interest of £500 bond due from the Testator 18 Dec. last	01 10 00
paid Simpson the Butchers bill	14 19 00
paid for the lamplight	00 04 00

paid Mr. Cooke for a years rent of his house in Conisford taxes deducted £2	18 00 00
paid Anne Peartree a Servant her wages	04 10 00
paid his mans wages	01 15 00
paid to Thomas Raylton Esq. what was due to Lord Sandwich for Aylsham Mannor & Mills . . .	48 11 00
paid for Probate of the Testators Will	04 15 10
paid Mr. Wm. Lovick the Apothecary's bill	22 11 06
paid to Mr. Norgate for the use of the well & close in St. John's Timberhill to Michas. 1714	00 04 00
Allowed on account of Frettenham Estate for pr[incipal] mony due to Mrs. Easton on Mortgages	600 00 00

It will be remembered that Edmund Themylthorpe was a successful attorney, hence there was an equally lengthy schedule showing considerable receipts and other assets, which included the following:

Cash in the House when ye Testator dyed	34 13 08
Of the Overseers of Tombland half a years rent . . .	18 00
Received for a horse sold	07 00 00
An Estate in ffrettenham was ordered by his Will to be sold and it was	1450 00 00
Moneys taken up at Interest towards payment of Testators Debts on the Estate at Northwalshamwhich is much more than the Reversion thereof is worth	700 00 00
Of Ash Windham Esq. A Bill of Charges	04 05 00
Of Jacob Preston Esq. for the like	03 08 06
A Barn sold . . . belonging to the Testator at Northwalsham	35 00 00

Included was an inventory of their 20-room mansion in which the plate alone amounted to £137 0s 6d.

The persistence shown by the Themylthorpe family, however, paid off when the court decreed that His Lordship 'saw no cause to give the Plaintiffs any relief in Equity and doth therefore Order that the matter . . . doe stand dismissed out of this Court . . .'. Nevertheless, some sympathy was shown to Wasey's claim, since it was ordered: '. . . but without Costs'. Equally, the Themylthorpes were not to be losers, having the order '. . . the ten pounds deposit on obtaining this re-hearing are to be repaid to this Defendant'.

Unable to use the legacy to help clear their father's debt to Elizabeth Coulson, Wasey and his sister subsequently decided, probably on the advice of their stepfather, to approach the agent of a fellow property-owner in the area: that great Whig statesman, Sir Robert Walpole. He it was who, in 1720, had the debt assigned to him, making himself Wasey's mortgagee.[6]

Hard working and ambitious, Wasey was soon in a position to pay off the mortgage and, before long, made a loan of over £2,000 to the landed Paston Herne Esq., of Heverland in Norfolk, a gentleman who had had recourse to borrow from the very same mortgagee as had his father, Elizabeth Coulson of Thorpe-next-Norwich. Herne thereby cleared his debt to Mrs Coulson, but over the years his debts to Wasey, with unpaid interest, increased, amounting, at one stage, to £12,000. Wasey never sued and it was ultimately left to his son and daughter to recover the loan.

HOSPITAL AND PRIVATE PRACTICE

At the hospital, work went ahead apace. One of the first cases, in the spring of 1720, was a widow whose 'condition was extreme moody and her distemper supposed to be the Sciatica'; it was ordered the surgeon 'be desired to visit her and a crown given for her relief'. Their first child-patient, a soldier's son of about 8 years, was diagnosed as having a 'carious bone on ye lower part of his knee'. A Mrs Cam, 'having been taken in upon tryall for a fortnight and being found to be incurable', was accordingly discharged.

It was resolved on 26 December 1721 that 'no person shall be admitted to serve as physician, surgeon or apothecary . . . without the consent . . . of our present physicians, Doctors Stuart and Wasey, and our principal surgeons, Amyand and Dickens'.

When a patient admitted with a 'bloody flux' was reported as 'behaving in a very rude and scandalous manner, cursing and swearing and complaining of the food', he was, on finding his defence to be drunkenness, discharged. Similarly, on 21 March 1722, Dr Wasey ordered one Samuel Moore be discharged cured, requesting that Mr Chairman 'do give him a reprimand for attempting to introduce a scandalous custom of extorting money from his fellow patients upon their admission into this house for Drinking-money and that the Matron take care to suppress such an irregular practice for the future'.

During those early years William would have been building up his own private practice and, to further his career, the influence of a distinguished patron (for a substantial fee) will have been necessary. One wonders whether this could have been Sir Edward Hulse, a founder of Guy's Hospital and eminent royal physician, who was, in the future, to witness Wasey's will. Contacts made in serving the infirmary – the governors, wealthy subscribers and supporters – would also have proved invaluable.

London and Westminster were cities of contrast, thronged not only with the poorest but also the wealthiest, hence the services of an able young doctor would be greatly sought in an era fraught with complaints, many of which were no respectors of class.

A young man of ability and purpose, William was aware he needed his degree in medicine to climb to the top of his profession. He returned therefore to Cambridge in 1723 where, having provided proofs of the required proficiency, and paid the substantial customary fee of £40, the doctorate was granted. Now in possession of a Cambridge qualification, he presented himself later that year for examination to the Royal College of Physicians and was admitted a candidate.[7]

It was an exacting time for Wasey: his stepfather, Mr Spencer Chapman, died at Worstead in November that year, necessitating a visit home. This may have been when, showing himself to be a conscientious practitioner at the infirmary, he introduced a Dr Wood to act as his locum for the period he was away, which set a precedent for the future.

In his will Mr Chapman named William's sister, Elizabeth, exonerating her from 'all sumes of mony which is or shall be due and owing to me . . . for her Board Educacon and Maintenance . . .'.[8] From thence, no more is heard of Elizabeth Wasey.

A REPROOF AND ADVANCEMENT

On 20 May 1724, we find in the hospital records: 'Mr Cheselden and Dr Wasey recommended Thomas Stevens, a stranger, to be cut for the stone'. He was admitted as an out-patient and Mr Cheselden (famed for removing gallstones) performed the operation, after which he became the infirmary's lithotomist. With his record of successful cases, the trustees must surely have been pleased that Wasey had introduced him and acquired his services.

A month later, however, Wasey was to elicit their disapproval when, on retaining the book of patients' prescriptions, he was requested to return it, as it was 'the property of the Infirmary', evoking the resolution: 'Resolved that Dr Stuart is the Senior Physician to this Infirmary'. This clash of personalities resulted in Mr Henry Hoare taking the chair at the following weekly board meeting, an unprecedented occurrence, when all passed amicably.

It was at about this time that new and more suitable premises were found in nearby Chapel Street. The rent was more – £35 per annum – but it was larger and when made 'wind tite and water tite' and the entrance whitewashed, it was ready to receive patients.

Later that year William was made a fellow of the Royal College of Physicians. Embarking, as he was, on a promising career, he no doubt caught the eye of many a fair young lady from the shires, in town with mamma, for the season. The daughters of London merchants, politicians and financiers, whom he met at balls, assemblies or while strolling in the royal parks, must also have afforded some mutual attraction. Fashionably dressed, he would have cut quite a dash, sporting a gold, hollow-headed cane, which served as vinaigrette against the pungent odours of the narrow, airless streets and courtyards of old Westminster.

His was the London of Steele, Pope and Swift. On first coming to town, he may well have seen Steele's play, *The Conscious Lovers*, at Drury Lane Theatre. Pope was frequently to be observed in the fashionable parks and gardens with ladies he admired. And others in this distinguished literary circle, such as John Gay, whose work, *The Beggar's Opera*, was extremely popular, were often found in London's fashionable coffee houses.

In the summer of 1727 King George I died. He had been unpopular, having no English and no queen (he imprisoned her for life) – even his mistresses were German. George II therefore could only be better. He spoke English, showed an interest in his kingdom, was prepared to lead an army when necessary, and, although he too had German and English mistresses, he thought highly of his charming and able wife, who patronized the arts and brought a sparkle to Court life.

A WIFE

It was probably in the late 1720s that William met Margaret Spearman. Thirteen years his junior, she was the daughter of a landed family from County Durham, descended in the female line from the Plantagenet kings.[9] At thirty-seven years of age, William's career was going from strength to strength, added to which his estates in Norfolk provided him with a comfortable private income. In July 1728 a draft of the marriage settlement was drawn up; the lady's portion was £5,000, while William settled 'all his Estate in the County of Norfolk now lett for three hundred & eighty six pounds per annum . . .'.[10]

The following year Wasey applied to register, officially, his arms with the College of Heralds, setting forth that: 'his ancestors were persons of good substance and lived in the reputation of gentlemen in the parish of North Walsham in . . . Norfolk and bore their arms . . . which are engraved upon their seals and also upon the tombstone of his father, William Wasey, in the church of North Walsham'.

Duly granted, they were registered on 12 August 1729.[11] The marriage settlement was completed a year later and the wedding took place in June 1730 at St Antholin's, one of the City churches said by Defoe to 'hold up their heads with grandeur and magnificence'. It was in Budge Row (old Watling Street), a busy thoroughfare near the Old Stocks Market, surrounded still by large merchants' houses. It may have been in one of these that the Spearman family took accommodation during their London sojourn that year when their son George entered Gray's Inn.

TAKING A HOUSE

Dr Wasey and his bride took 16 Gerard Street, Soho,[12] a newly-built house in this still-fashionable district, about 500 yards from Piccadilly. Four-storeyed, it sported good fireplaces, painted chimney-pieces and marble hearths. At the rear was the kitchen, fitted with a buttery, and 'new river water' was supplied by a pump. (Later the house became the Mont Blanc restaurant where, in 1900, G.K. Chesterton met Hilaire Belloc.)

It was a sizeable house, on the north side of the street, having a frontage of about 18 feet, with a small yard or garden at the rear. The poor-rate paid on it by Dr Wasey that year was £1 9s, only a shilling less than that paid by neighbour and colleague, Mr Amyand, sargeant-surgeon to the king. In addition there were water, cleansing, highway and watch rates which provided for scavengers in winter, water-carts to lay the dust in summer and a watchman to patrol at night. On his rounds the latter checked for fire and crime, called the hour and 'all's well' at regular intervals.

Another neighbour was hospital subscriber, Lord Scarborough, who lived in the mansion, once the Earl of Devonshire's, at the end of the street. There were also Mills' Coffee House and the 'Rumer' Tavern (later the Bear & Rummer) in which weekly concerts were held. Many occu-

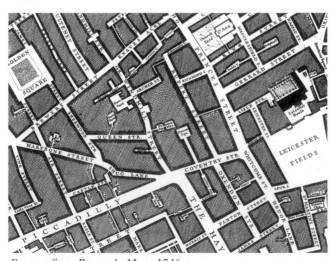

Extract from Rocque's Map, 1746

pants of the smaller houses were tradespeople serving the great Leicester House, the gardens of which backed on to the south side of the street (until recently, known as the 'alternative Court', where the Prince of Wales had held Court in opposition to his father).

In 1731 Wasey was appointed censor of the College of Physicians[7] and on 19 August the Waseys' first child, Margaret, was born. She was christened at St Anne's, the relatively new and fashionable church about 100 yards away, between King and Macclesfield streets (long before the construction of Shaftesbury Avenue). It was something of a royal parish then: when the Prince of Wales had lived with his family at Leicester House, several royal infants were christened there. Two years later, on 18 December 1733, Dr and Mrs Wasey celebrated the birth of a son; he too was baptised at St Anne's and was named William John Spearman Wasey.

SCHISM AND THE BIRTH OF A NEW HOSPITAL

This had been an extremely eventful year for Wasey and his colleagues at Westminster Hospital. The building in Chapel Street was said to be 'old . . . could not stand long and might soon tumble down . . .'. There was sufficient money, and the trustees were anxious to find a 'larger . . . more substantial . . . airy building to entertain their patients . . .'.[13] In June, Mr Green, the society's vice-president, offered houses he was prepared to let nearby and a committee of 'thirty gentlemen of distinction', including Drs Teissier, Stuart, and Wasey and Sergeant-Surgeon Amyand, was appointed to inspect the premises.

In the meantime, it had been ascertained that Lanesborough House at Hyde Park Corner was available on lease. At the next board meeting, Dr Stuart reported these developments, saying that Mr Lane, one of the overseers, desired 'that they would deferr for a few days their agreeing about any other house'. But, record the minutes, 'the Board thought fit to refuse . . . till they had first resolved that Mr Green's houses were most convenient . . .'. Only then would they hear the proposals regarding Lanesborough House, resolving that they were 'not proper' and appointing a committee to agree terms with Mr Green. Soon after, however, the medical men decided that Lanesborough House, at a rent of £60 a year, would suit their purpose more and proceeded accordingly, a lease being granted to Drs Stuart, Wasey and Teissier.

Despite opposition from the board when next they met, all the medical staff and many concerned in the founding of the hospital decided to proceed with the lease of Lanesborough House on account of the 'largeness and strength of the building and the airyness of its situation . . .' and resolved to open a subscription to this end. Plans went ahead and when made known to the general board there were 'some heats and differences being occasioned thereby'.

Differences regarding organization had occurred in the past. The siting of new premises provided the reformers with an opportunity to set up a new administrative structure involving delegation of responsibility and more efficiency. They were convinced that the hospital's needs would be better served in the more healthy, rural and affluent area of Hyde Park Corner. Both sides proceeded to distribute pamphlets in order to put their case to wealthy subscribers, and the outcome of it all was beneficial, since, with the founding of what became St George's Hospital, there were now two establishments serving the Westminster area.

The first general board meeting, held at Mr Carey's house in Golden Square, Soho, was attended by Drs Stuart, Wasey and sixteen others. It was resolved that they, together with further promoters, having subscribed five guineas and given an equal amount as a benefaction, should be trustees or governors.

Early contributors, whose wealth and position made their support a valuable asset to the new hospital, were Queen Caroline; Frederick, Prince of Wales, and the royal princesses; almost all the bishops; sixteen dukes and many of their duchesses; Lord Chesterfield; Lord Burlington; the architects, Kent and Ware; Richard (Beau) Nash, Bath's master of ceremonies; William Maitland, London's historian; Michael Rysbrack, the sculptor; David Garrick, the actor; and a host more.

A committee for by-laws was formed consisting of Drs Teissier, Stuart, Wasey and Mr Sergeant Dickins, Mr Sergeant Amyand and six others to refer to the by-laws of St Thomas' Hospital. Before long they had about 150 subscribers, most of whom were Whigs, one being Lord Walpole: his subscription of £10 10s was paid in on 13 March 1734 by Dr Wasey.[13]

An election took place in Norfolk that year and Wasey, as a Worstead freeholder (the largest in the 'market' area[14]), voted for the Whig candidates, both of whom were beaten by Tories.[15]

TOM'S COFFEE HOUSE

Hospital committees met during the first year at Tom's Coffee House, St Martin's Lane, north of Chandos Street. It was considered more convenient to the majority of members than Hyde Park Corner, then some distance from the limits of the town. Orders and by-laws were drawn up: 'That Doctors Teissier, Stuart and Wasey be appointed physicians to this Society', followed by the appointment of Doctors Broxholme, Burton and Ross. It was then agreed that 'no more physicians be added without their consent, they having all declared that they would serve without fee or reward'.

Matron was to ensure that 'no patient be allowed out of the house without leave of the physicians, surgeons or apothecaries; and that leave be not given to any patient to go into St. James' Park or the Green Park, called Constitution Hill [frequented by royalty and the aristocracy] upon any pretence whatever, to avoid offence'.

This was the London depicted so vividly by Hogarth, when the great evil was gin, the consumption of which helped to obviate the misery in which so many lived. Matron, therefore, was required to see that 'no gin, or other strong liquors shall be brought into the house . . . and if any such be found, it shall be taken away'.

Thirty tester bedsteads were ordered which were not to exceed six feet in height, as were breadths of cloth for the making of longcloth sheets and pillow-beres. Ordered too were blankets, bedcurtains and cover-lids. A clock was purchased for £4, a ballot-box for 15s and a sedan chair for £3.

The hospital building, once the country mansion of Lady Lanesborough, had a good entrance and grand staircase. The large main rooms on the first floor lent themselves to their new purpose, two of which initially housed 15 four-poster

St George's Hospital, Hyde Park Corner

bedsteads with hanging curtains to exclude the draughts and, beneath, a box to contain the patient's linen. Floorboards were bare and those outside, running along the gallery, were sanded. There were no curtains at the windows and in each ward the only piece of furniture, apart from the beds, was the reading-desk, to which were chained a Bible and Common Prayer book.

Breakfast was at 8 a.m., when those on a full diet were to have 1 pint of gruel (later altered to milk pottage) or broth, plus part of the 14 oz loaf of bread allowed each patient daily. Dinner was to alternate between 8 oz of boiled beef or mutton, and 1 pint of peas or plumb pottage. When pottage was provided, the meal was complemented with 4 oz of pudding. Supper, at 6 p.m., was to consist either of 2 oz of cheese or 1½ oz of butter to be eaten with the remainder of the bread. Their daily allowance of small beer was two pints in winter and three in summer.

Resident paid staff were engaged: an apothecary at £20, a matron at £10 and five day and five night (untrained) nurses, each at £6 per annum. There were also a housemaid, messenger and cook, the latter valued rather more highly than the nurses, receiving £7 per annum: all with full board and an annual gratuity.

The hospital opened punctually on 1 January 1733/4 with the admission of four patients by Dr Stuart, the senior acting physician. Twelve more in-patients and seven out-patients were admitted on the next receiving day by Dr Wasey, the name, address and disorder of each being recorded in the Minute Book.

Each of the five physicians attended weekly in rotation. On Wednesdays at 9 a.m. they received patients and prescribed for urgent cases. They visited again on Saturdays and Tuesdays, reporting those who were fit for discharge and passing to the surgeons those requiring dressings and surgical treatment. Cases considered surgical had symptoms discerned externally, whereas those exhibiting no outward signs were usually the province of the more skilled physician.

By the end of the first month, 43 patients had been admitted and 25 out-patients treated, their conditions ranging from consumption, rheumatism, jaundice and ulcers (some described as foul), to tumours of various kinds, ringworm, rupture, scarbutic eruptions, flux, palsy, fever and scrofula (the king's evil). Five died, and three 'returned thanks' on being cured.

PRIVATE CONSULTATIONS

It was usual for physicians practising privately to visit wealthy clients in their homes, whereas the less affluent were required to come to them. The consulting room in Wasey's smart Gerard Street home, however, would surely not have resembled that visited by Dr Johnson during an illness: 'they [patient and doctor] sate down on each side a table in the Doctor's gloomy apartment, adorned with skeletons, preserved monsters etc . . .'.[16]

Alternatively, patients could see an apothecary who, in turn, sometimes consulted physicians during certain hours at specified coffee houses, taking with them, quite often, a sample of their patient's urine! The physician would then, for half the usual fee of a guinea, give the prescription he thought appropriate.

Leading physicians used either Batson's or Child's coffee houses, depending on their politics. Child's, in St Paul's Churchyard, being the Whig house, would be that used by Wasey. Described by Boswell as 'dusky, comfortable and warm' with plenty of good conversation, this was a place where physicians could discuss cases and talk politics with eminent men such as Doctors Hulse, Richard Mead and, the latter's friend, Samuel Johnson.

Physicians in general were not highly thought of in 18th century society and when friends were aggrieved at the high fees they charged, Samuel Johnson once countered: 'produce one instance of an estate raised by physic in England'.[16] Nevertheless, the more distinguished of their profession were well regarded, living and dressing in the style of men of quality and fashion, often seen driving around London in their chariots and four or six.

Among the more notable medical men in London at this period was Dr George L. Teissier. Although he had been junior to Doctors Stuart and Wasey at Westminster Infirmary, he was appointed to the Household of George I in 1716 and attended various members of the royal family. He too was a founder physician of St George's, but was not actively involved, his attendance at Court preventing it; his inclusion on the staff roll, however, will have been of great benefit, due to his influence with royalty and the aristocracy.

Dr Alexander Stuart, a colleague of Wasey's throughout their years at Westminster and St George's, was appointed physician-in-ordinary to Queen Caroline and, it is said, to King George II. Dr Noel Broxolme, another of Wasey's colleagues, had been a student at St Thomas' under the great Dr Mead; he was appointed physician to the Prince of Wales in 1734 and was to assist at Queen Caroline's last illness. Dr Simon Burton, another of St George's six original physicians, had practised in Warwick for some years before settling in London. He too seems to have been royal physician-in-ordinary and he attended the poet, Alexander Pope, during his last illness.

Other notable physicians were Dr Charles Peters, physician-general to the army; Dr Benjamin Hoadly, physician to the Royal Household and to Frederick, Prince of Wales; and Dr Addison Hutton, subsequently another colleague at St George's. Also foremost in their field were sergeant-surgeons Dickins and Amyand; the latter, Wasey's neighbour, was an early advocate of inoculation for smallpox, who treated successfully two of the young princesses.

It may have been at about this time that Wasey sat for his portrait in miniature. His face is unlined as yet and the brows are dark, with no hint of grey. He wears a blue-grey coat of fine silk or woollen cloth with long, embroidered button-holes, a yellow waistcoat, white stock and shirt ruffle.

Dr William Wasey

HIS CAREER ADVANCES

Again Wasey was appointed censor of the college and his career continued to flourish, as did St George's. Frederick, the Prince of Wales, had become president after the death of the Bishop of Winchester and both Doctors Teissier and Stuart had retired.

After extensions, the hospital could now accept many more patients. At Sergeant-Surgeon Amyand's instigation a new wing was made available as a lying-in ward 'for the relief of poor pregnant women'. Money collected in the poor-box was used for redeeming patients' clothes from pawn, paying expenses to return them to their homes on discharge, the purchase of wooden legs and trusses, etc., and for conveying to Bath those who might benefit from the mineral waters of that city, a spa, incidentally, which Wasey must have visited on several occasions.

Among the cases admitted were those suffering from 'atrophy with violent pains and eruptions; nervous spitting with paralytic tumours; tumour of the heart [and] luxation of the spine'. The treatments were equally dubious, one being the administration of 'Mr Woord's pills'. Dr Hoadly prescribed them for consumption and Dr Wasey for fever and ague.

These pills were prepared by a Mr Joshua Ward who, dabbling in medicine, succeeded in introducing to the gullible public and medical world, among other things, his 'liquid sweat; dropsy purging powder; essence for headache' (a compound of camphor) and a paste made from pepper 'for fistula and piles'. He was much acclaimed when, after taking his pills, the Princess Caroline found relief from her rheumatism, and other notables such as Sir Robert Walpole and Lord Chesterfield found them to be efficacious.

Such remedies were often no less bizarre than those prescribed by the top medics. The spitting of blood, for instance, might be treated with 'a compound of dried horse's hoof' and ingredients such as 'viper's flesh, woodlice, human fat' and 'bone from the stag's heart' were sometimes used, in addition to the more usual laudanum (opium) and calomel. Bleeding and blistering were regarded as advantageous for any number of complaints.

When Queen Caroline was taken ill at St James's Palace on 9 November 1737, Dr Teissier was called to attend; he treated for colic and prescribed Daffy's elixir. This being ineffectual, the opinion of Dr Broxolme was sought and it was decided to administer snake-root and 'Sir Walter Raleigh's cordial'. Dr Ranby, the king's house-surgeon, apparently thought little of this, as well he might, having in all probability a more intimate knowledge of the queen's physical condition.

The queen remained in agony, and it was decided to bleed her twelve ounces. The pain increased, and on 10 November she was bled again, when the fever and nausea abated. However, to be on the safe side, two physicians of the highest rank were called: Sir Hans Sloane and Dr Edward Hulse. They were hampered in that they, through the niceties of etiquette, were unable to give the queen a proper examination. They ordered Her Majesty to be blistered and purged, after which she was again bled.

The following day it was established by two surgeons, Messrs Ranby and Shipton (who, presumably, were able to give the queen a more thorough examination), that she was suffering from an umbilical hernia of long standing.

Having unsuccessfully taken 'Daffy's elixir', 'usquebaugh' (whisky), 'mint water', 'snake-root' and 'Sir Walter Raleigh's cordial', Queen Caroline now underwent daily incisions and probings. These resulted finally in a rupture of the hernia which began, on the 13th, to mortify. On the 20th the poor queen, distraught with pain, asked Dr Teissier how much longer he thought she would have to suffer before, mercifully, that night, she was released and died.

A LARGER HOUSE

36 Gerard Street, Soho (interior)

During that year Dr Wasey moved to a more commodious and stylish residence. It was one of four built on the site of two earlier houses on the south side of Gerard Street, where the largest and best patronized houses were, their gardens extending to those of Leicester House. All were designed as a uniform group externally, but No. 36, that taken by Wasey, was planned, unlike the others, with the staircase placed between the front and back rooms[17]. It was of four storeys, had a frontage about 23 feet in length and was three windows wide. The front door, crowned with a fanlight, opened to a wide, panelled entrance-hall flanked by Doric pilasters with fluted shafts. And, from a spacious oblong inner hall, lighted by a roof lantern, rose a handsome staircase, the well-moulded hand-rail curving its way from the third to the ground floor, ending with a delightful circular flourish.

36 Gerard Street, Soho (exterior)

The panelled doors to the principal rooms were deeply recessed and crowned with an ornate pediment; the ceilings too were ornate, heavily moulded in the baroque manner. Most of the rooms were panelled, alternating wide and narrow in heavy mouldings, with a projecting dado below and a dentilled cornice above. The long wall opposite the windows of the largest room were divided into three equal bays by fluted pilasters in the Doric style. It was a handsome house, furnished no doubt in as elegant a manner, and William Wasey and his family must have been well pleased with it when they removed there in 1738.

Wasey was now among the commissioners of the vestry, attending meetings regularly with other principal parishioners. Their neighbours were the occupants of Gerard House; once Lord Gerard's, it was let variously to the Duke of Norfolk; Lady Mohun and, latterly, to Lieutenant-General Charles Mordaunt. At No. 37 was Catherine, the widow of Thomas Green DD, Bishop of Norwich and Ely.

Perhaps it was at about this time that the silver-headed ebony walking-stick, bearing the royal coat of arms and the inscription 'Presented to Dr Wasey by HM George II' came to be given to William. Was it, we wonder, on being summoned to give a second opinion on the treatment of a member of the Royal Household? Or was it given years before, when the king was Prince of Wales?

Again in 1739 Wasey was censor of the college. That year saw the advent of the Great Frost. After a fall of snow in January, no thaw came throughout the rest of that bitter winter and the snow remained until spring: conditions which

The Royal Walking Stick

heralded many more burials than normal at the hospital burial ground.

In May 1740, Wasey and his wife decided to sue her brother, George Spearman. This state of affairs came about because two years previously Margaret's father, Mr Gilbert Spearman, had died leaving large amounts of his daughter's portion unpaid.

When George Spearman and the other executors proved the will, making no attempt to pay off these debts and legacies, it caused discord. They 'ought' claimed the Waseys, 'to have sold . . . so much of . . . the . . . estate . . . for the remaining part of the mortgage money and interest due . . .' as well as for the 'further sum of one thousand pounds . . . secured . . . in trust . . .' which, said Wasey, they 'have hitherto neglected or refused so to do'.

Given a month to answer the charges, Spearman appears to have complied without the matter going further: as a member of Gray's Inn, he was conversant in the law and aware of his position.[18]

DOCTOR WASEY'S RESIGNATION FROM ST GEORGE'S

On 6 April 1745, at a hospital board meeting presided over by the Earl of Shaftesbury, Dr Wasey gave notice that he was obliged to resign on account of his private business. Before taking his leave, a vote of thanks was accorded him 'for his punctual and diligent attendance on the patients of this Hospital'. He had served St George's now for twelve years and was the last, except for Dr Ross, of the six original physicians.

Wasey's career continued to advance. He was named an elect of the college in 1746, was censor again in 1748 and nominated consiliarius in 1749. Then, on the death of Dr Jurin in 1750, he was elected president. On this auspicious occasion, Wasey will have donned the customary apparel of the office, a gown of the kind worn by the highest in the kingdom. It was of black silk, with full sleeves, liberally worked in gold braid and was worn with a neckerchief and frilled shirt cuffs.

Wasey was re-appointed in each of the four subsequent years, during which time the controversy which had started some years before continued to simmer unsolved. It had begun because of the custom of allowing licences-to-practice only to those with, or about to acquire, Cambridge or Oxford doctorates. When Jacob de Castro Sarmento, a medical author of note, fellow of the Royal Society and licentiate of the college, complained that a Dr Meyer Schomberg had interfered in a case of his, telling a surgeon at Janeway's Coffee House by the

Royal Exchange that he, Castro, was 'an ass and a fool', he felt the college should take action, which it did, imposing a fine of £4.

Later, Schomberg's son, Isaac, whose doctorate was from Leydon, began to practise in London and was summoned to the censor's board of the college. He replied in writing, asking to be indulged in practice until he had become a Cambridge doctor. Unwisely, he added that he would have made his request in person, but that 'he did not choose to meet a man who was disagreeable to the whole profession'. This was considered inexcusable, since none of those on the committee had been present when his father was admonished. Consequently the board adjudged his behaviour 'improper' and prohibited him from practice.

When, finally, Schomberg obtained his Cambridge doctorate, the president and censors were prepared to remove the veto. However, Dr Schomberg arrogantly announced he was unwilling to undergo the customary examination, demanding to be admitted 'as a matter of right'. He was claiming not, as had been sanctioned in the past, the right to practise without a licence, but the automatic right to become a fellow. This, in short, was denied, and it was 20 years before he was eventually admitted a fellow.

These and other matters, including dealing with discontent from licentiates who felt they gained little in return for their annual payments, were the concern of the college during Wasey's years as president.[19]

HIS LAST YEARS

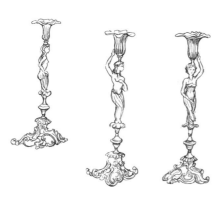

Dr Wasey's Candlesticks

When Dr Wasey retired from the college in 1754 he received the customary presentation, comprising 30 oz of plate. Wasey chose four silver candlesticks, each in the form of a female figure, nude to the waist, the arm supporting a flower-shaped sconce on the head. Each has a triangular base, on one side of which Wasey had the arms of the college engraved and, on the other, those of Wasey.

Wasey was now widowed. When he made his will the previous year he referred to 'my late wife', although no record of her death can be found. Since Wasey bequeathed her wearing apparel as well as her lace and jewels to his daughter (who in 1753 was aged 22 years), it suggests that she had died relatively recently. His son had not then reached his majority and so he appointed as guardian and trustee 'my good ffriend and cousin William Greenaway, Attorney at Law at Norwich', to whom he left 30 guineas 'to buy Mourning with'. Sadly, William Greenaway, his Norfolk cousin and boyhood chum, died in 1756. He was buried in Scottow Church, where Wasey would almost certainly have been present, with their other loyal cousin who commissioned the inscription for his tomb: 'In gratitude to whose memory Thomas Blake placed this stone'.

A year later, after 40 years spent in the medical world, Wasey himself died. Unfortunately his resting place is unknown. To his daughter, Margaret, he bequeathed a legacy of £8,000 in addition to the £2,000 secured to her by his marriage settlement. She was also to have the silver, china and household linen, as well as his 'Rings and all my Jewellery and Lace and also my two best Bureaus to put or keep her things in and also such Books as she shall chuse out of my Library not exceeding the number of sixty'. It was specified that these legacies: 'be immediately paid out of my real and personal Estate . . . [adding] this I do that there may be no dispute about it'.[20] The doctor was well aware of his son's extravagant nature.

Nevertheless, all the real estate and the remainder of Wasey's personal estate were bequeathed to his son, now aged 23 years: the 'money, public funds, mortgages or other securities' as well as 'the remainder of my household ffurniture Books Linnen Apparrell Coaches Horses Gold Watch and Chain and also all the Residue and Remainder of all my Goods and Chattels . . .'.

William Wasey, this orphaned son of a country attorney, had risen to the top of his profession, bringing credit and esteem to his name. Now, at his death, he left his son and daughter very comfortably placed to make their way in the world.

Chapter Three: The Soldier

At 23 years of age William John Spearman Wasey had enjoyed every advantage, but, like many another indulged and only son, he showed some fecklessness from an early age. At 18 he was admitted to Clare College, Cambridge, and appointed a Freeman Scholarship but in less than three years he left, without gaining his degree.[2] This was in 1754, the year his father retired from St George's Hospital 'in consequence of his private business'.

That he caused his father concern as he grew to manhood is evidenced from the remarks recorded by a grandchild: '. . . on account of his expensive habits his father was not on ye best of terms . . . [and] it is said [his father] refused a baronetcy on that account at the same time when his colleague, Sir Edward Hulse was made'.[1] This, at least, was doing the doctor's son an injustice: when Sir Edward Hulse was created baronet in 1739, William John (known as John) was a boy of only 6 years.

John and his sister Margaret had grown up in London during the colourful era of King George II with its masques, plays, pleasure-garden concerts, firework displays and gambling. Later, in Gerard Street, their childhood home, the 'Bear and Rummer' became the 'Turk's Head', first home of the renowned Literary Club, where Sir Joshua Reynolds, Dr Samuel Johnson, Oliver Goldsmith, Richard Sheridan and Edmund Burke met regularly. The world and his fashionable wife were still to be seen passing along the streets and squares of Soho during this part of the century.

On the death of his father, Wasey considered his future and, with a smart and prestigious career in mind, chose the army. He was in a position now to apply for a commission in that splendid regiment, the 2nd Troop of Horse Guards (later, Life Guards) and on 15 July 1757 was accepted cornet, for a fee of about £1,200.[3]

He was required to provide his own horses and possibly the long regulation sword, two pistols and a carbine. His scarlet coat was lined with blue, embellished with gold lace facings, and an epaulette of gold ribbon adorned the right shoulder. A cuirass of pistol-proof armour was worn and a loose red cloak, to which a small cape was attached; buff leather breeches, jack boots, spurs and leather gauntlet-gloves completed the outfit. Mounted on a well-groomed and accoutred gelding, his hair in a soldier's queue crowned with black tricorne hat bound in gold lace, he was certainly a figure to be admired.

This was a career to which Wasey was suited. His love of good living and tendency to extravagance was characteristic among his fellow officers, many of whom had known each other from childhood having shared the same preparatory schoolroom, public school dormitory and university refectory.

Although no training establishment existed then, these men came from the county and gentry families who hunted regularly, knew how to assess the lie of the land when it came to battle and were conversant in the running of their estates. Rigorous public school and university education made them used to receiving and dispensing discipline, while a private income supplemented their officer's pay. Their families provided endless dinner, card, country-house and hunting parties and, of course, balls and 'drawing rooms' from which daughters could be launched into the social scene for their 'coming out' at eighteen or thereabouts.

Wm John S. Wasey as a young man

Later that year, as heir to his father's Norfolk estates, John appointed his kinsman, Thomas Blake of Scottow, his attorney, and through him, at North Walsham's Court Baron, was admitted to property in 'Worstead, Westwicke, Smallburgh, Northwalsham, East Ruston, Felmingham, Swanton Abbott, Scottow, Dilham and Sloley'.[4]

An attractive young man with good features, large brown eyes and pleasant expression, Wasey looked no further than his own family for his bride. He proposed marriage to his cousin, Elizabeth Honoria (known by her second name), co-heiress to Spearman estates in Co. Durham. She was the 16-year-old, eldest daughter of his mother's brother, George Spearman of Bishop Middleham: the uncle with whom, years before, his father had instigated a lawsuit. Her mother, Anne (née Sneyd),[5] had died of smallpox when Honoria was only 10 years old. The marriage settlement was drawn up, dated 19 August 1758, and the wedding took place, at Bishop Middleham, five days later, thereby combining Wasey's own

No. 36

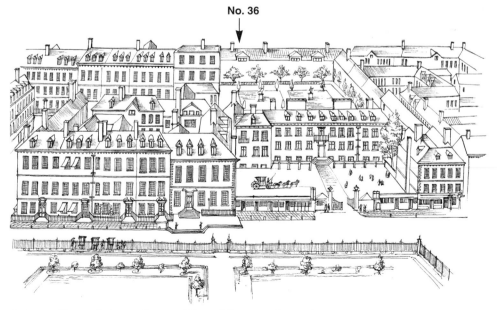

Leicester House, Leicester Square (Gerard Street at the rear)

fortune with that of his mother's family. The couple took accommodation in Leicester Square, along one side of which, set well back, was the great Leicester House. London, then, was at once colourful, romantic and squalid, with the brutality of the bear-gardens, bull-rings, cock-pits and gin-shops as evident as the popular coffee houses, elegant ballrooms and well laid-out pleasure gardens.

In August 1759 Honoria and her sisters learned of their father's rapid romance. He had met a Miss Webb of London, a young lady aged about 18 years, 'of great beauty, merit and accomplishment, with a considerable fortune', and, at 45 years of age, on the strength of a week's acquaintance, went off to Scotland and married her.[6] Soon after, Mr Spearman decided to demolish the Old Hall at Bishop Middleham and rebuild.

This was probably when the *Family Book* passed to Wasey and his wife. Bound in tooled and gilded black leather, Honoria's father had made it a present to his first bride in 1741. Inscribed 'The gift of Mr Spearman to Anne Sneyd now his much honoured wife Mrs Anne Spearman', details of their children were recorded on the first page. The hand of John Wasey takes over, recording the births and deaths of his children. His son George continues, with entries of his family, but the most copious notes were by one of his grandsons who made transcripts of family records, collateral pedigrees, etc., not only on the blank pages but on the preceding ones, interlining and interleafing those already inscribed.

The book therefore is often difficult to read in a coherent way; nevertheless it is of enormous value, since the original records from which much of the information is taken were evidently discarded. Newspapers, in time, of course recorded the usual family events, and these cuttings and more bulky items continued to be pushed between its pages, forcing off one of its handsome covers.

AN EXECUTION AT TYBURN

Public executions drew huge crowds at Tyburn, and Wasey's regiment was on duty in May 1760 when Lord Ferrers met this end, the last peer of the realm to do so for felony. Was Wasey in the contingent of Guards which escorted Ferrers in his own landau from the Tower? If so, he will have witnessed one fall, when his horse's leg became entangled in a wheel of the carriage, and may have heard Lord Ferrers exclaim, 'I hope there will be no death today but mine'.[7]

The duties of the 2nd Troop of Horse, apart from Household and ceremonial, were mostly preserving public order when peace on London's streets was threatened. Its barracks were on the Knightsbridge side of Hyde Park, a lonely area beset by footpads, where royalty still occasionally hunted deer. A turnpike, St George's Hospital and a few houses clustered round Hyde Park Corner, but much of the ground was open towards Piccadilly. Not all the men were housed in barracks; some were billeted 'within the sound of the trumpet call' and officers, to be on hand when called out, had their houses within easy riding distance.

John and his bride had their silhouettes in miniature taken at about this time: his hair is in a queue and he sports a dress-hat, while Honoria wears her hair swept high. In August that year Wasey improved his situation when he sold his commission and purchased a lieutenancy, with an increase in pay from 8*s* 6*d* to 11*s* a day.

That October, in common with his fellow officers, Wasey must have been greatly shocked to learn of the king's sudden death at Kensington, only five days after holding a review attended by many of the regiment. Although during Wasey's period in the regiment no part was taken in campaigns, the Blues fought at Warburg, Kirk Denken and Wilhelmstahl, and the whole army, to a man, was proud of its king's gallantry at Dettingen. There had been glory too, with Pitt at the helm, when Wolfe in Canada gained the lucrative trade in furs and fish; and in India, Clive won Bengal with huge benefits to the East India Company. Now, with the king's death, a new era was to begin. Frederick, the Prince of Wales, had predeceased the king and so his 22-year-old grandson, George, succeeded, heralding a major change in politics.

The Horse Guards went into mourning: their scarlet coats were trimmed with black, their hats, swords and sashes decked with black crepe. On 26 October they took part in the proclamation of George III who, soon after, gave instructions regarding the escorts who were to attend the royal family. The Princess Dowager of Wales was to be attended by a subaltern, two grenadiers and eight Life Guards. The dukes of York and Cumberland and the Princesses Augusta and Amelia were each allotted two grenadiers and seven Horse or Life Guards.[7]

The king's funeral was not held until 11 November when the coffin, hung with purple amid silver lamps, emerged from the chapel of St Stephen's, Westminster, to the tolling of bells. The procession to the abbey moved through a line of Foot Guards, every seventh man bearing a torch, while the Horse Guards lined the outer sides of the route, their officers bearing drawn sabres.

Before long there was also to be a family funeral. Mr Spearman, Honoria's father, did not long enjoy his second marriage: on 14 April 1761 he died and was buried at Bishop Middleham, next to the recently demolished hall. A month later, Lieutenant and Mrs Wasey's first son, William George, was born. They christened him at St James' Church, Piccadilly, having recently removed to that parish, taking a house in Great Poulteney Street.[8]

On 8 September that year the country celebrated the marriage of its new king. Princess Maria Charlotte was escorted from Romford by the Life Guards, one hundred of whom were on duty during the ceremony in the palace itself. Later that month, at the coronation, they undertook their customary ceremonial duties and were criticized for obscuring the view of onlookers, who claimed they were beaten back with broad swords and muskets.[9]

A COURT CASE, ILLNESS AND PROMOTION

Wasey and his wife were currently experiencing difficulties regarding the trust set up by Honoria's parents at their marriage in 1741. This was because the last surviving trustee, Charles Howard Esq., of The Cathedral Close, Lichfield, was failing to administer it. The estates involved were those at Bishop Middleham and elsewhere in Co. Durham. Consequently the Waseys sued,[10] setting forth that Charles Howard, second proctor in the ecclesiastical court of Lichfield (a friend and schoolfellow of Dr Samuel Johnson[11]) refused to act in the execution of the trust.

Wasey claimed that, on the death of Honoria's father, the freehold premises comprised in the marriage settlement ought to have been sold and the proceeds divided between the three daughters of the marriage. The portions for the younger daughters, Anna and Margaretta, he claimed, should be placed out at interest towards their maintenance and education until they were 21 or married. Many requests were made to Mr Howard either to appoint another trustee or adminster the trust by selling the freehold part of the property (valued at £12,000) and arrange renewal of leases, collection of rents, etc. on the remainder, to no effect.

Howard claimed he lived at so great a distance from the estates that he could not 'without the greatest inconvenience to himself' attend to the trust. Consequently the court appointed a new trustee and ordered the defendant to 'convey . . . and assign all the Trust Estate vested in him' to this family friend and kinsman, John Cuthbert Esq.[12] The case, however, dragged on for some time.

This was not the first occasion on which Wasey had had recourse to the courts. Four years previously he had joined with his sister Margaret to recover loans made by their father many years before to the Herne family of Heverland in Norfolk.[13]

Wasey and his wife were blessed with a daughter in 1763. This joyful occasion, however, was soon to be followed by the death of Honoria's youngest sister, Margaretta, aged 13 years.[14] When another daughter arrived the following year, she was named after this and Honoria's surviving sister.

Wasey was ill from the summer of 1764 to the spring of 1765 and was put on lieutenant's half pay[15]; when he returned to duty it was with promotion to exempt and captain, which rank he held for the next six years. The orders of rank were different from other regiments, although changes were to be made later in the century.[16] A gentleman, if fortunate enough to be accepted an officer in the Horse Guards, could start with the rank of sub-brigadier and cornet, rising to brigadier and lieutenant, followed by exempt and captain, a commission which cost £2,700 in Wasey's day. Next was guidon and major, followed by cornet and major, costing £4,300. To gain promotion to 2nd lieutenant-colonel and then to 1st lieutenant-colonel (both referred to as 'Colonel') an officer needed not only distinction, but the means to pay £5,100 for the former and £5,500 for the latter commission.[7]

In 1765 London's Spitalfield weavers rioted. Horace Walpole described how a well-disciplined mob congregated at Westminster, assaulting Bedford House where the duke headed a clique known as the Bedford House Whigs. After reading the proclamation, the gates of the court were opened and sixty soldiers marched out. The mob fled, but were met by Horse Guards and 'much trampled and cut about, but no lives lost'. On the following Sunday, though in his chariot, Walpole 'found so large a throng that I could scarcely get through' and, he said, Bedford House was 'a perfect Garrison, sustaining a seige – the court full of Horse Guards . . .'. The mob, he said, 'grew so riotous that both Horse and Foot Guards had to parade the Square before the tumult was dispersed'.[7]

Another son, John, had been born to Captain and Mrs Wasey on 19 August 1765, only to die five months later. Perhaps theirs was an unfortunate combination of genes, being so closely related: of their eight children, only one was to survive them. Smallpox was one of the greatest scourges: if it did not kill, it frequently blemished and marred one's looks for life.

The decision to have the children treated with the early form of inoculation would, therefore, seem to have been a wise one. It involved pricking the arm and rubbing into the puncture a piece of material on which the smallpox germ had been introduced, resulting, usually, in a mild attack, thereby preventing a serious one. However, alarming results often occurred and so it was a calculated risk when Mr Bromfield, the well-known man midwife,[17] was engaged to inoculate all the children in October 1766.[1]

Nevertheless, their little daughter, Anne Elizabeth, died the following spring. The *Family Book* records that 'she had ye Chicken Pox at her birth [and that] when she was about 6 months old she had ye whooping cough', but makes no mention of the cause of her death. She was taken to be buried at St Anne's, Soho, where most of the children were christened and several were buried.

Captain and Mrs Wasey had moved again by this time to a more commodious house in Soho Square. Many embassies were occupying the larger houses and among their neighbours were 'The Spanish Minister' and 'His Excellence the Venetian Resident'.[18] Almost next door was the Soho Academy, run by Dr Barwis, among whose pupils were the sons of James Boswell and Edmund Burke. In the square, too, was the renowned Carlisle House where the celebrated Mrs Cornelis staged the most glittering public events 'for London's nobility and gentry'.[19]

COUNTRY CONNECTIONS AND MORE RIOTS

Regular journeys to Norfolk were made by the Wasey family over the years to visit their many connections and to discuss the administration of property with Blake cousins. As freeholder of the Worstead property Wasey was eligible to participate in Norfolk elections and in 1768 he cast his vote for the Whig candidates.

Meanwhile, the lawsuit regarding the Durham estates still dragged on.[10] The pleadings had required alteration in 1763 when Honoria's young sister Margaretta died. Wasey, in right of his wife and her other sister, now became entitled to her share. Earlier, Wasey had borrowed the sum of £3,000 from *his* sister, Margaret, and he used this debt as leverage, a customary ploy, to attempt to bring about a conclusion to the case.

Another alteration was necessary when Honoria's surviving sister Anna Susanna reached the age of 21 years and became entitled to her share. In due course the court decided that as the:

> estates . . . to be sold . . . lye very much intermixed with [others] . . . not comprised in the . . . Settlement, so that [they] . . . cannot be sold without great loss . . . it will be much more for the benefit of the Plaintiffs to have the . . . Estates conveyed to them than to have [them] sold under the . . . decree.

This was no doubt a wise conclusion since the yearly rents were worth nearly £400. It was eventually ordered that the new trustee, Mr Cuthbert, should vest one moiety for the use of Anna Susanna Spearman and the other should go to Wasey, subject first to the repayment of the £3,000 loan and interest to his sister, Margaret. Before long, however, in 1769, the property *was* sold, despite all, to Ralph Hopper Esq., barrister at law.[20]

Although anxious to convert the estate into capital, perhaps it was John who wished to keep at least a memento of the family's Durham seat. It was not of

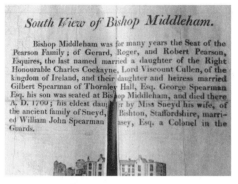

South View of Bishop Middleham.

Bishop Middleham was for many years the Seat of the Pearson Family ; of Gerard, Roger, and Robert Pearson, Esquires, the last named married a daughter of the Right Honourable Charles Cockayne, Lord Viscount Cullen, of the kingdom of Ireland, and their daughter and heiress married Gilbert Spearman of Thornley Hall, Esq. George Spearman Esq. his son was seated at Bishop Middleham, and died there A. D. 1700 ; his eldest daughter by Miss Sneyd his wife, of the ancient family of Sneyd, of Bishton, Staffordshire, married William John Spearman ...sey, Esq. a Colonel in the Guards.

Bishop Middleham Hall with text, from the
Family Book

course the Old Hall, home to his wife and mother: that had been demolished soon after his father-in-law's second marriage. Nevertheless a sketch was made of the rebuilt hall, and a few lines of text added to further the tradition of its having anciently been the seat of their ancestors' family, the Peirsons, and inserted into the *Family Book*.

More riots occurred in London during 1768/9, the cause being the notorious John Wilkes who, despite his scurrilous journalism and scandalous private life, was favoured by the London mobs. Consequently, when rioting began, the peace was maintained by having the Horse Guards 'brought out ostentatiously each day till . . . the new Parliament met'.[21]

The Waseys had two more sons within the next two years – Clement John, who grew to manhood, and Spearman – but they also suffered the loss of their other little daughter, aged only five years.

At Carlisle House Mrs Cornelis continued to bring lustre, if not notoriety, to Soho Square. She held glittering balls and assemblies which at first were said to scandalize, but soon drew 'both the righteous and ungodly', attracting crowds who gathered to see the fine dress and equipage of attenders. Fanny Burney, the well-travelled diarist, made a visit in 1770 and, although she expressed disappointment because 'the Rooms were so full and so hot', she declared the 'magnificence [and] splendour of the illuminations and embellishments, and the brilliant appearance of the company exceeded anything I ever before saw'.

In 1771 the family again resorted to the law courts. This time Wasey supported his sister against Northumbrian William Heath Esq., of Hawkwell. It seems that, on receiving the rents and profits of property in Co. Durham, Heath '. . . applied the same to his own use' without paying the interest on the £6,000 loaned by her. And, it was claimed, 'he suffers the same to run greatly in arrear'.[22] Their counsel was evidently sound, because the outcome appears to have been to Margaret's advantage.

Wasey was now promoted guidon and major with, two years later, further promotion to cornet and major. At about this time he and his wife sat for their miniatures. John, wearing his uniform, has a solemn expression. Honoria, her powdered hair dressed with ribbons, wears a gown with deeply frilled neckline.

Wm. John S. Wasey and his wife Honoria

When another son, George, was born in 1773, a sponsor was Richard (later General) Vyse, the widowed husband of Honoria's now deceased sister Anna.[23] Married two years previously, Anna had sadly died in childbirth. In 1778 the Waseys' last child, Willoughby John, was born, only to die a year later. A godfather, Sir Willoughby Aston, was a fellow officer in the Guards for a while, but appears subsequently to have left the regiment.[24]

William George, the eldest son, was now aged nearly 17 years and deemed old enough to be launched upon a career. Through family patronage a place was found for him in the service of the Hon. East India Company as a 'writer'.[25] The opportunities this afforded were considerable: progress could be made to 'merchant', and then to 'factor', all three grades being in a position to carry out trading on their own account. A successful factor could expect to return to Britain a wealthy man, procuring a large and pleasant estate for his retirement. To this end then, young William sailed for Madras on 7 February 1778 in the *Osterley*,[1] Major and Mrs

Col. Wm John Spearman Wasey

Wasey no doubt waving him off. As fate decreed, it proved to be the last they were ever to see of this, their first born.

In 1779 Wasey received further promotion in the regiment. He had been lieutenant-colonel on the Army List already for two years when he was promoted to 2nd lieutenant-colonel in the regiment. The holding of dual ranks was then the practice: Lord Robert Bertie, colonel of the regiment, had held the rank of general in the army since 1777.[16]

Now a senior officer, Wasey served another seven months before retiring. It is likely, since the *Family Book* records it, that when deputizing for the officer commanding the troop – Silver-Stick-in-Waiting to King George III – Wasey himself undertook these important duties. A highly responsible and privileged position, it involved close liaison with the palace: indeed 'Gold-Stick' was said by Sir Robert Walpole to have been the most influential position at Court. On ceremonial occasions Gold- and Silver-Stick were stationed at the right wheel of the monarch's carriage, ready to convey orders, or defend their king if necessary.[7]

During the colonel's last few months in the regiment it was called upon to 'disperse a great assemblage of the populace in St. James' Square'. This was on the night of 11 February 1779 when several of the nobility and ministers of state had their houses destroyed. The Horse Guards recorded: 'a number of the ringleaders were secured; and the remainder then dispersed'.[26]

In the year following Wasey's retirement the infamous Gordon Riots occurred and, although no longer actively involved, he will have witnessed the tumult on the streets of London recorded by the Regimental Diary: 'These riots were occasioned by the removal . . . of certain restrictions from His Majesty's Roman Catholic subjects; and the people were, by the speeches and writings of designing men [Lord George Gordon and his followers] induced to believe some great national calamity would result . . . The populace assembled in great numbers near the House of Lords and insulted many members of Parliament.'

They began to set fire to Roman Catholic chapels, but magistrates were slow to call out the Guards who, records their diary, were 'not sufficiently numerous to reduce the multitude to obedience' and it was the king himself who ordered out the troops.[27] But '. . . while they were proceeding in one direction, havoc was going on in another; and such a scene of uproar, confusion and destruction followed as cannot be described. The houses, chapels, and schools of the . . . Catholics were soon in flames. Many . . . rioters were . . . sent to prison; but. . . were . . . rescued, and the prisons set on fire. The King's Bench Prison, the Fleet . . . New Bridewell, St George's Fields, and the New Gaol, were in flames . . . and, on the nights of the 5th and 6th of June, London presented a dreadful scene of conflagration and bloodshed.'

It was not, continues the diary, 'until about twenty additional regiments had arrived that order was restored' and 'great numbers of the mob were killed'. Many others, 'having broken into cellars and become intoxicated, perished in the flames . . .'.

LAUNCHING THE OTHER CHILDREN

Colonel Wasey decided his younger sons should go into the navy, where the sea would benefit their lungs and the discipline their souls. All three were entered as captains' servants, a euphemism for midshipmen when too young to be entered officially as such. Spearman, aged 9, was entered first: on 13 April 1780, on the books of 'ye Fortified'[28] by Sir Richard Bickerton. Two weeks later, followed 10-year-old Clement John 'on board ye Canada 75 guns by Sir George Collier', and the following month, George, aged 7, was entered 'on board ye Buffalo . . .'.

The earlier a boy was entered on a ship's books, the sooner he would be eligible for a lieutenancy. Strictly, boys could not be accepted as midshipmen until 15 years of age, hence their entry with appropriate interest as captains' servants, some never going near a ship, but gaining time towards the coveted lieutenancy. Although entered in 1780, Clement appears to have been at Cheam School during this period and it was nearly two years later, after the promise of 'future patronage of Cn. Cranston & Captn. Rowd. Cotton', that he was again entered, 14 December 1781, and 'Sailed from Portsmouth in ye Inflexible . . . Feb. 6 1782 for India'.[1]

Britain, now at variance with France, Spain and Holland, was fighting for supremacy at sea and HMS *Inflexible*, a two-decker, 64-gun ship of the line, was lying off Portsmouth waiting to sail with a convoy to India, when Clement, now aged 12, joined her. There was some disturbance, however, before they could get underway.

On 3 February, when the convoy's commodore 'made the signal to unmoor',[29] the crew of HMS *Inflexible* made ready and 'unspliced the small Bower cable to clear Hause'. But the seamen staged a mini-mutiny and 'refused doing any more duty til they were payed all arrears of wages'. At this, their commander, the Hon. John Whitmore Chetwynd, 'retired to the Bay forward, lowered down all the Ports and took away the ladders from all the hatchways'.

Next morning, however, the men capitulated when 'the Agent came on board & payed P[rize] Money'. The log adds: 'when on deck fixed Marine Centinels at the Hatchways to prevent them going below'.

On Tuesday the commodore came on board and, ordering all hands on the quarter deck, 'convinced the Ships Company of the impropriety of their Conduct & requested they would return to their duty'. Having now been paid, this 'they consented to do', giving three cheers. Two days later they 'came to Sail in

Company with Commodore Sir Richard Bickerton in the Gibraltar, several Men of War and a fleet of East Indiamen . . .'.

VOYAGE TO INDIA

On 8 February, the commodore 'made the signal for the Order of Sailing' and soon after, they got under way, '50 Sail in Company'. From time to time 'strange sails' (unidentified vessels) were sighted, and they were given the order 'to Chase'.

The weather became rough off the Scilly Isles and they 'saw one of the Indiamen with her main topsail carried away'. A few days later: 'saw the Commodore with his M. top Mast carried away [and] got the Canvass in the storeroom up on deck to dry . . . the sailmakers employed mending the sails . . .'. The storms raged and 'the Comm. made the signal for the Convoy to keep close to him'.

The fleet continued on out into the Atlantic and, in very heavy seas, HMS *Inflexible* 'opened the Scuttle of the Bread room, found some of the bread much damaged by the deck leaking [and] Lost the Barges covering overboard when washing it'. Later, the 'Ship pitched the head under water [losing] 20 Pieces of Pork out of the Steep [salting] Tub'.

On 4 March they parted company with 'His Majesty's Ships Alexander, Agamemnon, Renown & Assistance on their return to England, and the Magnificent, for the West Indies'. Before turning eastwards, the rest of the fleet continued on towards Rio de Janeiro, the crews performing everyday activities such as 'washing and smoking between decks, exercising great guns and small arms' and watching for 'strange sails'. Continual reefing and furling of sails was necessary in making manoeuvres to keep their station in the convoy, while seamen were constantly employed carrying out repairs and maintenance to sails, boats and masts destroyed in the storms: 'found the Fore top yard sprung in the slings; got it down & a new one put up'. They painted the ship and made netting for the quarter deck, while misdemeanours such as theft, insolence or neglect of duty were punished, usually with twelve lashes.

At last, on 25 May, 15 leagues off Cape St Thomas, one of the convoy made the signal for seeing land. During the following week, while in Rio harbour, there was sickness aboard, for the log recorded a seaman and a second lieutenant of marines had 'departed this life'. On 27 May 'the Comm. made the signal for the troops to embark' and at 4 p.m. another seaman died. Having 'supplied the Griffin Cutter with provisions & water', they made ready for sea themselves, receiving 'Brooms & water by the Boats' and got underway on 3 June, 'as did the rest of the Fleet. . .'.

They sailed round the Cape of Good Hope fairly uneventfully, albeit with their spirits allowance cut to two-thirds, and, half a mile from the island of Johanna (off Madagascar), they 'hoisted out the Long Boats & sent the empty casks on shore for water'. On board, they received the 'Prince of Joanna', saluting him with eight guns. Three days later, the surf running very high when the seamen were returning from the shore, the 'Cutter overset by which accident lost a . . . mast, sails, oars and boathook . . .'. On rejoining the fleet, a seaman was punished with 12 lashes 'for running the boathook into one of the inhabitants of Johanna'.

Seven months after leaving England they reached India and moored off Bombay, landing occasionally to receive provisions: 'one hundred barrels of powder and 13 head of cattle . . .'. On board too came 18 soldiers from the 'Morse Indiaman'. They sailed south, then north through the Palk Straits to Madras, where, during October, they spent some time moored off the coast. Christmas Day, unacknowledged, came and went; orders now were received from 'the Admiral' (Sir Edward Hughes) commanding that area.[30]

SIGHTING THE FRENCH FLEET AND BATTLE

While patrolling the waters between India and Ceylon during June 1783, the French fleet was sighted bound for Cuddalore, which was under seige from the British, and, on the 17th, was logged: 'the French Fleet coming down in a Line of Battle abreast'. The British fleet now continually manoeuvred to get the advantage, the admiral ordering that they 'form the Line ahead at two cables length assunder' and, on drifting apart, 'tack Leewardmost & Sternmost ships first [followed by] the Fleet to tack together'. HMS *Bristol, Naiade, Chosen* and *Isis* joined them and all continually tacked and filled to keep their station and to 'endeavour to work to windward of the enemy'.

During the next few days they logged, 'the French Fleet NBN 3 miles', only to drift apart and then nightfall intervened. Again they 'saw the French Fleet bearing West four Leagues' when the admiral signalled to form the line ahead and then to chase. But as dawn broke the opposing fleets had drifted apart yet again. It was not until Saturday 21 June that, after constant manoeuvres, the *Inflexible* finally received orders to 'close too one cables length assunder'.

The French fleet, now to the south, 'wen[t] and stood for us [and] . . . hauld their wind to the northward when their headmosts ship fired a shot'. Ten minutes later, 'they bore up & came nearer us' and, in another ten minutes, the admiral made the signal to 'engage the Enemy immediately, when the Action became general. . .'.

The fighting went on for nearly three hours until, just after 7 p.m., '. . . both Fleets ceased firing'. The admiral signalled to continue in the line of battle, while the enemy 'twisted their distinguishing lights'.

There had been roughly 100 men killed on each side during the engagement, the last to be fought between Sir Edward Hughes and the Bailli de Suffren.[31] During the next few days HMS *Inflexible*'s crew repaired 'the damages sustained by the Action' and Clement watched as they committed to the deep the bodies of those who lost their lives: two seamen, a lieutenant of marines and the purser.

THE MOVE WEST

The family moved house once more at about this time: Soho Square was becoming less fashionable. Wasey purchased No. 4 Queen Anne Street,[32] a street intersected by Wimpole and Harley streets just north of Cavendish Square. The house, three windows wide and four storeys high,

4 Queen Anne Street

plus basement and attic, has ground- and first-floor windows now projecting into three window bays and across the first floor is a wrought-iron balcony. There are attractive railings at pavement level, where the door was once no doubt as elegant as the rest of the house. It was the type of residence aspired to by people of quality, where kith and kin could be entertained, many of whom also had their town establishments in the area.

This life-style was supported by the effective management of country estates. In Co. Durham, the remainder of Wasey's interests were administered by John Cuthbert. In Norfolk, Thomas Blake renewed leases, collected rents, saw to maintenance and paid the land tax which, in 1781, on the North Walsham property alone, amounted (at 4s in the £1) to £18 16s.[33]

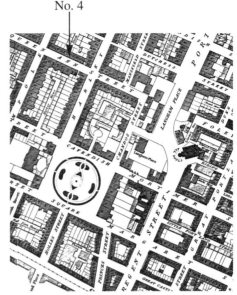

No. 4

Extract from Potter's Plan of St Marylebone, c. 1832

Leases to neighbouring landowners were for varying periods and rentals, as in 1782: 'that Messuage . . . & ffarm with the Houses, Outhouses, ... Barns, Stables, Yards, Gardens, and Orchards . . . situate . . . in North Walsham . . . by estimation 164 acres . . . now in the . . . possession of William Artiss . . .' for a yearly rent of £110.[34] One lease in 1767 incorporated an attractive plan of a Swanton Abbot estate with 'perspective view of the church'.[35]

THE SONS

William George, the eldest son, was doing well. Reaching Madras on 12 June 1778, after a journey of four months, he progressed in the service of the East India Company and before long was appointed paymaster at Palamcottah. Here he met Hannah Johnson, an attractive young widow, and proposed marriage. Consequently his parents consented to the sale of some Norfolk property entailed by their marriage settlement, in order to raise his portion of £4,000,[36] and an indenture was duly drawn up with the prospective purchaser, Berney Brograve, Esq.

The documents were shipped off in February 1784, being received 'about the month of September' that year, when they were 'executed and perfected' by William at 'ffort Saint George in the East Indies'. But 'no opportunity afforded of returning them from hence to England til the month of February 1785'.

Meanwhile, his brother Clement, still serving in the navy, had been transferred in September 1783 to HMS *Juno*, a 32-gun frigate. On sailing to Bombay, they found riding in the harbour there 'Commodore Sir Richard Bickerton and his Squadron and several Company's Vessels'. They returned again early in 1784 to the Madras Road. Did Clement, we wonder, meet his

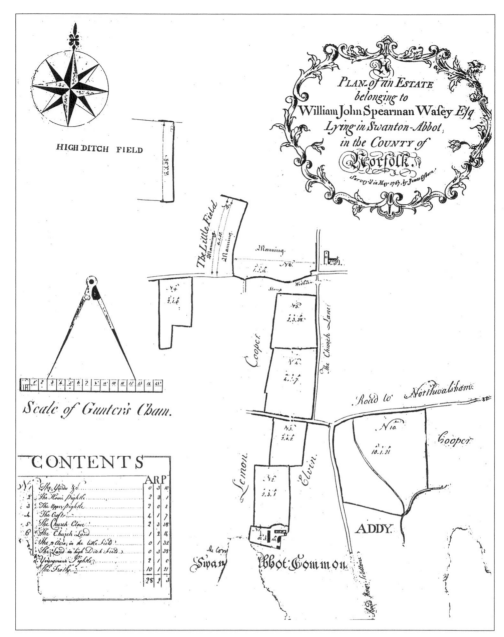

'Perspective View of the Church'

brother William at Fort St George or at Palamcottah during the years he was sailing in Indian waters?

The two youngest boys, George and Spearman, now aged 12 and 14 years, had been sent away to Rugby School. Here they were both making good headway and impressing their masters; their school report that spring was gratifying to receive:[1]

Rugby
May 14 1785

Sir

It gives me great satisfaction to write that your eldest son Spearman is an exceeding clever boy, and of manners unexceptionable & that your youngest is a very able and good scholar for his place in the school. The eldest is now in the Upper Remove of the 3rd form & the younger brother is in the middle remove of the 3rd. Spearman will go into the 4th form about three weeks after the June Holidays. I am, Sir, with great respect.

Your obliged & humble serv[t]

T. James

The school holidays over, Colonel and Mrs Wasey must have been devastated, at the end of August, to receive news from the school that Spearman was ill with a violent fever. Did they reach Rugby in time, or was it already too late? He died on the 23rd of that month. His memorial, now high in Rugby Church, was composed by the headmaster, Dr James, who had signed his school report only three months earlier.[37]

In October, Colonel Wasey received the signed deeds from his eldest son, William, eight months after their despatch from India. With them was a request that he should accept bills drawn on him amounting to £2,000 which was to be part of the amount raised. Now the documents had been received, the agreement to purchase for £3,390 by Mr Berney Brograve of Worstead House, Worstead, could be finalized[38].

This family estate, almost certainly that purchased by Colonel Wasey's grandfather 100 years before, consisted of 'a messuage wherein John Ashmul then dwelt' with brewhouse, malting office, barns, stables, dove houses, building yards, gardens, orchards, lands, meadows, pastures and grounds in Worstead and Westwicke, 'containing in the whole by survey 112 acres'. Also there were several cottages in Worstead, a malting office in North Walsham and The Crown, in Smallburgh. Although the purchase money, at 4 per cent interest, was not due for another year, Brograve was to take possession in October, receiving the rents and profits: during which time the conveyance was to be prepared.[38]

As cruel fate would have it, however, before this could be done, Colonel and Mrs Wasey received the terrible news from Lord Macartney in India that their son had died. His death had occurred thirteen days after his 24th birthday and was attributed to 'ye gout in his stomach'.[25] The impossibility of conveying such news, quickly, from halfway across the globe, meant the arrangements to procure his marriage portion had been going ahead long after his death.

These dreadful tidings probably arrived with news of the marriage, which had already taken place between William George and Hannah on 18 January that year,[39] and, even more poignantly, that a child was expected at the end of the year. One can imagine the pain and anguish suffered by Wasey and his wife, so soon after the loss of their other son, Spearman.

LEGAL DIFFICULTIES

At Worstead, Mr Brograve was having second thoughts about proceeding with the purchase of the property now that one of the chief vouchees was dead. Although, since 10 October 1785, he had been 'in possession . . . of the rents and profits', his counsel had advised that 'by the . . . death of . . . William George Wasey' the conveyance had become 'wholly ineffectual to Bar the Entail', and Brograve refused to complete his purchase unless 'Wasey would obtain an Act of Parliament to re-settle the estates . . .'.[38]

So now, in addition to the traumas recently suffered, Wasey was obliged to take lengthy and expensive procedures to set right again the legal situation regarding the Norfolk estates. He had been advised that by the death of his son before the recovery was finalized, this in itself cancelled it. But, 'being . . . desirous of removing all possible objection by . . . Berney Brograve Esq. to completing his . . . purchase', he consented to the expense and trouble of preparing and obtaining an Act of Parliament.[38]

To prevent further objections, the wording of the act was laid before Mr Brograve's counsel for approval prior to it being 'referred by the House of Lords to the Judges . . .'. Even this, however, was insufficient to allay Brograve's fears, who one suspects had other reasons now for preventing the transaction.

Could this be, one wonders, because Thomas Blake, Wasey's attorney, was greatly concerned at his breaking the entail of this family estate now that the eldest son was dead? Did Blake perhaps have a word in Brograve's ear? Certainly Mr Brograve did everything he could to make matters difficult. As loyal advisor and trustee, Blake may have recognized his duty to preserve, and not jeopardize, the rightful inheritance of the two younger surviving sons. Perhaps it was for this reason that, when Wasey resorted yet again to Chancery, claiming he had repeatedly applied to Mr Brograve to complete the purchase, his kinsman, Thomas Blake, and his own two sons, Clement and George, aged 17 and 13 years respectively, were now 'confederating' with Brograve against him.[38]

Whether Mr Brograve was ultimately obliged to complete his purchase is not known, but sold it was with more of the Norfolk property. The proceeds, £6,033 5s 5d, Wasey invested in Consolidated Bank Annunities at 3 per cent, and the Trustees, Messrs. Sneyd and Batt, had the same power to provide for the Wasey heirs as when their inheritance had been in real estate.[40] Over the years leases, etc. on the rest of the Norfolk property continued to be made for various terms to the Berney Petre family and others.[41]

Robbed of their eldest son, the family commemorated him in the *Family Book*: '[he] was always a lad of ye strictest probity . . . & Universally esteemed'. In due course they learnt of the handsome monument, a 20ft-high plinth erected by his friends, Messrs Kindersley and Torin, at the New Burial Ground at Palamcottah bearing the epitaph composed by Mr Erwin[25] which began: 'Rais'd by Friendship | And hallow'd by affection | This Pillar | The Monument of Willm. Geo. Wasey | Records the Vanity of human Wishes |While Youth regards it with a sigh |the Virtuous and the Happy shall ponder on their Lot.'

News of their granddaughter's birth will have arrived after the usual interval of at least four months, pleasing them perhaps with the choice of names bestowed on her: Eliza Honoria Margaret 'in compliment to her grandmother and aunt'.[1] One of her sponsors was N.E. Kindersley Esq., also of the East India Company, who, before long, became the third husband of Hannah, her mother.[42] Little Eliza was brought back to England where, we learn from the *Family Book*, she was brought up by Colonel and Mrs Wasey.

FRIENDS AND KINSMEN

Preserved in the family is a silhouette of friend and kinsman, the Hon. William Cokayne, son of the 5th Viscount Cullen. A copy letter from Barbara, his wife, addressed to Colonel Wasey's wife has survived between the pages of the *Family Book*. Dated 1789 and postmarked Kettering, it is reproduced here, the spelling and punctuation unaltered.

Mrs Wasey	M A	Rushton Hall
Queen Ann St. West	4	
Cavendish Square	8 9	
London		May ye 2ᵈ

My dear Mrs Wasey

When we parted in Town you were so kind as to express a wish to know our future destination since that time we have been almost constantly stationary here & Lady Cullen is too good a correspondent for me to take that employment from her – but now we are going to remove hope to renew my claim of hearing from you de tems en tems.

After many *pro's* & *con's* Mr Cockayne has fixed on York chiefly for the sake of education as we are informed that the schools are good & some excellent masters for our girls I believe we shall stay some few years there 'till it will be necessary to give them more polish than a Country Town can afford & possibly shall then change our situation for Paris or London was it not for the expense we certainly should now have preferd the capital but we have heard of the cheapness of York & do not despair of finding a tolerable society Mr C has a relation settled in the town & my old friend (Miss Englefield that was) is married in that neighbourhood & about half a dozen pleasant families who constantly reside besides *tabbies* but as I shall not enter into cards hope to escape that set your old friend Mrs Fairfax has procur'd us a good house in the Minster Yard till October & then she tells me we shall have choice of most of the furnishd houses in York & it is certainly most agreeable to settle ones own habitation we do not think of leaving this place before the end of the month & believe we shall rest a *very* few days at Stapleford as I shall be anxious to be quite arranged in June as I expect to be confined the middle of July & have quite a *horror* of being caught on the road – we flatter ourselves tho: at a great distance from our friends that we shall not be entirely deprived the pleasure of seeing them, there are so many things worth visiting in the North besides Scarboro & Harrowgate that are sufficient to induce them to travel our way & York itself I am told merits much attention – we do most sincerely wish that you & Coll. Wasey will when you settle your summer plan think to take us in yr way as it would give us great pleasure de vous faire les honneurs de York – I saw Mrs. Lodington lately she always makes many enquiries & begs me to say some kind things for her this severe winter has shook her greatly indeed most old people have sufferd much, even Ld. Cullen tho wonderfully strong seems hurt from the intense cold I hope you & yrs have escaped cold. Lʸ C. desires her best Compᵗˢ & hopes her little Beau Clem will not forsake his old flirt, she is recovering from a sore throat which has been here almost universal & has left her low, are you not tho very loyal almost tired of illuminating I think I shoud was I in Town tho none can rejoice more sincerely my paper reminds me to conclude which I do with assuring you that I remain ever yrs affly

B Cockayne

Mr. C. unites with me in Compts & best wishes to ye Coll & desires I will tell you if you come to us at York he will shew you a book he has been collecting from his pedigree where the Spearmans Piersons do make a considerable figure in short he is a complete herald

The Hon. William Cokayne was the only child of the second marriage of Charles, 5th Viscount Cullen (third cousin to both Wasey and his wife, described as 'wonderfully strong' at 78 years of age). Cokayne and his wife, the writer of the letter, had ten daughters, but no sons. One daughter became the mother of G.E. Cokayne,[43] Clarenceux King of Arms, renowned for his *Peerage* and *Baronetage*.

The celebrations marking the recovery of George III's sanity will have been observed by the Wasey family, albeit with muted appreciation, if of the same opinion as their Northamptonshire kin. And one wonders whether Mrs Wasey, too, disliked card parties made up of 'tabbies' or, in today's parlance, 'hen parties'![44]

The allusion to their son, Clement, as Lady Cullen's 'little beau Clem' is charming and is an indication of his pleasing personality. He had left the navy after five years' service and, at 18, had gone up to Oxford – the year before the date of the letter. From its tone, we may assume that visits to and from Rushton Hall had often been exchanged.

If, later that year, Wasey and his family accepted the invitation to York and travelled via Norfolk where friends and relatives still lived, they may, in reading the *Norwich Mercury*, have happened upon any number of interesting topics. There was correspondence regarding 'the Man in the Iron Mask', said to be the son of Louis XIV's mother by Cardinal Mazarine. Norwich bakers, due to the distress of the poor, decided 'to bake at 30s per coom, which is 2s per coom less than the act allows'. Wasey's cousin and attorney, Thomas Blake, was advertising property to let from his address near Tombland; and Joseph Saul, a kinsman, was selling yet more of his property at Worstead. Stewards were announced for the various assemblies. At Aylsham, for instance, George Wyndham Esq., Squire Custance and Sir Thomas Durrant did the honours. Sir Thomas could also be found, as JP, committing to the Castle Prison a Coltishall man for stealing a plated bit and bridle.

Sir Thomas Durrant (made Baronet in 1784) would be a cousin visited by the Wasey family during sojourns to Norfolk. He had been godfather to one of their children in 1764[1] and interestingly (in 1787), he became godfather to John, son of Mr Custance, squire of Weston Longville (whose sister was Sir Thomas' wife). On that occasion the renowned Parson Woodford was officiating clergyman and dined with them at Weston House.[45] Scottow Hall, the Durrant family seat, was tucked away next the church where Colonel Wasey's grandfather had married Bridget Durrant in 1688.

Another letter preserved in the *Family Book* takes us to the Waseys' West End home in the 1790s. It was from a friend of their son George recalling the days when he still lived mostly at home: '. . . The Rev'd George Wasey of All Souls was . . . a very old friend of mine when he lived at

Col. Wm. John S. Wasey with his wife and granddaughter

No.4. Queen Anne Street, West. I have spent many happy Sundays in that house in the last Century about the year 1794 . . . I have a dear recollection of the kindness of old Mr & Mrs.Wasey with their son & their very pretty grand daughter Eliza.'

This description of their deceased son's child is confirmed by the miniature of a charming group, with the now white-haired colonel seated with his wife, and Eliza, aged about 5 years, between them. Her pleasing appearance accords with the sweet nature she was to display throughout her life and she must, in part anyway, have compensated for the two little daughters they lost many years before.

THE DEATH OF MISTRESS MARGARET WASEY

News arrived in 1794 that Colonel Wasey's sister, Margaret, now living in Bath, was ill. She died on 24 November and a notice appeared in the *Bath Chronicle* announcing that she had died after a long illness 'at her house in Bladud's Buildings'. From the Church Rate Books, however, she appears to have been living two doors away, at No.1, The Paragon, the house to be frequently taken, during Bath visits, by Mr and Mrs Leigh Perrot, notorious aunt and uncle of Jane Austen.[46]

Margaret was buried, as she wished, at picturesque Bathampton, two miles away. Her will, making Wasey her executor and residuary legatee, was proved by him nine days later, legacies being left to his two surviving sons and his granddaughter, Eliza, now 9 years old.[47]

In addition to the legacy, Margaret left Clement, 'who is just going to house keeping', a third of her household linen, 100 oz of plate and 'my two patch work window Curtains and the Covers for Chairs which I am now making'. George also received a third of her linen and 100 oz. of plate. To Honoria she left 'all my Trinkets and jewels of every sort . . . in order that she may dispose of the same . . . as I have already informed and desired her . . .' together with 'such of my Laces and fine worked muslins as [she] may think worthy her acceptance and will condescend to wear for my sake'.

CLEMENT TAKES THE CLOTH

Having left the navy, Clement took his BA degree at Oriel College, Oxford, in 1792 and was ordained at about the same time. The year he took his MA degree and 'began to house keeping', was also when his poem of more than twenty pages, 'Corsica', was published, setting out the island's history.[48] Corsica's fate attracted the sympathy of many, not least James Boswell, who had endeavoured to persuade Pitt to participate in the conflict against France on her behalf. All, as Clement versifies on page 19:

Beheld the cruel war, the deadly rage,
When the fierce battle Gaul and Britain wage.
At length to fortune, and to British skill,
Cyrnus submits, and yields to Albion's will;
The galling pain of Gallia's heavy yoke
With joy disclaims, and long allegiance broke:
No more the Coral with the Lily twines,
But with the Rose in sister tints combines;
To George presents her long-contested Crown,
And decks his brow with Honour and Renown . . .

Also in 1795, Clement made his will; perhaps, like many of his family, his was not a strong constitution. As it transpired, however, he had a few more years to serve the Church and, in 1805, in addition to his South Shoebury living, he took the rectory of Ulcombe, in Kent.

Colonel and Mrs Wasey were to enjoy the wedding of only one of their progeny when, in 1810, their son, George, married Anne Sophia, the daughter of Captain Frodsham, RN. This happy event was, the following year, however, to be overshadowed by the death of Clement, now aged 42 years.

Clement had expressed the wish that his funeral be 'conducted in a private plain and decent manner void of all unnecessary expense or ostentation . . .'. He left his brother his plate, his mother £20 worth of books from his library, and legacies to four friends. Half the residue was for his niece, Eliza; a quarter for his parents; and the remainder was to be shared.[49]

FULL OF YEARS

Colonel Wasey lived to enjoy not only England's glorious victories at sea but also to share the country's delight in Wellington's achievement at Waterloo. Full of years, he and Honoria had seen all but one of their eight children die before them; but they had experienced the pleasure of watching their first granddaughter grow to maturity, and their youngest son and his wife present them with four more grandchildren, before the colonel passed away at their home in Queen Anne Street soon after his 83rd birthday.

The trust remained from the sale of Norfolk property[40] and in his will Wasey made further provisions for his wife, son and granddaughter.[50] The proceeds of the house were to be shared as were the plate, linen, wines, spirits, furniture, pictures and books, except for 'my largest silver Waiter or Tea Table two caddies the picture of Servantes Jervis edition of Don Quixoth and Edwards Birds and Flowers' which were for Eliza. Although not specified, included was the royal walking stick and his father's retirement gift from the college, the 'Wasey Candlesticks'.

He left to 'James Ibbotson my own servant . . . two hundred pounds . . . my Metal Watch and all my cloaths Linen Wearing Apparel and Mourning'. To his coachman, Richard Keen, he left £20. Mary (?Ayers) 'who looks after my house when I am out of Town' received five guineas and 'every other servant who shall have lived with me a year', a year's wages and mourning.

Differences with his cousin appear to have been resolved: bequests of one hundred guineas each were made to 'Mary Blake the daughter of Thomas Blake of Scottow [and to] Mary Blake the younger now both resident at Norwich . . . as a mark of my remembrance to them'. A witness was N.E. Kindersley, his granddaughter's stepfather, whose town address was Upper Seymour Street, West. Here, Eliza would now be spending much of her time.

Honoria lived on for another seven years to enjoy the company and gratification of George's growing family, bringing comfort and fulfilment in her remaining years.

Chapter Four: The Georgian Parson

George Wasey was five years old when his eldest brother, William, sailed away to make his fortune in India, and it was two years later when he and his other two surviving brothers were entered in the navy as captains' servants. Since the *Family Book* says of both George and Spearman that 'Mr Painter at ye Navy Office can satisfy all points about ye boys [and they] had ye whooping cough at Southampton 1781', it seems possible that they were actually sent off for a while to sea. Certainly it was not unheard of for boys of such tender years.

George had his silhouette taken at about this time. Angelic looking, his hair reaching to below his ears, he wears a jacket with wide, frilled lace turnover collar, revers and cuffs. The *Family Book* tells us he was 'Entered as C^{ns} serv^t on board ye Buffalo Captn Cotton May 30th 1780 – Discharged July 30th 1780 & enter'd on board the Inflexible C^n Cotton July 31st 1780'. This was about 18 months before his brother Clement had sailed in the *Inflexible*, and the reason for the change of ships can be found in their respective log books.[2]

Young George Wasey

At the end of July that year HMS *Buffalo* was sailing off Portland Bill with a convoy when a 'strange vessel' was sighted and the order was given for HMS *Thetis*, *Southampton* and *Alarm* 'to chase' whereupon they 'brought the chase too'. She proved to be a French privateer lugger and was sunk by the *Southampton*, four prisoners being taken on board HMS *Buffalo*.

On board HMS *Inflexible* the following day they sighted five enemy ships and 'got the ship cleared for Action'. Then disaster struck: their captain, John Raynor, was taken with a 'Paralitick Stroke' and died. Next morning the log records: 'came on board Rowland Cotton Esq., Captain of HMS Buffalo & had his Acting Orders read to the Ships Company. . .' – which explains how George's name came to be taken off the musters of HMS *Buffalo* and transferred, with that of her captain, to HMS *Inflexible*. Five years later, George and his brother Spearman were sent the seventy-mile journey to Rugby School.

It was probably something of a novelty finding themselves, after the bustle of Southampton and sophistication of Marylebone, in this small country town where the ancient and noble school dominated affairs. At 12 and 14 years of age respectively, George and his brother were doing well; they had not long been pupils, however, when Spearman was suddenly taken ill and died. This was probably the greatest loss George had known during his short life and it would

Rugby, May 14 1785

Sir,

It gives me great satisfaction to write, that your eldest son Spearman is an exceeding clever boy, and of manners unexceptionable; & that your youngest is a very able & good scholar for his place in the school. — The eldest is now in the Upper Remove of the 3d form, & the younger brother is in the middle remove of the 3d. — Spearman will go into the 4th form, about three weeks after the Stone Holydays. I am, Sir, with great respect,

Your obliged & humble servt.
T. James.

Rugby School Report, 1785

certainly have had more effect on him than the news, soon to follow, of the death in India of his eldest brother, William.

Remaining at Rugby, George himself suffered the following year from measles, the potentially dangerous illness which may well have caused Spearman's fatal fever. George recovered, however, and continued 'a very able and good scholar', going up to Oriel College, Oxford, at 18 years of age. In November 1794 he was elected a fellow to All Souls, obtaining his BA degree the following year. Four years later he gained his MA degree, becoming Dean of Arts in 1800,[3] an office which circulated among the fellows, involving responsibility for the services in chapel and the presentation of candidates for degrees.

ROYAL CHAPLAIN AND INCUMBENT OF THREE LIVINGS

In 1799 Wasey was presented to the living of Whitington, Gloucesterhire, by patrons, Mr and Mrs Hanbury Tracy. Charles Hanbury Tracy, later raised to the peerage as Baron Sudeley, had been at Rugby with Wasey and they remained good friends all their lives.

Wasey became chaplain to the Prince of Wales in 1801, a position he retained until 1820.[4] The prince had more than one hundred chaplains at any one time and although they had no regular duties and were not salaried, the honour was a mark of the prince's favour and very desirable, being of great benefit socially.

A year later, Wasey received the livings of Albury in Oxfordshire and Wytham in Berkshire, both being 'no more than thirty miles' distant from the rectory of Whitington and in the gift of the Earl of Abingdon, with whom there were distant

Whitington Church and Court

family connections.[5] Because, by law, a royal chaplain was only able to hold three benefices in plurality (each worth £8 or more) provided that one of them was in the gift of the king,[6] it was necessary to obtain a dispensation from the Archbishop of Canterbury with royal confirmation by Letters Patent.

These impressive documents, comprising two large sheets of vellum, were held together by the 'tail' of the enormous royal seal (a horsed figure on one side, the seated monarch, surrounded by courtiers, on the other) and duly despatched to Wasey in metal containers with hinged lids. For some time now, Wasey had experienced difficulties regarding the Whitington living. It seems that Richard, then Bishop of Gloucester (subsequently of Bath and Wells), had disputed Mr and Mrs Hanbury Tracy's right of presentation and had instituted a friend of his own, one Revd Warre Squire Bradley. Mr Hanbury Tracy therefore brought an action against them both 'for the purpose of dispossessing' Bradley and compelling the bishop to institute Wasey 'upon the Presentation . . . executed . . . on 6 December 1799'.

In 1800 the case came before the Gloucester Assizes when the Bishop claimed, among other things, that he had not received relevant papers sent by Hanbury Tracy. On enquiry, it was found they had gone astray, being 'dropped out of the coach in the streets of Bath'![7] The outcome was a verdict for Mr and Mrs Hanbury Tracy, which caused the bishop and Bradley to appeal, hoping to have the verdict set aside and a new trial granted. However, this was refused and early in 1802 Hanbury Tracy and his wife 'obtained judgement . . . and Warre Squire Bradley was thereby dispossessed'.

Hanbury Tracy now ordered a writ to be served on the bishop commanding him to institute Wasey – which was finally carried out, in what must have been a very highly charged atmosphere, on 10 February 1802. Subsequently, Wasey sued for the rectorial rents, profits and dues which should have been his during all this time; they amounted, he said, 'to a very large sum of money' which the bishop and Bradley 'have applied . . . to their own . . . use and benefit . . .'.[7] The upshot was, when put before the Lord High Chancellor and Council in 1803, that the evidence brought by the defendants was adjudged insufficient and Wasey won the day.[8]

MARRIAGE

During this decade, trouble in Europe and elsewhere was being fermented by Napoleon, and there was great rejoicing in England when Nelson's victory at Trafalgar thwarted French invasion plans. Reports of these and other events, though much delayed, were recorded by newspapers and brought to the quiet cloisters of Oxford. Wasey, at All Souls, will have resided in college during the first year of his Fellowship and, although not compulsory thereafter, probably continued to do so for much of each year. In 1809, at 36 years of age, he gained his BD degree, by which time he had probably met his future wife, Anne Sophia, the 28-year-old daughter of Captain John Frodsham, RN.[9] They married on 2 June the following year at St Marylebone[1].

Anne's father had died nineteen years previously, aged 54 years, after 38 years' service in the Royal Navy. On his memorial and on the reverse of his portrait 'done at Bath 1774', it says of him: 'he was no less remarkable for his learning and amiable manners, than for his abilities and gallantry as an officer on many occasions tried and distinguished, particularly his famous action in the "Aligator" sloop of 14 guns against the French frigate "La Fee" of 40 guns'. This and other gallant exploits are recorded in the *Family Book* with the information that: 'Captain Frodsham's health, which had suffered much . . . was for many years in an inferior state and he died May 28 1791'.

Also recorded is that: 'his widow, in consideration of his services, received a desirable appointment of housekeeper at the Navy Office, Somerset House, where she resided til her death'. This was in the days when the main government department at Somerset House was the Admiralty, and the river, then unembanked, lapped the south wing where three great arches allowed boats and barges to penetrate to landing places within the building. This, then, had been home to Anne from the age of ten and explains why St Mary le Strand is given as her parish.

JANE AUSTEN'S ERA

The *Family Book*, from which much of the biographical information comes at this period, reads like something out of Jane Austen; it was her era and her scene. One can almost identify many Wasey personalities with hers, fancying them attending the assemblies, card routs, cotillion balls, picnics and boating parties enjoyed by Austen's characters.

Anne Sophia, as it happens, was descended from the same ancient family as that much loved author: the Leghs of High Legh in Cheshire. Much of her time will have been passed, during the years her father was at sea, in the cultured circle of family and friends found surrounding the Cotswold village of Broadwell, home of her maternal grandparents.[10]. It is only two miles from the Gloucestershire seat of Jane Austen's branch of the Leigh family, Adlestrop, where she visited on at least one occasion.

The Leigh family, from which both of Anne's parents descended (being second cousins once removed),[11] were, like the Spearman and allied families, well-connected, affording a wide choice of influential godparents for the Wasey children. Their first son, William George Leigh, was born in May 1811, four days after the death of Clement, George's elder brother, and the christening was postponed until the end of July.

Later that year Wasey resigned his fellowship of All Souls, convention allowing it to be retained for only a year after marriage. This was the year too that he succeeded to his deceased brother's living of Ulcombe in Kent, resigning his three former preferments, although the family christened their next child, Willoughby Clement, at Albury in 1812.

Wasey does not appear to have been very active in his Ulcombe parish during the ensuing years; he signs the registers during the summer of 1813, after which curates take over. The comments recorded by his son in the *Family Book* provide the reason: '. . . after a few years [he] was compelled by ill health to leave that fertile, but damp neighbourhood, having reduced to the point of death by an illness which rendered him unfit for active duty ever afterwards'.

Perhaps as a result of this illness, or possibly in fulfilment of duties as royal chaplain, the family made an extended visit to Brighton, recognized for its bracing qualities and made famous by the attentions of the Prince of Wales, now Regent. The town at that time was described by an appreciative traveller as 'surpassing in beauty all other towns in the world [and as presenting] a scene of evident wealth, of pleasure and of luxury'.[12]

The prince had become very unpopular in London, due largely to his treatment of his wife, the hoydenish Princess of Wales, for whom he did not scruple to show his dislike. To alleviate criticism from all quarters, he resorted more and more to drink and to extravagant building projects; all of which alienated him even more from the populace who, in London, gathered in crowds, hissing and jeering when he drove out in his yellow chariot.

In 1814, when the prince arrived in Brighton during the last week of August, however, he was to find its residents pleased, as usual, to see him: his presence brought life and prosperity to the resort. After a few weeks he had regained his geniality sufficiently to invite his mother, the queen, for a visit. She, too, was warmed by the loyalty she found there as she paraded on the Steyne with her family.

When Wasey or another royal chaplain attended to take a service or preach, it was usual to dine with the Prince's Household[13] and one can imagine the splendour of those occasions, especially on completion of the fabulous Pavilion three years later. Sophia Elizabeth, the Waseys' first daughter, was born on 27 December that year and christened at Brighton[14] on 4 March the following year by her father, their address being the New Steyne.

THE OLD HOUSE AT SWANBOURNE

Wasey's signature appears again in Ulcombe parish registers during the summer of that memorable year, 1815; but thenceforth there are few visits made by its rector, a succession of curates being employed. The memoir in the *Family Book*

Betsy's drawing of Swanbourne

telling of Wasey's illness adds to our knowledge: '. . . on his recovery, he rented a house at Swanbourne, Buckinghamshire for three years, til the death of its owner, Sir T. Fremantle, when his widow returned to it'.

Sir Thomas Fremantle and his wife Elizabeth had met romantically when she, as a young girl, with her parents and sisters, fled from the Continent before the French revolutionary armies, making their escape on Captain Fremantle's ship HMS *Inconstant*. 'Betsey' Wynne and the captain fell in love and were married in Naples, with Nelson and Lady Hamilton for witnesses. On their arrival in England the couple set about looking for a home and decided upon the house at Swanbourne which, as 'Betsey' noted in her diary, '. . . is two miles from Winslow, about two miles from the turnpike road . . . very agreeably situated on a hill. . .'.[15] A day or two later she comments gleefully 'we are to buy for 900 guineas – it is worth £1,200', and a little later, 'there is three little fields with the house and a good kitchen garden'.

It was in 1816, when Fremantle was given command in the Mediterranean,[16] his wife and family accompanying him, that the Wasey family rented 'The Old House'. Here they remained for three years or so, during which time their last three children were christened at Swanbourne Church, Wasey himself officiating.

Soon after the death of his father in 1817, George Wasey and his mother brought an exparte suit to Chancery. The outcome was an order requiring the last remaining nominee of the trust set up by Colonel Wasey to transfer its management to the trustees of George's own marriage settlement. George was also to receive his entitlement of £2,000 from his parents' settlement and the use, with his mother, of the residue.[17]

George's mother and niece were currently residing with him and his family for much of the time. Eliza, now a young woman of 24, 'much admired for her beauty and still more so for her excellence',[1] spent long periods, also, with her mother and stepfather, Mr and Mrs N.E. Kindersley, whose town house was in Upper Seymour Street. Eliza's half brothers and sister were Richard (called to the Bar in 1818 and later knighted); Nathaniel, of the HEICS; Edward, a Cambridge MA; and Henrietta, married, in 1816, to the Ven. Henry Lloyd Loring, DD, Archdeacon of Calcutta.[18]

A MOVE TO WALES AND A FORTUITOUS MEETING

News of the sudden death, in December 1819, of Admiral Fremantle at Naples came as a great shock, and necessitated the Waseys' removal from the house at Swanbourne. Wasey's old friend, Charles Hanbury Tracy, came to the rescue and offered the loan of Gregynog House, the family's Monmouthshire seat situated in the hills near Newtown.[1] It was of red brick, with a blue slate roof: very old and in a poor state, but redolent of its historic past.

The magnificent carved parlour, built in the reign of Charles I, was richly ornamented with the 'coats of arms of legendary Welsh chieftains and princes to whom the Blayneys [the family's ancestors] related themselves . . . the lion rampant of Cynwrig ap Rhiwallon, the fleurs-de-lys of Collwyn ap Tango, the spearheads of Caradog Freichfas, the three eagles of Owain Gwynedd, the wolf of Bleddyn ap Maenarch, and the red hand in the dragon's mouth of Rhys Goch'.[19] If comfort was lacking, atmosphere certainly was not!

During a visit to the south coast one year when the children were young, the family met, at Southsea, a gentleman who, attracted by George and Anne Wasey's young sons playing on the beach, enquired their name. To his astonishment it was the same as his own. The gentleman, John Thomas Wasey Esq., of Priors Court, near Newbury, was a wealthy bachelor who had, to his knowledge and regret, no male kin bearing his name. He became more closely acquainted with the Revd Wasey and his family and, over the years, a bond of friendship grew between, not only himself and his namesakes, but also between them and his sisters.

Visits were exchanged, the Wasey children enjoying the freedom of Mr J.T. Wasey's large estates at Chieveley and elsewhere in Berkshire. Their pleasure in each other's company was such that Mr Wasey endeavoured to prove a relationship between the Revd George Wasey's family and his own which, although wealthy, appeared to lack the illustrious ancestry of his clergyman friend.[20] The name was rarely encountered outside East Anglia and, although J.T. Wasey's parents' marriage had taken place but a few hundred yards from the Soho home of George Wasey's childhood, no kinship could be found. He delayed making his will, however, hoping to find a family connection, with a view to making them his heirs.

EDUCATING THE CHILDREN AND ANOTHER MOVE

Of the Waseys' six children, four of them were sons and their education had now to be determined. The eldest, William George Leigh, gained a place at that esteemed London school, Charterhouse. Was this, one wonders, when he sat for his silhouette? The tilt of his head, his regular features and short curly hair give the impression of an intelligent, eager young boy.

Their next son, Willoughby Clement, was 'educated with a view to his going to India but was disappointed of a Writership by the death of Sir Walter Farquhar'.[1] Sir Walter was physician to the Prince of Wales and, since it was through his interest that Willoughby's appointment was to be made, his death in 1819 completely changed Willoughby's future prospects. John Spearman, the third son, was sent to Wasey's old school, Rugby, while Edward and his two little sisters probably took lessons from their father or tutors until old enough to be sent away to school.

With the death in 1820 of the old king, the unpopular Prince of Wales, for many years Regent, was at last crowned. It was probably an occasion when all royal sinecures were reviewed, because this was the year Wasey's appointment as royal chaplain ceased.

In about 1822 the family removed again, this time to Oxfordshire, entering 'upon Mr. Chamberlain's house at Wardington, five miles from Banbury [where, records a son] at different periods . . . my father officiated as curate to the Rev. J. Ballard, both at Wardington and Mollington but [he adds] his health was never strong'.[1] This property was in Lower Wardington, part of an estate owned by another schoolfellow, Revd T.C. Hughes Chamberlain.[21] Although unidentified, it was one of the three most highly taxed houses in Wardington, the highest being the Manor House.[22]

FAMILY CONNECTIONS

Visits continued to be exchanged with the Leigh family of Broadwell, Gloucestershire, and of High Legh in Cheshire. One such occasion was at the death of Anne Sophia's aunt Elizabeth, a much respected resident of Knutsford. The erection of a monument to her memory in the parish church there was arranged:

> To the memory of | Elizabeth Leigh | Daughter of the Late Revd. Peter Leigh | of the West Hall, High Legh| She died on the 25th June 1823 aged sixty nine | After a residence of above fifty years in this Town | Where her fervent and cheerful piety | Her daily attention to the wants and distress of the Poor | Her useful endeavours to promote the religious | And moral education of the rising generation | And her uniform kindness to all | Will be long remembered with affectionate regret.[1]

Her property was bequeathed to Miss Frodsham, Wasey's sister-in-law, charged with certain annuities and a payment of £1 per annum to 'the singing girls of Knutsford Church for ever'.[1]

Intimacy was still preserved with the Spearman family of Thornley and of Old Acres, Co. Durham. Wasey appears to have stood godfather in 1808 to the son of his kinsman, Major Alexander Young Spearman of the Woolwich Garrison, the child being christened George Wasey. Sadly he was to die in 1824 as a 15-year-old midshipman when the frigate *Delight* was thought to have foundered at sea.[23] It was Major Spearman's eldest son, Alexander Young junior, who, in 1817, was sponsor to the Waseys' third son and was to assist in finding a place in the Customs Service for yet another of their sons.[24]

Ties with the Kindersley family too were fostered. Hannah, the widow of Wasey's deceased elder brother and mother of his only niece, having remarried to N.E. Kindersley Esq., had another daughter and three sons, the eldest of whom, Richard Torin Kindersley (who became a master in Chancery and was knighted), became godfather to the Waseys' youngest son.[1] Later there were to be even stronger affiliations.

THE OLD GREY

A charming story recorded years later by Wasey's eldest son brings the flavour of the family's life at Wardington into focus. By way of introduction he enters into the *Family Book* some verses of his father's, bearing the date 15 May 1828, about a well-loved horse stolen and feared lost for ever:

And art thou gone, my aged gallant Gray
My ever willing, well beloved Steed
Who through the course of many years hath gained
Thy master's steady praise, how poor a meed
For all thy labours and unceasing toil
Yes, thou art gone, but not to pasture green
Or manger filled with odiferous oats;
To bed high bolster'd up with wheaten straw
Or gentle slumber on the verdant mead

A different fate awaits thee now, I fear –
Hard knocks, hard fare and exercise of strength
Beyond your powers. Methinks I see thee now
Crouching beneath some shed, or harder fate
Sinking beneath the weight of the Pot-man's car
Or linked in infamy with gypsey horde

These sad forebodings pain thy master and
Call forth his sorrow – Yes, my old Gray
By me thou surely wert most prized – and long
Shall I deplore thy loss of comfort; and
That thy future years must pass away
In Squalid wretchedness perchance in want

He then comments thus:

The above lines, composed by my father, I find in his handwriting. They are connected with an incident of no great importance, but so very remarkable as almost to be called providential and to justify its being recorded in the Family Book.

A favourite fleabitten grey mare of my father's had been stolen from a field at Wardington near Banbury. No trace of her could be obtained for some time, and my father wrote the above lines when, unexpectedly, he received a letter from Mr. Carter of Edgcote, our nearest country squire, who was then in London, at his house in Brook Street (I think) to say that his coachman had just come to him and said he was sure Mr. Wasey's old mare was at that time in their mews. A man had brought her in with a load of sand. He could tell her out of a thousand in London, and as he was sure Mr. Wasey would never have sold her, there must have been some 'foul play' so he had kept the man under some pretext while he went to his master. Mr. Carter immediately went to a police magistrate, Sir Benjamin Hall, I think it was, who he knew, and who happened to live close to him, and asked whether, under such circumstances, he could give authority for detaining the man. He said he'd detain the *mare* so as to allow time for identification, provided the coachman was quite sure about it. The man, on being questioned, stated that he had bought her from a boatman on the canal, which added to the suspicions, so she was detained, and my father sent a servant to town to swear to her and bring her back. The sandman, the fellow, was not heard of again. Whoever had stolen her, she no doubt had been worked up the canal, 80 miles to London. The poor thing neighed several times when brought into our yard. She was in a miserable plight from ill-usage and died with her lungs completely diseased, some months after.

That she should have been taken into the only mews in London where the only man in London who could have identified her happened to be at that time. That his master should have been at home. That a police magistrate, with whom he was acquainted, lived close to him, and was himself at home, were such remarkable coincidences as almost to justify the application of the text: 'What hath God wrought without whom not a sparrow falls to the ground!'

The peaceful village of Wardington, not far from the canal, is less than a mile from the picturesque village of Edgcote, seat of Mr Carter 'our nearest country squire'. On the south external wall of the chancel of Edgcote Church a tablet had been erected to commemorate the passing of Wasey's mother, Honoria, when she died four years previously. More poignant is the inscription on the adjacent stone covering the family vault, made when they laid their daughter Emma to rest, aged only 11 years: 'Behold the harvest when the bud is perfect'. And in the *Family Book* Wasey wrote: 'this sweet child died October 1 1827 at Oxford'.

A EUROPEAN TOUR AND A VISIT TO BATH

Wasey took his family abroad for the year in 1830 and they were in Brussels during the uprising – which began in an opera house. The audience gathered forces and, during the three days' streetfighting that followed, resisted occupation by Dutch troops sent during negotiations for their independence.

It is exasperating to find in the *Family Book* meticulously recorded details of births, sponsors and childhood illnesses; yet all it conveys of their presence during this turbulent event (from the eldest son) is: 'spent the next year with my family abroad, was at Brussels during the revolution'! Their European tour evidently continued eastwards, since he adds: 'and afterwards in Germany'.

Later that year Wasey's mother-in-law died. She had been resident since her widowhood mostly at Somerset House, but now her body was returned to Broadwell and buried in the church there with her husband, Captain Frodsham.[25]

Early in 1834 Wasey and his wife visited her unmarried sister, Emma, now living at Bath, where, according to the *Family Book*, she 'passed the chief of her latter years with her very dear and valued friend Mrs. Harriet Bowdler, well known for her Christian excellence and literary pursuits'. Mistress Bowdler had died in about 1830 when Emma Frodsham took (or was bequeathed) her friend's house, No. 2 Park Street, St James' Square.[26]

While there, Wasey received a letter from his curate Mr Burkitt, at Ulcombe, telling of a petition presented by his parishioners to the House of Commons.[27] It was, he said, 'signed by everyone in the parish and . . . of the most radical cast . . . stating that the tithe absorbed "the whole profit of the Farmer" and overwhelmed him with the expense of the poor by rendering him unable to employ the labourers he would etc . . .'.

The subject of tithes and the Poor Law was presently being much debated in Parliament, a special commission having been ordered to investigate its applications throughout the country. To help alleviate the plight of the poor at Ulcombe, Wasey had offered allotments for cultivation. The letter from his curate reported:

on the 17th I let the whole of the remaining quarters[28] [but, he said, within] a day or two some of the best of your new tenants came to me for advice . . . [The farmers] had declared that they wd do all in their power to oppose their labourers renting land and . . . some had told poor fellows who had been all round the parish to ask for work, and having *got none*, were going to dig their own land, that if [it] should be cultivated . . . by themselves or by their boys even, or wives, [the benefit from this] . . . should *at once* be deducted from their weekly allowance (to labourers unemployed) the value of the work done on their land.

So the farmers were threatening to have the out-relief allowed to the unemployed of the parish stopped, should they dare to work, or even have their families work, the ground they rented to help alleviate their distress. The farmers, said Mr Burkitt, asserted the men were giving too much for their land, and making it pay, so that the farmers' landlords would expect more of them. He said the men knew the farmers were unwilling that the landlords should find out how productive the land could really be, one reasoning thus: 'I gave Mr. Day 10*s* last year for a quarter of an acre of inferior land, to this I raised 22 sacks of potatoes. If Mr. Wasey had taken his right, he would have taken at least 6*s* for his tithe; but Mr. Wasey took only 1*s*, so that a ¼ of an acre of inferior land would have stood me in 16*s* instead of 12/6 which I am to pay for Mr. Wasey's field.'

Mr Burkitt said the men were willing for the parish to take a tithe after they had obtained a crop from the land, but it was to the farmers' advantage to ensure their rector should not know its value and thus they were afraid the poor, by their efforts, would reveal its true worth. Burkitt points out that the system of parochial allowance (dependent on the size of family) often made it impossible for a man to earn, at the low rates paid by the farmers, more than two-thirds of his allowance in parish relief. '. . . I am happy to say [he continued] that I find on the more near acquaintance which this allotment system has given me with ye labourers, that *the desire* of being independent of the Parish is still strong – and that if our farmers were possessed of half the good feeling of the labourers, labour wd find its *due* reward . . .'. In his last paragraph he appeals: 'If I had any friends in Parliament who would be likely to make use of the . . . circumstances of this Parish . . . for illustrating . . . the senseless character of the clamour against tithes and the clergy, the supineness (or worse) of Landlords and the extreme abuses of the Poor Law system I would certainly address a letter . . . on these subjects, and your allotments should have their proper place in my statement.'

To this, Wasey responded by writing to Sir T.F. Fremantle (son of Admiral Fremantle)[29], a politician much concerned with the tithe and Poor Law question:

2 Park Street, St. James Square, Bath   Feby 28 1834

My dear Sir, Knowing you to be active . . . in your . . . endeavours to bring about a better state of things in the country respecting the Poor Laws, and my Parish having lately brought themselves before the House in the form of a Petition . . . for the Commutation of Tithes, I am encouraged by the obliging note you favoured me with in Feby last to recur to a statement I then took the liberty of troubling you with, relative to the Living of Ulcombe in Kent, if such a benefice can be called a Living, which, though comprehending a considerable number of Acres, and a comparatively small Population, is yet so circumstanced as to yield scarcely anything to its possessor.

The accompanying . . . Letter received . . . from my Curate . . . who is . . . anxious for a better state of things in the Parish, will give you some insight . . . – which he will fully enlarge upon for your better information if you will allow him so to do.

In the hope that this will find you, and Lady Fremantle quite well, I Remain, My dear Sir

    Y^rs very sincerely   George Wasey

From the Lime Cliffs near Bath

As absentee parson, Wasey appears to have been subject to the disregard, if not actual animosity, of Ulcombe farmers; his phrase 'if such a benefice can be called a living' demonstrates his frustration. Some years before, it had been necessary to sue one yeoman farmer, Thomas Bates the elder, for an unpaid debt.[30]

The Revd George Wasey

On 5 April (her illness no doubt the reason for their stay in Bath), Wasey's sister-in-law, Emma Frodsham, died. She bequeathed the Park Street house to his wife, and a family bible dated 1693 is another of her possessions which came to the Wasey family. Emma was buried at Box, opposite the grave of her friend, Mrs Harriet Bowdler, and in the *Family Book* is a drawing of the tombstone with, on the adjacent page, a charming sketch of the village of Box, 'taken from the Lime Cliffs nr. Bath' showing Brunel's elegant entrance to the new and famous tunnel.

It was probably while in Bath that Wasey and his wife sat for their silhouettes. George, clean-shaven, his hair cut close to his head, appears to be wearing his cassock. Anne has her hair swept up and has it crowned with a cap or ribbons. From the *Family Book* we learn that George's health remained delicate and '. . . in the spring of 1836 [he was] severely attacked by influenza, from which he never completely rallied'. Two years later, he died.

In his will Wasey commends his soul to God and prays, 'He will of His infinite goodness guard protect and take under his particular care my beloved Wife my children and my Niece . . .'.[31] Having provided for his children, he

His wife Anne

specified that Anne, in addition to her legacy, should have his household goods, furniture, books, plate, linen, china, carriages, horses, stock and interest in 2 Park Street, Bath, during her lifetime.

Domestic matters were left to her, who, he said, 'I feel sure . . . will . . . do all that is right about my servants'. Eliza was clearly worthy of the love and affection shown by all members of the family. To her, 'my beloved niece', he left one hundred guineas, 'a poor insufficient but grateful return for her ever kind love and attention to me'. He adds, 'I could wish much to leave several remembrances beyond the above named but forbear the Gratification fearing they might bear too heavily on the limited means I am enabled to leave my beloved wife Anne Sophia and my five children.'

George was buried at Edgcote which, as his son records, 'from its quiet beauty he had chosen as the burial place of my grandmother Wasey'. And, he says, 'in a secluded nook . . . on the south side of the chancel . . .within the communion rails, my mother erected a small tablet of beautiful taste and workmanship to his memory'.

George Wasey, we may feel sure, would have been content with the epithet his son wrote at the bottom of the page allotted to him in the *Family Book*: 'He was throughout life a most popular man amongst a large circle of friends and acquaintances and left a good name to his children'.

HIS WIDOW

Spared the pain and sorrow of future events, Wasey was also denied the joy of his daughter's marriage in the spring of 1840. Sophia Elizabeth was engaged to marry the Revd George Wingfield, rector of Glatton, Hunts. He was the youngest son of

Wasey's Memorial (a page from the Family Book*)*

J. Wingfield Esq., of Tickencote, Rutland, descended from an old and knightly family in Suffolk.[32] The wedding took place on 21 April, the bridesmaids being Caroline Kindersley, Fanny Loring, the two Miss Holbecks and 'the two Miss Leighs'.[1] The latter were cousins, mentioned in the diary of a clergyman, the Revd F.E. Witts,[33] whose home, Upper Slaughter, was but a few miles from Broadwell: 'We dined at Mr. Leigh's at Broadwell and met Sir Charles and Lady Imhoff, Miss Chapuset, Mr. & Mrs. Vavasour of Stow, Messrs. W.B. and Mundy Pole; with the family party we sat down fifteen to dinner. Music in the evening, the Misses Leigh playing and singing . . .'.

The Mr and Mrs Vavasour at the gathering had sent their son to Rugby School in August 1832, making him a fellow pupil of Sophia's young brother, John Spearman, entered at the same time. An earlier diary entry, made in 1827, records a visit to a neighbour and his new bride: 'We took a drive to Adlestrop to pay the compliment of a wedding visit to Mr. & Mrs. Twisleton, the young rector having lately married the Hon. Emily Wingfield. The lady possesses more blood than beauty . . .'

If the lack of good looks perceived by Mr Witts was prevalent on the distaff side of the Wingfield family, they must surely have been charmed by the beautiful Sophia Wasey when she married George Wingfield that spring. A portrait was taken to commemorate the event. Her hair is drawn smoothly back from a centre parting and her lovely heart-shaped face has a straight delicate nose, large liquid eyes and well-formed mouth. She wears an off-the-shoulder gown, fitting well into her tiny waist, with double bows on each shoulder and flowing lace sleeves; draped over her arms is a dark taffeta stole edged with lace. Her hair is liberally dressed with jewellery and she wears drop earrings, a brooch, and a large chunky bracelet. News reports describe the festivities: 'Wardington . . . presented a scene of very joyous animation. The church was crowded with . . .villagers . . .'.

Sophia Wingfield, née Wasey

On the following day, to celebrate the event, Mrs Wasey gave a dinner to 194 poor of the neighbourhood who were, we read: 'hospitably regaled with roast beef, plum pudding etc., on the lawn at Mrs Wasey's residence' One account continues: 'Loyal . . . toasts were . . . responded to, followed by loud cheering and songs, concluding . . . with God Save the Queen which . . . was well given in full chorus and sung in the good old English style. Dancing in which the family and visitors all joined . . . commenced, which was kept up with great spirit til dusk. The happy party then broke up highly delighted with the reception . . . which was rendered additionally cheerful by the auspicious weather of the day' Another report concludes: 'It is only proper to add that this is of a piece with the general habits of the Wasey family who, from their first coming to the village about 20 years ago, have always pursued a course of active and unremitting benevolence to the poor'.

BAD NEWS FROM HOME AND ABROAD

Mrs Wasey must have been delighted during the summer to hear that Sophia was to become a mother, happiness which turned to anxiety when her daughter 'fell, soon after her marriage, into a state of continued sickness, the latter part of her time, confined wholly to her bed'.[1]

Meanwhile, her second son, Willoughby, who had fallen ill after going into the Customs Service, subsequently '. . . went to Corfu in the Commissariat Department'.[1] Then came the dreadful news: struck down, suddenly, with the Ionian fever, he had succumbed and died. Next to a drawing of his memorial in the *Family Book*, it tells us, 'He bore a high character for gentlemanly conduct [and displayed an] active, conciencious performance of his duty'.

Willoughby Clement Wasey's memorial

This was not the only reason for Mrs Wasey's anguish: her lovely young daughter's condition was worsening. We learn that 'her beautiful composure and cheerful patience were the admiration and comfort of all who attended her'. But, 'after giving premature birth to a child who died instantly, she also sank exhausted, on the 5th November 1840'.[1] One can scarcely imagine the grief created by these two tragedies in such a short space of time.

Mrs Wasey had five more years to live, much loved by her three remaining sons, one of whom was to marry, before she passed away on 1 December 1845.

Chapter Five: Two Clergymen and a Sailor

After Willoughby's death there were still three brothers to further the name and fortunes of the Wasey family. The elder two, very different in character, were to take the cloth and the other chose a naval career.

William George Leigh, the eldest (known as George), is he to whom we owe so much for the biographical snippets preserved in the *Family Book*. In it he tells us he spent four years at Charterhouse, but left 'on account of ill health [and] went to Revd. Dr. Radcliffe's at Salisbury' where he remained 'in perfect health and great enjoyment til 1827'. Later, he tells us, he 'went to Revd. William Allen's, Peel Hall, near Bolton for a year's private tuition' and, having entered Christ Church, Oxford, in December 1829, he spent the following year abroad with his family.

On returning to Oxford he took his BA degree in 1834 and later that year, the curacy of Mollington. Soon after, he was appointed domestic chaplain to Lord Bridport (with whom there was a family connection)[2] and on gaining his MA in 1836 was ordained priest, taking the curacy of Condover, Shropshire, and subsequently of Herstmonceux, Sussex. But he 'only held it three months, having received from Lord Sudeley, my father's old and firm friend, the . . . Curacies of Morville cum Aston Eyre . . . and Quatford'.[1]

Meanwhile, in August 1832, his younger brother John Spearman (known as Spearman) was entered, aged 15, at Rugby School and placed in the esteemed 'School House'. If he took the coach called the Regulator, which passed that way from Oxford, the 30-mile journey would have taken the best part of the day, travelling at about six miles an hour with stops for meals and to bait the horses. Dressed in petersham coat with velvet collar, Spearman reported with his trunk to the housekeeper who will have allotted him a small, shared, partly-wainscoted study furnished with table, chairs, sofa and bookcases. Soon it was time to assemble in 'big school' for 'calling over', when each of the three hundred boys, called by name, would answer 'here' before taking his leave.

As a new boy, Spearman was excused fagging for the first month while settling into Rugby's way of life, and before long he was initiated into the school's revered sport, its unique form of football. Schoolwork started early and finished at 5 p.m., but numerous leisure periods allowed for the usual schoolboy pastimes of bird-nesting, fishing and swimming, as well as cricket, fives and 'hare and hounds', a form of cross-country running. Here, Spearman was privileged to spend the next few years under the influence of the renowned Doctor Arnold. The following term a now-famous, though younger, contemporary joined them: Thomas Hughes, author of *Tom Brown's Schooldays*.

Three years later, the youngest Wasey brother, 15-year-old Edward (known as Ned) 'entered the Navy [and] went out to Rio de Janeiro to join his distant cousin, Sir Graham Hamond,[3] Admiral of that Station in Dublin'.[1] When Sir Graham returned to England (having been promoted vice-admiral), Ned went with his son, Andrew Hamond, to the Pacific in the *Rover*, returning to England in 1838. That same year he sailed to the West Indies under Captain George Ramsay in the *Pilot*, subsequently going on to the North America Station where, during the five years he spent there, he suffered from yellow fever. From the *Family Book* we learn that on 31 January 1842, after six years' service, Edward passed his examination, going on to serve as mate in the *Pilot* and subsequently in the steam frigate *Penelope* under Commodore William Jones.

CAPTURE OF A SLAVE SHIP

It was on Ned's return from an extremely perilous, 89-day journey crossing the Atlantic that he was promoted. The sloop *Alert*, on which he was acting-lieutenant under Commander Bosanquet, had captured, at Cabenda, an unnamed Brazilian slave ship, without colours, having between 70 and 80 slaves on board. The story continues, as reported in the *Herald*:

> . . . having put Mr. Wasey and a prize crew on board, he was ordered to proceed to Sierra Leone for adjudication. The gales, however, were unpropitious, and he was driven by their force on the south coast of America. He managed . . . by almost superhuman exertions to reach Maranham, one of the northern presidencies of the Brazils, although he had frequently seven feet water in the hold, with fresh leaks breaking out at intervals, and only kept her afloat by dint of extraordinary perseverance, in working with great difficulty the pumps, and baling.

On arrival, the British Consul 'rendered every assistance' and an endeavour was made to locate government officers to protect the slaves until a vessel could be found to take them. But:

> . . . whilst Mr. Wasey was engaged on shore with the President in endeavouring to effect his object, a body of about 40 or 50 armed men, in the uniform of the national guard, proceeded to the vessel, saying to those on board that they were instructed to take the slaves and crew, and conduct them to a place of safety for the night it being then impossible for any one to remain on board as the water was washing over the decks. [However] the English seamen refused to leave the vessel in the absence of their officer; but all the slaves, together with the captain and crew of the slaver, landed with their visitors.

On Wasey's return he found the 80 slaves and the prisoners gone. The 'Brazilian soldiers' proved to be a party of brigands in disguise 'who had made themselves masters of the cargo, and had marched them off up the country . . .'. The government's attempt to recover them was unsuccessful and so Wasey, with his men, embarked on board a merchantman for Liverpool where, on arrival, he 'immediately reported himself at the Admiralty'. His intrepid conduct, we read, not only during this incident, but while acting-lieutenant on the coast of Africa, and while in the West Indies when the *Pilot* was afflicted with severe sickness, brought promotion to the rank of lieutenant.

PIRACY IN THE MEDITERRANEAN

Life for Ned continued hazardous. He was appointed, on 24 April that same year, 2nd lieutenant to HMS *Polyphemus*, a steam sloop commanded by Mr MacCleverty on the Gibraltar Station. Exploits on her also made headlines. A press cutting dated 20 November 1848 declares:

> It is not often . . . we have to record a . . . case of piracy in the vicinity of a British fortress, but the Pasha, from Gibraltar, brings us details of an extraordinary piratical attack on an English brig, on the part of the Moors . . . chastised by the energy of Captain M'Cleverty of H.M. steamer Polyphemus. It appears . . . the English brig Three Sisters . . . arrived at Gibraltar . . . from Glasgow . . . was becalmed about 12 miles off Cape Tres Forcas, coast of Morocco, when six piratical boats filled with armed Moors put off from the shore and attacked the vessel. . . .[4]

From a letter sent by the captain of the *Three Sisters* to the consignees we learn:

> . . . they were nothing else than pirates, each boat pulling from 12 to 14 oars, with an additional lot standing in midships, with their long muskets, all ready for action; they also had large guns on their gunwales. After witnessing all the formidable weapons I thought it was high time to look for the preservation of our own lives; . . . I ordered the small boat to be got out, in order to keep without the reach of their guns, but . . . no sooner had we put off from the ship, than a volley of shot came tumbling about the boat, but . . . they all fell a few yards short; and I am confident had I remained five minutes longer, there would be no person to tell the tale . . . .[5]

Having made their escape in the jollyboat, Captain Forster and his crew of eight were picked up about 12 hours later by an English brig, the *Dawn*. They last saw their vessel being towed by the pirates in seven launches towards the shore, about ten miles distant. On board, in addition to other merchandise, were 800 barrels of gunpowder. The letter from Commander MacCleverty to the Admiralty tells of what took place when his ship, with Wasey its 2nd Lieutenant, became involved:

Moorish Pirate

> We started the same evening to the Rif Coast, and . . . discovered her [the *Three Sisters*] anchored close to the shore in a small bay, partly surrounded by an amphitheatre of precipices, high rocks, and ravines, all of which places were crowded with men armed with long muskets, evidently for the purpose of protecting the brig, which lay considerably within musket-shot range. Their boats . . . were hauled up on the beach . . . with a strong party of armed men lying under cover for the protection of part of the cargo, which they had landed. Their whole force appeared to consist of at least 500 men. On approaching . . . the brig they opened fire of musketry from all points, which we immediately returned with grape, canister, and musketry, doubtless with very good effect, as a very large number of them began flying about in all directions, and taking up more secure positions. Having dislodged them from the beach, we

HMS Polyphemus *and the* Three Sisters *on the Rif Coast*

proceeded to take the vessel in tow . . . performed by Lieutenant Gardner, who volunteered to take the cutter, with a hawser, and weigh the brig's anchor. Just at this time a fire was opened from a gun, supposed to be a six or nine pounder, and as unavoidably, our stern was towards the nearest point of low rocks, and therefore could make no return, encouraged them to approach us quite close, and open a well-directed fire of musketry, which, I regret to say, severely wounded Lieutenant Wasey and slightly two seamen . . . .

It was the captain's intention to land and burn the boats, but:

from the secure position taken up by so numerous a body of well-armed men, I deemed it very imprudent to risk so severe a loss as must have . . . taken place, particularly as the fire from our great gun had rendered them unserviceable . . . [and so] Having now taken the brig in tow, we steamed to sea . . . .

Captain MacCleverty's account concludes:

. . . it would be invidious . . . to point out any individual where every one behaved so well; but I cannot omit bringing to your notice the zeal displayed by Mr Gardner, First-Lieutenant, who volunteered to board the brig under so severe a fire . . . also the able support I received from Lieutenant Wasey, in command of the foremost gun, and the coolness and skill displayed by Mr. Taylor, the Master, in conducting the ship in so intricate a place.

A letter from the Albion Office gives additional information:

. . . The captain of the Polyphemus . . . fortunately would not take the bad advice of our governor to proceed at first to Tangier and consult with the Consul-General, but started direct for the coast of Riff in search of the brig, which he found anchored in a little creek . . . with hardly room for the steamer to turn in . . . and preparations were made to give him a warm reception . . . [It tells of the waiting armed men] to the number of several hundred. [Nevertheless, it continues] the prize was brought out, but not until four of the crew . . . were wounded. Lieutenant Wasey received a ball in his arm, near the elbow . . . .

The story also appeared in the *Illustrated London News*, with an artist's impression of the two ships. The report ended thus: 'This circumstance had created some excitement at Gibraltar, and it was supposed that Her Majesty's Government would demand satisfaction from the Emperor of Morocco for this wanton aggression on the part of his subjects.'

THE ROYAL YACHT *VICTORIA AND ALBERT*

After spending some time in a Gibraltar hospital, Wasey returned home in the *Polyphemus*, the ball still in the bone of his, now almost useless, right arm.[6] Despite this handicap, we learn from the *Family Book* that he was appointed, in March 1849, second lieutenant to the Royal Yacht *Victoria and Albert*. This was the year the queen paid her first visit to Ireland, suffering still, after four dreadful years of famine. Its people, however, could not have welcomed their queen with more jubilance.

One visit was to Cove, renamed 'Queenstown'. The hills around blazed with fires and the guard-ships 'ran out white lamps along their spars and rigging . . . throwing up rockets . . .', while every vessel in the harbour 'vied with the other in splendour of illumination'. 'Never' claims a news report of 3 August, 'was there such a night of rejoicing . . .with all its cannonading-cheering – addressing and Queenstowning'.[7] It was 'meagre and petty', however, 'in comparison to the displays which awaited her Majesty and the royal suite on their return from the "Beautiful Citie". . .'.

The queen wrote to her uncle the King of Belgium: '. . . our entrance into Dublin was . . . a magnificent thing. . . . Our visit to Cork was very successful; the Mayor was knighted on deck . . . like in times of old. . . . We had previously stepped on shore at Cove . . . to enable them to call it Queen's Town; the enthusiasm is immense, and at Cork there was more firing than I remember since the Rhine.'

Having been made commander in September 1850, Wasey remained on the yacht for two years.[1]

A WEDDING

The first of the three Wasey brothers to marry was George, the eldest. He took as his bride Elizabeth (Eliza) Lenora, the daughter of Philip Monckton Esq., of the Bengal Civil Service. Both he and his brother, Edward of Somerford (by whom Eliza was brought up after her father's death), were grandsons of the 1st Viscount Galway and many of the press cuttings kept by the couple relate to the Monckton family.[8]

George and Eliza married at Brewood, Staffordshire, in April 1844 and soon made their home in the vicarage at Knowle Sands, on the banks of the Severn. Wasey's other living was across the river at Quatford: reached by ferry, or by a

Revd Wm George Leigh Wasey

drive of about four miles via the ancient arched bridge at Bridgnorth.

Miniatures of the couple were painted soon after their marriage. George's handsome features are crowned with dark wavy hair and sideburns reach to his chin; he wears a white frilled shirt with high stock beneath his morning coat. Eliza too has good features and her hair is sleek with a centre parting. She is wearing an off-the-shoulder gown with tight-fitting bodice, topped with a deep band of lace, which shows to advantage her tiny waist.

The Revd George and Mrs Wasey were to have two daughters but no sons, which was regrettable, since, judging by the way they valued and updated the *Family Book*, they had a strong sense of family.

His wife, Eliza

Their first daughter, Sophia Honoria, had her details entered in the time-honoured way: 'Born at the Knowle Sands parsonage . . . 18 January 1847. Christened at Quatford Church . . . . On the same day, the Queen's . . . sermon was preached there for the Irish famine. The noble collection of £50 was made. Her sponsors were Edward Monckton Esq. . . . of Somerford, her mother's eldest . . . uncle; Elizabeth Honoria Margaret Wasey, my 1st cousin [she was to die in December that year, her memorial erected in Wardington Church[9]]; Charlotte Sophia Whichcote Lizzie's sister. Her names were chosen after my sweet mother [she had died the previous year] and sisters.'

The following year another daughter arrived and Wasey recorded: '. . . Christened . . . Leonora Sabrina, in honour of our beautiful river, which flows close under our windows, and the county in which I have received so much kindness, and by God's mercy, have been so abundantly blessed . . .'.

PASTORAL BENEFACTOR

A conscientious and dedicated clergyman, George enjoyed the loyalty and affection of his neighbours and flock. Although he held three livings, he was not, claimed a neighbour writing of him years later, a rich pluralist: 'the income of Morville and Aston Eyre together was £227 10s 6d, and of Quatford was £59, with seven acres of land, out of which he employed a curate'.[10]

He lived comfortably, however, employing, in 1851, a groom, four servants and a nursemaid, and was in a position to travel, both in England and abroad, visiting and being visited by a wide circle of family and friends. One such holiday was when the family toured Ireland by that new mode of travel, the railway, noting '. . . to the right of the Line from Dublin . . . the ruins of Lea Castle which once was the property of Lizzy's maternal Gt. Grand-father. . .'. In the *Family Book* there is an account of it, dated 7 September 1852, 'cut out of the Irish Chart of Dublin & Cork Railway'.

Knowle Sands Parsonage

Over the years, with the help of friends and relations, many of them wealthy, George raised sufficient funds to expend the sums of £664 2s 1d on the restoration of Morville Church, £280 on Aston Eyre's and a further £951 1s on his beloved Quatford Church.[10] In December 1856 the *Bridgnorth Journal* carried a report on the reopening of Morville Church, mentioning the reroofing of the chancel carried out two years previously at 'the joint expense of Lord Sudeley and the Rev. G.L. Wasey'. It continued:

> The church was . . . ornamented by . . . parishioners, with wreaths of evergreens winding over the arches, round the pillars, and hanging in rich festoons from the wall . . . [A] procession . . . headed by the children . . . with banner . . . proceeded to the church, which was completely filled by . . . the chief gentry and farmers of the district . . . Amongst the clergy . . . were the Ven. Archdeacon Waring; Rev. G.L. Wasey, incumbent; [and 26 named clergy from far and wide]. The solemn manner in which the . . . service was conducted . . . the elegant though simple decorations . . . leave a lasting impression on those . . . present. The sum of £44.13s.9½ was collected . . . towards the building expenses, and the erection of a handsome stove [it was Christmas] . . . appeared well to answer its object.

A year later, in the *Shrewsbury Chronicle*, an article appeared telling of the restoration and enlargement of Quatford Church when extensive alterations and repairs were carried out, including additional seating for 270 and 'a handsome west memorial window to the mother of the present incumbent' (Anne Sophia Wasey).

The church was full, attended by 'the clergy and principal gentry of the neighbourhood', of whom at least 80 were named, including the Ven. Archdeacon, Rural Dean, the residents of Quat Castle and the mayor of Bridgnorth. A collection of £48 12s was made and after the service, Wasey 'entertained a party at lunch in the Schoolroom'.

Not content with restoring the churches in his keeping, Wasey worked towards other building projects: a schoolhouse and residence for a teacher at Eardington, amounting to £618 6s 11½, £300 for the same purpose at Quatford and at Morville the magnificent sum of £748 12s 9d was raised. He also built, with typical Victorian double standards, the parsonage at Morville for the disproportionate cost of £1,359 17s 4d. Beneath these sums Wasey noted in his account book: 'The above very important works have been effected, thanks to Almighty God, and to very kind and liberal relations, owners of property and friends'.[10]

LOCAL POLITICS AND HISTORY

As elsewhere, there was a great deal of antipathy in the Bridgnorth area against the formation of turnpike trusts enabling groups of local gentry to build roads and charge tolls for their maintenance and use. It bore heavily on farmers and tradespeople needing to transport goods and produce to and from the towns, reducing their profits considerably.

Aware of their plight, Wasey took action, and the gratitude of neighbours was expressed by a presentation made to him and his wife at their home, Knowle Sands, as reported in the local paper: 'An interesting meeting of neighbours took place at the parsonage . . . when twelve principal gentry and farmers . . . presented the Revd. G.L. Wasey with a beautiful token of their esteem and . . . approval of his persevering conduct in lowering the tolls at the Oldbury Catchgate, which for so many years pressed most unfairly on the district skirting the south bank of the Severn. The testimonial took the very pleasing form of a charming miniature of Mrs. Wasey, by Reginald Easton Esq., and is a remarkable faithful likeness . . .'.

Presentation painting of Eliza

Eliza is shown seated in what must be Knowle Sands parsonage, for in the background can be glimpsed the river so loved by the family. Forty-five friends and neighbours contributed to the gift, which was enclosed in a Morocco case, bearing the inscription: 'Presented by his neighbours of . . . Eardington, Chelmarsh and Highley to . . . Rev. William George Leigh Wasey as an acknowledgement of his persevering efforts in carrying through the House of Commons a petition against the Oldbury side turnpike gate and obtaining a reduction of more than half the tolls January 1st 1858.'

George Wasey was fascinated by the history of the Bridgnorth area. Having studied the subject he prepared a lecture to be delivered to 'The Bridgnorth Society for the Promotion of Religious and Useful Knowledge' and began by saying: 'let me not . . . imply that antiquarian lore is . . . a dry pursuit; on the contrary, those who give themselves to it find it peculiarly engaging; it brings us acquainted with men of other minds and habits than our own; it accounts for many of the things we see around us; it shows us to whom, under God, we may be thankful for our ancient institutions, . . . it opens our minds . . . removes us for a time from our own daily cares and selfish feelings and carries us away to live with past generations . . . and when it is directed to objects in our own neighbourhood, it tends to increase our patriotism and warm our local affections, and make our homes dearer to us.'

He refers to the foundation charter of Quatford Church and quotes: 'In the time of William the King . . . and Adelaysa, the Countess built a church in Quatford . . . . They gave . . . that land which is between the water (i.e. the river) and the mount (i.e. the opposite bank) nigh to the bridge. . .'.

No bridge had existed at Quatford for hundreds of years! For a parson with a living each side of the river who found it necessary, as did many of his parishioners, to regularly traverse in a small boat that often treacherous water, a bridge was the ultimate dream and Wasey comments: 'It is curious that to this day thirty five acres on the Eardington side of the river should belong and pay rates to Quatford township, and in the exact position thus marked out 770 years ago, between the river and the opposite rising ground . . .'. He adds wistfully:

in those . . . times . . . communication between the two parts of the Parish was so much more convenient than it is now: there was no need of an experienced and stalwart ferryman to put people safely 'over Severn'; no timid females were alarmed, . . . no idle parishioners could make the dangers of the passage an excuse for not attending Divine worship; no mischievous boys were tempted to rock the boat . . .; no affectionate clergyman . . . [and] ministering canons were made nervous after an unusually good congregation by the . . . possibility of danger to their flock from . . . crowding into the boat . . . in . . . their reckless haste to dinner – but the . . . bridge . . . spanned fair Sabrina's stream . . . near the Deanery public house, now a mere approach to two fields, was then the high road . . . to Quatford bridge (O name! the desire of one's heart).

Wasey continued to long for the convenience and safety of a bridge, an ideal which remained with him until his dying day. The lecture was so successful that, with additional information and acknowledgements to sources used, it was published in 1859.[11]

WINTERING IN THE SOUTH OF FRANCE

When his daughters were aged 9 and 10 years respectively, Wasey had their portraits painted in miniature and in the *Family Book*, he comments: 'though only ten years old, Sophia was 4ft 10 inches high'. Both girls were pretty but, although tall for her age, Sophia was of a delicate constitution and suffered much ill health. For this reason the family went abroad during the winter months on more than one occasion: 'In consequence of Sophy's delicate health after the whooping cough, our kind Archdeacon Waring insisted on our going to the South of France for the winter of 1859 and we did not return til May 23 1861' (her sister's entry).[1]

Leonora and Sophia Wasey

While there, George Wasey preached, when invited, as was the custom for visiting clergy. His sermon, 'The Spirituality or Reasonableness of the Church of England Public Prayers', preached at Christ Church, Cannes, on Sunday, 28 April 1861, was so well received that it was suggested he publish it, and friends 'saw it through the press' for him after his return to England.

News cuttings tell of the excitement generated on the family's return: '. . . five to six hundred people . . . assembled at Quatford Toll Gate, to give their pastor a truly hospitable . . . reception'. When the family drove up in their carriage, there was 'a burst of hearty cheers that made the welkin ring . . . [and also] at the Tollgate, [where] a triumphal arch, composed of flowers and evergreens, was erected . . .'. As the carriage passed through, the band struck up and after hearty cheering, a welcoming address was made: 'Reverend Sir, it was with extreme regret that we . . . had, nearly two years ago, to bid you farewell on your departure from this to another country. It is today . . . our privilege to bid you welcome home again, and to offer you our hearty congratulations on the safe return of yourself and family . . . '.

Wasey replied at length:

> . . . I . . . thank you truly for the trouble you have taken in assembling to bid Mrs Wasey and the children welcome home; and hope not to be obliged to leave you again. It is quite in character with the kindness I have received since I came into Shropshire . . . I hardly think that any person born in it can love it better than I do. . . . You have . . . hardly been a day out of our thoughts. A little book that was given me at parting, with sketches of Quatford, has been continually in our hands, and I saw nothing which gave me such. . . pleasure and true comfort, even . . . at the far-famed city of Rome, as an old Quatford schoolgirl who was so good as to speak to me in the Vatican. . . . I do not mean that there are not many other sources of pleasure and delight, for we have . . . seen a great deal, and seen it thoroughly, working hard at it; but with all the beauties of scenery and the novelty abroad, our English home and your parish welfare have been the things dearest to our hearts . . . .

The procession to accompany the Wasey family to the school, headed by the Band of the Rifle Corps, formed thus:

> Herald with Banner. Herald on Horseback. Herald with Banner.
> Banner containing the following motto –
> 'A People's welcome to their Pastor'.
> Band of the 4th Shropshire Rifle Volunteers, playing
> 'Auld Lang Syne'.
> Churchwardens, Overseers, Sexton and Parish Clerk.
> Carriage containing
> Mr. and Mrs. Wasey and Family.
> School Children with Banners.
> Villagers and Visitors.
> Banner – 'Old England for ever.'
> Carriages.

On arrival: 'in a . . . tastefully selected spot a range of tables had been placed, at which the children and visitors partook of tea and other refreshments . . . the tables were then cleared, and replenished several times; the supply of good things being supplemented by a provision of excellent beef and ale for the felicitation of the coarser sex . . .'.

A long list of the attending gentry was made and the report, evincing the elan with which they celebrated, concluded: 'After every one had partaken of the good things provided, the children and visitors, who had now increased to nearly a thousand, proceeded, headed by the band, to a large field, kindly lent for the occasion . . . . Here the votaries of Terpsichore had ample opportunity of "treading a measure" to the "sweet sounds" of Mr Sewell's corps, whose performances during the afternoon and evening elicited unqualified admiration; while racing, football, cricket, and other athletic games were carried on with the greatest spirit, exhibiting . . . the prowess of those who had not troubled themselves to learn the intricacies of the dance . . .'.

In 1870, again because of Sophia's ill-health, the family spent the winter at Hyeres. Was it on their return, perhaps, that their younger daughter, Leonora, met her future husband, Lieutenant Digby of the Royal Navy?[12] He was with them the following summer at Quatford when the family's carriage overturned on their return from a visit to friends: one of the horses kicked the other and broke the pole, causing both horses to bolt. George Wasey suffered a dislocated shoulder, Eliza a broken arm, and they were all badly bruised and shaken.

Just before Christmas 1872, Leonora went to visit their distant relative, Lady Hamond, aged 80, at Norton Lodge, Isle of Wight. Perhaps it was on that occasion, while talk of matrimony was in the air, that the old lady recalled the day she married Sir Graham in her home town, Fowey, Cornwall. They had been married, recorded Leonora,[1] by special licence, at 4 a.m. on 30 December 1806 and had set out for the London house of her husband's father, Sir Andrew, immediately. The journey took four days, although, said Lady Hamond, they posted all the way, with four horses, making Exeter their first resting place. Two days after Leonora's return, the family learned of Lady Hamond's death, on Christmas Eve.

A GREAT DAY AT QUATFORD

Nearly two years later, during a visit to Wolverhampton, Henry Almarus Digby, son of the Hon. and Revd Kenelm Digby,[13] rector of Tittleshall and Hon. Canon of Norwich, asked Leonora to marry him. Her Italian singing master had given her a lesson that day and the poem he wrote on the occasion of the couple's engagement was thought worthy of entry in the *Family Book*. With this verse were two others: one, by Egerton Leigh, written from the Gd. Jury Room, Chester (he was High Sheriff), went thus:

> Say Irish muse, Why is this lass
> Christened 'Sabrina'? By the mass
> The reason for the name is plain
> As 'Venus' once sprang from the Main,
> So sprang this maid from the Say-brine
> That's why her look is so divine

Beneath, signed G.L.W. (her father), are these words:

> And why, unless the Fates should fail her
> She's given her word to wed a sailor

Not to be outdone, a friend added: 'For "L.S.D." fm. Mrs Mosley':

> The wife the 'better half' ?
> Oh yes, as the initials well express
> Hers the Pounds; Shillings – in L S
> His but the pence – Nevertheless
> Tho' so unequally this sounds,
> None can depreciate the Pence –
> The proverb gives us the true sense
> That Pence well cared for, turn to Pounds

When the wedding took place, on 26 September 1874, the local press proclaimed it: '. . . a great day in the parish of Quatford . . . from early dawn, numbers were . . . engaged in erecting arches composed of evergreens and flowers, with banners bearing appropriate mottoes at various points along the road . . . a very elegant one was opposite the house; another at the Oldbury turnpike gate; opposite Quatford

Castle; at Gen. Shepherd's; at the Quatford School and at the top of the long flight of steps leading to the beautifully situated . . . church . . . decorated with choice greenhouse and other flowers and plants and was crowded with the families of many neighbouring gentry and well-wishers . . .'.

Quatford Church

The wedding party arrived and the bride: 'attired in rich white silk . . . trimmed with lace . . . approached the altar on the arm of her father . . . attended by four bridesmaids – Miss Wasey [her sister], Miss Rosa Boddington, Miss Eliza Wasey (of Compton) [her cousin], and Miss Alice Monckton – who wore very pretty white muslin dresses, figured muslin flounces, light blue sashes and bows, bonnets to match, trimmed with blackberry leaves and long veils at the back. . .'.

The service, during which several voluntaries were played, was impressive, taken by the groom's father, assisted by the bride's uncle, the Revd Spearman Wasey. When the happy couple left, they were followed by guests in ten or more carriages and 'the leading parishioners and a host of friends', who afterwards 'assembled at the parsonage for 5 o'clock tea and to inspect the presents . . .'.

Having 'left . . . at 3 o'clock under a remarkably beautiful double arch', the bride and groom drove to the railway station 'which was decorated in a like manner' and were 'heartily cheered' on boarding the train for Chester and a tour in Ireland. That evening, on the short grass of Camp Hill, there was dancing by moonlight 'in which some of the visitors at the parsonage joined . . . with great spirit', followed by a display of 'red and blue Bengall lights and rockets . . .'.

The celebrations ended when: '"God Save the Queen" was sung . . . and cheers were given for some of the principal personages, after which the Eardington contingent, to the number of some 150, wound down the very picturesque hill with their flags, to the ferry, where they were safely punted across the Severn . . .'.

The following day: '. . . a tea drinking was given at Quatford by the vicar, to the women and children of the parish from both sides of the river. The weather . . . was perfect which enabled it to take place on that lovely spot, Camp Hill, where tables and benches . . . were laid out and where the scene on such occasions is always so picturesque and happy.'

This romantic little village was so idyllic, and so kind were its residents that, having won the hearts of the Wasey family, George purchased, probably for his retirement, a house there, called Roccabrun, which he later willed to his elder, unmarried daughter.

A SAFE CROSSING

During the spring of 1877 George Wasey became more and more anxious about the question of a bridge to connect Eardington with Quatford. The ferry boat had been in use for many years and was now in a very unsafe condition, a circumstance which weighed much upon his mind. It became clear, however, that, despite all his efforts, sufficient funds could not be raised for a bridge, and so he directed his energies to obtaining a new, safe boat.

Hearing, one day, that one was for sale at Tewkesbury, he took the train and went to ascertain its details and cost to put before the parish meeting. He had to hurry to catch his return train and became overheated, whereupon he appears to have taken a chill which brought him to, what transpired to be, his death-bed. 'Till he became unconcious', wrote his daughter in the *Family Book*, 'his people were his constant care and thought.'

Ill and feverish, unable to attend the parish meeting a day or two later, he disobeyed doctor's orders to dictate this letter:

> . . . to the Parishioners of Quatford assembled in Vestry,

> Gentlemen, Do not I pray you be persuaded by anyone to patch up for a 12 month the old punt . . . . At the Tewkesbury Ferry boat there are two attached to the chain bridge, in one of which I was pulled over by a little girl, as a quicker means of getting across to catch the train . . . . 'Have a new Boat!' and then, have up a blacksmith . . . and let him see the working on Sunday, and let him see the traffic. He told me he was willing to put up a smaller boat of the kind used at Tewkesbury for from £40 to £50. If when he thinks it will work well, you wish for a larger boat . . . but mind there is danger with that, not of people going down wholesale, but of walking over at the edge. My attention was called to it by seeing two life-buoys attached to the bridge, and a poor drunken fellow walked into Severn last winter along the bridge – and our tattling boys might go over two or three at a time. I hope I may live to hear what the engineer says. He told me also there was a smaller boat . . . lately put down some miles above Gloucester . . . . God bless you all . . . . NB William is to take this to Quatford tomorrow . . . and attend the meeting, and bring an account of what passes.

HIS LAST JOURNEY

Three days later George Wasey was dead. With his obituary was a letter from the Revd Bellet, rector of Whitbourne, who said of him: '. . . His loss to the parishioners of Quatford, Morville and Aston . . . is greater than can be easily estimated . . . . He had laboured among them for more than thirty-seven years, with an earnest diligence which never seemed to tire, and with a zeal for their spiritual and temporal interests that continued unabated to the end . . .'.

Having selected a quiet spot for his grave at Quatford, Wasey left instructions that his funeral be conducted in an unostentatious manner, with neither hearse nor mourning coach and no hatbands or scarves to be worn. The following Wednesday afternoon his body was placed on board the ferry boat, taken down river and landed on the Quatford side.

Here, the coffin, covered with wreaths from countless friends, was met by mourners and fourteen bearers to be carried along the familiar footpath and up the steps Wasey had climbed so often. 'Although the funeral was of [a] strictly private character,' said the newspaper report, 'great numbers . . . followed, desirous to pay a last tribute . . .'. And after the service, school children 'walked past the grave, each one dropping a bouquet of white flowers upon the coffin . . .'.

George Wasey's widow and their elder daughter were not among the many mourners. 'His death', wrote Mrs Digby, their younger daughter, 'was such a

Quatford Ferry and Camp Hill

shock to our beloved mother, that within twelve hours, she had a terrible stroke of apoplexy and paralysis, and after lingering a few weeks, she followed on July 29th 1877.' Eliza's remains, followed by many of the same mourners, were also taken down river to Quatford's peaceful churchyard to be buried with her husband.

In his will George Wasey bequeathed money first and foremost: 'towards the erection of a Footbridge over Severn from the Eardington side to Quatford Church . . .'. Sums were left for Salop and Bridgnorth infirmaries and after legacies for his daughters, brothers and godchildren, one of whom was Arthur Frodsham Wasey, the residue was for his daughters, with the proviso 'that the Wasey Diamond Earings; the four Figure Candlesticks given to my Great Grandfather by the College of Physicians; the large silver waiter . . . and silver cup and cover which all came from my Grandfather Colonel Wasey shall be kept as Heirlooms by my daughters during their lives and afterwards by my Brother Spearman and his eldest descendants of the name of Wasey in succession . . .'.

A NEW FERRY BOAT

Some years later it was decided by the parishioners that their departed parson's memorial should take the form of a new ferry boat and that improvements should be made to the paths on both sides of the river. Eventually, in March 1885, when these arrangements had finally been completed, a ceremony took place: 'The Choir met at the old Ferry . . . and walked along the river bank . . . singing the hymn "the Church's one Foundation", to where the New Boat the "George Leigh Wasey" was moored. They then, together with some of the chief inhabitants of the Quatford portion of the parish, embarked and crossed over to the other side, where they took on board a number of the Eardington people. The Boat was then swung out into midstream, and remained there while a short service was held . . .'.

Mrs Digby was called upon to dedicate the boat, and a brass was placed in the church (near that in memory of her sister, who had died in 1881), commemorating their father:

> This Brass was placed here to Record
> The completion on March 8 1885 of the
> New Church Ferry
> And Also the Augmentation of this Living
> By the sum of £1,000
> which were undertaken in
> Loving and Grateful Remembrance
> of the faithful administration of
> the Rev. W. George Leigh Wasey
> for 37 years Vicar of this parish

Despite all, then, sufficient to build a bridge was never raised and eight years passed before a new ferry boat was procured.

THE OTHER TWO BROTHERS

After leaving Rugby, Spearman Wasey had gone up to Trinity College, Oxford, and having passed 'Little Go' in June 1838, he was subsequently taken ill and went abroad until September 1842.[1] He returned to take his BA in 1844 and, after gaining his MA the following year, was ordained deacon to the curacy of Hertingfordbury, becoming priest in 1845. Two years later, due no doubt to the family connection, he was appointed domestic chaplain to Viscountess Hood.

Spearman subsequently took the curacy of Needwood in Staffordshire, but, 'in consequence of ye death of his old rector, he removed to the curacy of Aynhoe, Northampton',[1] not far from his childhood home. In November 1853, however, he was offered the cure of Compton Parva, Berkshire, by its patrons, Mrs Stacpool and Miss Wasey, the two sisters of J.T. Wasey, Esq., the family's old friend and namesake, whom they had met at Southsea many years previously and who, in 1852, had died intestate.

This living was accepted gladly. Pleasantly situated on the Berkshire Downs it was within easy distance of London, to which one could travel, now, by train. The vicarage house, however, was in a poor condition, damp and out of repair. Spearman therefore set about building another: £900 was borrowed from Queen Anne's Bounty, Mrs Stacpool and Miss Mary Wasey of Priors Court each gave £100 and Wasey provided the rest; the whole, including the cost of the road, amounted to over £1,700.[1]

During that same year Spearman married. His bride was Harriet Jemima, the daughter of Edward Cockburn Kindersley Esq., of Harley Street, through whose veins flowed Plantagenet blood.[14] She was also the granddaughter of Hannah, who, before marrying N.E. Kindersley, had been married to Spearman's uncle, William Wasey, dead for many years in India. Over the years the couple were blessed with a large family. Their first child, Elizabeth Mima, was born at Aynhoe and her Quatford uncle, the Revd George Wasey christened her, his wife, Eliza, being one of her godmothers.[1]

The family probably continued to live at Aynhoe while the house at Compton was being built, but, before long, it was ready for occupation. Soon after, Mrs

Compton Vicarage

Stacpool and Miss Wasey, now mistress of Priors Court, built a national school and masters house for Compton parish, although the estate and advowson were subsequently sold. Both ladies remained close friends and were sponsors to two of the older children. Priors Court became to the next generation of Wasey children what it had been to the last.

Perhaps during one such visit Miss Wasey related the story of the alarming journey made through Savernake Forest in March 1787 by her parents, Mr and Mrs John Wasey. Travelling from Marlborough to Newbury in a one-horse chaise, at about one o'clock in the afternoon, they were stopped in the forest by two genteel-sounding young men dressed in mourning, one of whom had a black mask over his face. They presented pistols, demanding money and Mr Wasey, apparently, gave them two guineas, whereupon they are said to have 'expressed themselves fully satisfied and returned thanks'. Nevertheless, they were apprehended a few hours later at Albourne and 'carried before Lovelace Bigg Esq., who committed them to Salisbury gaol . . . to take their trial at the next Assizes. . .'.[15]

When, in 1859, Mrs Stacpool died without surviving issue, her only son having been killed while hunting, her sister, Mary Wasey, was bereft indeed. She had no close male relatives, certainly none bearing the name Wasey, and it was to the three brothers, her namesakes George, Spearman and Edward Wasey, and their families that she turned.

Two daughters arrived before a son was born to the Revd and Mrs Spearman Wasey; this event was noted at Quatford in the *Family Book*: '. . . His third child, the first boy in our family, was born April 4th 1857 at Compton, Edward John Spearman . . .'. One of his godfathers was his other uncle, Lieutenant Edward Wasey RN, appointed in 1855 Inspector Commander of Coastguard at Ballycastle.

COASTGUARD

Subsequently, Edward Wasey was appointed to the command of coastguard at Fleetwood where, as in the past, he continued to court danger. In the *Family*

Book, beneath a dramatic newspaper illustration depicting a lifeboat launching in heavy seas, with the date 1860 inked above, we read the following: '. . . the Silver Medal . . . [was awarded] to Captain Wasey R.N., Inspecting-Commander of the Coast-guard, and John Fox, chief boatman . . . in putting off and rescuing, after several attempts, one man of the crew of the schooner Ann Mitchell, of Montrose, which was totally wrecked, during a heavy gale . . . off Fleetwood on the night of . . . 22nd Jan.'

Another records the award of the Second Service Clasp 'for putting off and rescuing the crew of 4 men of the schooner Catherine, of Newry, . . . wrecked off Fleetwood during a gale of wind and heavy snow-squalls . . .'. Details concerning the rescue of the schooner *Jane Roper* were recorded and yet another cutting tells more of the crew's gallantry: 'Oct. 20 – The Fleetwood life-boat, commanded by Captain Wasey, R.N., and manned by 11 men, had gone off and rescued the crew of 15 men and a pilot from the barque Vermont, of Halifax, Nova Scotia, which, during a heavy gale of wind, had stranded on Barnett's Bank, three miles from Fleetwood. – Reward, Third Service Clasp to Captain Wasey, R.N., in acknowledgement of his intrepid conduct on the occasion . . .'.

In noting these incidents about her uncle, Mrs Digby adds: '[he was] at Fleetwood til 1860 where in consideration of his valuable services in saving life . . . the Lords of the Admiralty were pleased to mark their high approbation by extending his term of service for an additional two years and removing him to Portsmouth. His time expired 26 April 1862. Went on half pay and bought a house in 18 acres of land at Foxleys, three miles from Maidenhead.'

A CHESHIRE FUNERAL

It is probable, since they had always kept in touch, that Captain Wasey and his brothers attended the funeral, at Rostherne, three years later, of their mother's cousin, Egerton Leigh. His obituary, kept in the *Family Book*, told of his colourful life: 'He represented two of the oldest families in this county – that of the Leighs of the West Hall, High Leigh, and of the Jodrells of Yeardsley and Taxall. . . . When six years old he was sent on the saddle before his father's coachman to Macclesfield School, celebrated at that time as one of the best in England. Amongst his schoolfellows were Lord Abercromby and his brother, the late Lord Dunfermline, formerly Speaker of the House of Commons, who married Mr Egerton Leigh's eldest sister . . .'.[16]

From there, continues the report, he:

> went to Eton . . . and was distinguished as an elegant Latin scholar . . . . One of his early friends . . . was Lamb, afterwards the Premier, Lord Melbourne . . . . He was Captain of Eton for more than a year, and went thence to join the 3rd Dragoon Guards . . . . Soon after he left . . . with his Regiment for Windsor, and while quartered there, he gave one of the proofs of that spirit and self-respect which distinguished him through life. The Prince of Wales, afterwards, George IV, [to whom George, father of the Wasey brothers, had been chaplain] gave a grand banquet to the officers of the 3rd Dragoon Guards . . . . The Duke of Clarence, afterwards William IV, was among those present. Many of the guests at the close of the banquet left for the Promenade, the remainder closed up from the bottom of the table, and Cornet Leigh found himself seated next to the Duke of Clarence, who was at that time a violent supporter of the

Slave Trade . . . . The Duke began to abuse Wilberforce in unmeasured terms. Cornet Leigh requested his Royal Highness to moderate his language, as Wilberforce was a connection of his own, but the Duke persisting in his abuse, the young Cornet . . . rose, left him, and seated himself on the opposite side of the table. In the course of the evening the Duke met him on the Promenade, and said 'Come, young Cheshire, you must not be angry with me: let us be friends, shake hands . . .' and afterwards apologised to the Colonel of the Regiment, for having hurt the feelings of one of his young officers.

Mr Leigh later married Wilhelmina, daughter of George Stratton, Esq., of Tew Park, Oxon., and went to reside at his Broadwell, Gloucestershire seat. Subsequently he removed to Cheshire where, at his death, Wasey cousins will have followed his remains 'from Jodrell Hall . . . for interment in the family vault in Rostherne Church. As the funeral cortege passed through Knutsford, the shops were partially closed, and the windows veiled . . .'.

In 1867 Edward Wasey was put on the Retired List as post captain. Now aged 50, he felt himself ready to settle down and, at St Marylebone Church, in August 1869, he took for his wife Maria Louisa, the second daughter of General Marriott[17] and widow of George Stewart Mackenzie.[18] The couple lived happily at their home, Foxleys, a large Victorian house at Touchen End in the idyllic countryside near Maidenhead, for more than twenty years before Maria's death parted them.

COMPTON'S PARSON

Over the years, the Revd Spearman Wasey's family increased to six sons and three daughters, the last being born in 1870. By this time his Quatford brother's two daughters had grown up: it had been in 1874 that Leonora married Captain Digby and chose her cousin, 'Miss Eliza Wasey of Compton', as one of her bridesmaids. Four years later, Eliza (known as Mima) herself married, taking the rector of Brightwalton, Berks., for her husband: Henry, the son of the Hon. and Revd Henry E.J. Howard, DD, of Lichfield.[19]

Photographs had now replaced paintings and all the Berkshire family were photographed over the years. Two photographs are of the bearded Revd J.S. Wasey, with his wife and six sons; another is of Mrs Wasey in hooped crinoline, and one shows two of their little daughters wearing buttoned boots, short paletots and frilled skirts.

In 1880 the family's firm friend and namesake, Miss Mary Wasey of Priors Court, died, aged 84 years. She had been patron and benefactress of many worthy causes during her life, including the gift to Fleetwood of a lifeboat, the *Edward Wasey*, and another to Deal, the *Mary Jane*. Now, large legacies were left to hospitals, to Chieveley Church and for the building and upkeep of schools. It was a measure of her esteem for the sons of the Revd George Wasey of Wardington, whom her brother had met at Southsea years before, that it was to them she bequeathed her large estates comprising the Priors Court, Bradley, Curridge and Faircross properties: in all about 1,100 acres.

As the elder of these sons had died at Quatford three years previously, leaving no male issue, it was to the next surviving son, the Revd Spearman Wasey, that they passed, together with a handsome legacy and the 'household goods,

Revd John Spearman Wasey, his wife, Jemima, two of their daughters, Mima and Hattie, and son Cyril

furniture, plate, oil paintings, linen, china, books and household effects, carriages, horses and live and dead stock . . . in and about my mansion house and premises at Priors Court . . .'. In addition were substantial legacies to two of his children: godchildren of Miss Wasey and her deceased sister. The daughters of his elder brother were also beneficiaries, while a residuary legatee was his young brother Captain E. Wasey.

This good fortune must have greatly eased the burden of educating and placing the Revd and Mrs Spearman Wasey's many children.[20] Their eldest daughter, Mima, was already happily married, but Harriet and Mary were still at home, and their six sons were between the ages of 10 and 23 years. In common with many of their generation and situation, it was felt desirable to encourage their sons, once educated, to go out to the colonies and elsewhere to make their fortunes and this they did: to India, to the Argentine and to Canada.

One son, Cyril Leigh, went into the navy, serving, in 1882, on board the *Achilles* during the bombardment of Alexandria. He became lieutenant in 1889, but three years later, while serving as junior lieutenant on the *Dreadnought*, he died of gastric fever in a Malta hospital. The obituary, preserved in the *Family Book*, records that his '. . . charming character and bonhomie had endeared him to all who knew him, officers and men alike'. He was buried in the family vault at Compton with another son, Willoughby Frank, who had died ten years previously, aged 18 years.

The Revd Spearman Wasey and his family continued to live in the picturesque vicarage at Compton, letting the properties recently bequeathed them, until, in 1890, due to failing sight, Spearman retired. They chose to live neither at Priors Court, Bradley Court, nor indeed at any of the farms on the estates, but took Speen Hill House, in Newbury, to spend their remaining years.

The only story to have survived of the elderly Spearman was of his fondness for taking the pony and trap to visit his old and valued friend the local doctor for a convivial evening. On returning, the pony, who knew his way well, never failed to bring his now sightless old master safely home completely unaided! After a long illness Spearman died in November 1899 aged 82 years. From his obituary we read that: 'Amidst every token of respect and in the presence of a large number of friends [his remains] . . . were conveyed to the . . . family vault in the . . . churchyard of Compton . . on the shoulders of workmen employed on the Priors Court Estate . . .'.

Among the many mourners were several who had attended his brother George's funeral at Quatford more than twenty years before. The house at Speen was left to Jemima, in addition to the contents of Priors Court, including the plate 'which I may not have given away in my life time . . .', indicating a disregard for

Prior's Court, Chieveley

such material items. Having provided for his children, he remembered, among others, his only surviving niece, Leonora Digby.

The last of the three brothers, Captain Edward Wasey, a favourite in the family, had no children of his own, but was able to regale his many nephews and nieces with stories of his full and adventurous life. His marriage, at 50 years of age, to Maria Louisa had been long and happy, making his loss, when she died in 1890, greater. He married again (at St James', Piccadilly) to Jane Mary Anne, widow of John Haig Esq. (said to be of the whisky family, and by whom she had sixteen children).

It was with his first wife, Maria Louisa, however, that Edward wished to be buried when he died in 1902: in his vault at Touchen End,[21] their home for so many years. After directing that his burial expenses should not exceed £40, he appointed his cousin, Francis Kindersley, and a fellow member of his club, the New University, St James' Street, executors of his will.

Five years on, in Compton Church, a plaque was erected to commemorate his brother: 'To the Glory of God and in Loving Memory of the Revd. John Spearman Wasey 37 years Vicar of this Parish. This Nave was reseated by his widow and children. October 1907.'

A few months later Jemima too died. An invalid for many years, she had resided latterly at Newbury, where also lived her two maiden daughters, Harriett (Hattie) and Mary (Polly). In addition to her eldest daughter, Mima, her four surviving sons had married and presented her with grandchildren, ensuring continuity of the line.

A sentence in her obituary illustrates the changes augured for the coming century: the emergence and importance of the new mode of transport used at her funeral. Her body, we read, 'was conveyed in a Washington car, covered with beautiful wreaths, to Compton, where it was interred in the family burial place by the side of her husband . . .'.

Chapter Six: The Twentieth-century Families

Edward John Spearman Wasey, the eldest of the four surviving sons, was educated at Forest School and Haileybury College. His first venture was tea planting in India but, suffering ill-health due to the climate, he returned to England. Subsequently he took up sheep farming and then ranching in South America and the Argentine where he met with success and remained for some sixteen years. In 1892, at Rosario de Santa Fe, he married Amy Florence, the daughter of William and Mary Ison, thought to be from Yorkshire, England.

Lionel Torin, the youngest of the four brothers, also made his way to Argentina where he too spent many successful years cattle farming. Like his brother, he met his wife out there: Edith Ann, the daughter of Robert Walter Traill[1]; they married, as it happened, six days before the Revd Spearman Wasey died in England. Their two children were Gladys and a son, Lionel Robert Traill, who was born in Donnington, Newbury, during a visit to the UK. After a further five or six years in the Argentine the family retired permanently to England where Lionel purchased 'Ecchinswell', an estate near Newbury with a large roomy house, stables, cottages and two hundred acres. It was an idyllic place, with lovely grounds, in the area where the film *Watership Down* was featured, and the family remained there for some years.

Edward, the eldest brother, had returned with his family to England at about the time of their father's death and, inheriting the Berkshire estates, now became lord of the manor of Chieveley.

Residing initially at Priors Court Farm, Edward exchanged ranching for English farming with aplomb and, as one of the neighbourhood's principal landowners, settled readily to the life of a country gentleman. He took a keen interest in land management and in his tenants, being recognized as an extremely considerate landlord. He hunted, he shot, became a guardian of the poor, a school manager, district councillor and zealous churchwarden. A staunch Conservative, he was an energetic supporter, and he sat on the Bench where, it is said, he administered justice in a straightforward and simple way. He was also said to have been endowed with great mental as well as physical energy, performing his numerous public and private duties with thoroughness, urbanity and efficiency.

It is a pleasure to know Mr Wasey [says a published profile[2]]. There is such a reassuring absence of hauteur about him, and such a courteous and cordial manner that at once makes one feel at home in his company; and yet, when occasion arises, he can be as firm as a rock, but he would be the last person to be unduly arbitrary or unnecessarily harsh . . . . In everything he does he has the laudable reputation of being as straight as a die; and he certainly is never afraid to express his opinions frankly and fearlessly, no matter whether they may happen to be at the time popular or unpopular . . . .

Edward J.S. Wasey (seated left) with his wife, Amy (centre) and family at Bradley Court

Their first son, born in the Argentine, had, alas, died aged only a few weeks. Two daughters followed at two-yearly intervals before another son, Willoughby Spearman, was born in 1899 and nicknamed Tom. Fourteen years went by before another son, Benjamin John Spearman, arrived, followed, a year later, by Amy (known as Dolly). A charming photograph shows young Ben leading his little sister on a donkey past the porch of Priors Court, where, being on friendly terms with the tenants, yet another generation of Wasey children were spending much of their time.

The family had by now moved to another of the estate properties, the much-loved Bradley Court, where, over the years, Edward Wasey took a keen interest in local organizations. He was a patron of cricket and keen follower of the Craven Hounds, in addition to being an active supporter of the Newbury Horse Show and the Agricultural Society.

CANADA AND INDIA

Arthur Frodsham Wasey, the second of the four brothers, went to Canada to make his mark. Here, at 40 years of age, he married Ethel, the daughter of G. Crawford of Swan Lake, Manitoba, and had two sons, Arthur and Edward. The family appears to have returned to England by 1910, Arthur's address being 6, Donnington Square, Newbury. Later they took a large house outside the town.

George Kindersley Wasey, the third brother, sought his fortune in India where he became chief engineer and director of the West of India Portuguese Railway in Goa. Here he met Sidney Jane, the daughter of Colonel C.W. Godfrey of the Bombay Staff Corps; they married in 1892 and within a year their first son Cyril was born.

Life in India, despite the heat, was perfect. There were tiger shoots, tennis parties, balls: a social life second to none. The climate, however, was unsuitable for children; in common with all British children born out there, Cyril was sent home to be educated. Sidney vowed she would never have another child from whom she would have to be separated. Nine years went by, George achieving success in his career, but seldom did the couple enjoy the company of their young son.

Then Sidney found she was to have another baby. Much as she loved life in India she knew she could never leave another child far away in England. She told George of her decision: either they must return together to England, or separate. The couple were devoted and George agreed to his wife's wishes, obtaining a position with the same company in

George K. Wasey

London. They looked for somewhere to live and took, firstly, Wolfhall, near Burbage, the historic home of Henry VIII's third wife.

Their daughter Sydney Joan was born in 1903 and George's cousin, Leonora Digby, was godparent. Happiness reigned. Cyril came home from Eton to spend school holidays, and their little daughter was fascinated with the dogs, horses and other animals to be observed on the adjoining farm. Sidney, however, used to the sophistication of life in India, found the proximity of the farm at Wolfhall disagreeable. She had always liked the charming dwelling, Leigh Hill House, in Savernake Forest and so, when it was vacated by Lord Aylesbury's agent, the Wasey family took it.

Sidney Jane

Mr and Mrs George Wasey were devoted, though firm, parents. The family always walked through the forest to church for instance; the use of a vehicle on Sundays, unless the weather was very bad, was unthought of. Another child, Geoffrey, arrived in 1907 and all three grew up loving the forest. George had some shooting rights there and during school holidays he taught his eldest son to shoot, mostly rabbits and pigeons. Their daughter adored ponies, but was permitted to ride only side-saddle, envying two friends who rode astride at the

Geo. K. Wasey, with his wife (left) seated, his father-in-law (far right) and friends, Goa, India

Tedworth Hunt. However, when invited by their uncle to ride with the famous Pytchley Hunt, they too were required to ride side-saddle before accepting!

Visits were exchanged between the Wasey families, favourites being Lionel, at his home near Newbury, and Edward, at Bradley Court, where family and friends made up shooting-parties. Their two maiden sisters lived in Newbury still, while their married sister, Mrs Howard, and her large family were not far away at Brightwalton, north of Hungerford.

Leonora, daughter of their Quatford uncle, also visited with her husband, Captain Digby, until his death in 1913. He had led a full and active life, his naval career beginning in 1857 as a cadet in HMS *Shannon* where he saw action during the Indian Mutiny. Four years after their marriage he was promoted commander and in 1891 he retired, taking for a while the command of the coastguard at Lynn. During his retirement Captain Digby was magistrate for Norfolk, having the reputation of being hard when appropriate, with a brusque, quarterdeck manner. But this, it was said, belied his real nature; he worked tirelessly on behalf of local charities, one being the West Norfolk and Lynn Hospital. When he died, reported the *Eastern Daily Press*, 'Prominent people of West Norfolk gathered in considerable numbers' at his funeral.

The couple had lived for twenty-seven years at North Runcton Lodge, not far from Lynn, and during visits, members of the Wasey family took the opportunity to visit North Walsham and places connected with their roots. After her husband's death Leonora Digby continued to visit George Wasey's family at Savernake, 'always with her maid', recalled their daughter, Joan.

It was cousin Leonora who continued to preserve press cuttings relating to the family and their connections. Did the 'Leigh' items, one wonders, remind her of visits made when a girl to Broadwell Manor in the lovely Cotswold Hills? A water-colour of it had been pasted into the *Family Book*, probably at the time when her eccentric great uncle, Admiral Jodrell Leigh, lived there. He and other residents were frequently in dispute over such issues as parish rates, changes in the church and diversion of roads and paths.[3] Visits there must have been memorable! Another fascinating item was about the husband of Leo's aunt Charlotte (née Monckton):

> General George Whichcote, the last surviving English officer who took part in the battle of Waterloo, died . . . [August 1891, in his 97th year]. . . He was present at the famous ball given by the Duchess of Richmond at Brussels on the eve of Waterloo,[4] and in the battle had charge of a company of the 52d Regiment. He marched with the allied forces to Paris, and was encamped in the Champs Elysees, close to the house occupied by the Duke of Wellington . . . . He was on duty at the . . . Louvre while it was dismantled of the many . . . treasures which Napoleon had appropriated when in the zenith of his power from various European capitals . . . . He retained almost to the last his physical activity and memory unimpaired, and was full of reminiscences of the Peninsular campaign . . . .

How entertaining must visits have been to this uncle and aunt. Clearly, Mrs Digby, in common with her father, the Quatford parson, had a great deal of feeling for family, and it was to her cousin, George Wasey of Savernake, who, she felt, shared this empathy, that she decided to leave the *Family Book* and other Wasey heirlooms after her death.

THE GREAT WAR

Arthur Wasey had returned from Canada with his family by about 1910, taking a large house at Altamont Wash Common just outside Newbury. War broke out on 14 August 1914 and, although unconnected, it was ten days later that the family tragedy occurred with such dire consequences. Arthur had taken his two sons, aged 14 and 12 years respectively, pigeon-shooting on Wash Common when the elder, his namesake, told to shoot a rising bird, swung round and accidentally shot him.[5] The injury was fatal.

Ethel subsequently returned with her two sons to her parents' home in Canada where she remained for some years, completely out of touch with the rest of the Wasey family. Arthur's will required his wife to sell his real estate in England and Wales, and his personal estate in Canada, for the maintenance and education of their children 'in a manner suitable to their station in life'. In addition to his wife, his brother, George of Savernake, was made executor, with a family friend, Harry Mowbray Merriman, who was evidently godparent to his younger son who bore the name Mowbray.

Lionel Torin Wasey

With the outbreak of war Lionel, the youngest of the adult Wasey brothers, became, as his son later observed, 'a bit patriotic', applying for a position which would help the war effort. Made agricultural officer for Essex, he and his family removed to Chelmsford.

Meanwhile, George Wasey's eldest son, Cyril, having completed his training at Sandhurst in 1913, had joined the Royal Warwick Regiment and, at the outbreak of war, went to France with the Expeditionary Force. Twice he was wounded. He held the Military Cross and was awarded the Legion of Honour for gallantry during the retreat from Mons, when he was mentioned in one of Lord French's dispatches. In the summer of 1917 he joined the RFC and, after completing his course as an observer, had only been back at the front about six weeks when he was killed.

His wife, Edith Anne

When the tragic news reached his parents they were devastated. Cyril had been all that they could have wished for in a son and was liked by all who knew him. His commanding officer wrote of him: 'I never met a more splendid or stout-hearted fellow. He was a thorough sportsman all through and afraid of nothing. He has done splendid work for me, but it will be as a friend I shall miss him most'.[6] His parents' anguish was heightened by the loss, only the previous year, of their other son, Geoffrey, while still at school.

George and Sidney Wasey were not alone in their sorrow. George's sister, Mima, married to the Revd Henry Howard, lost two sons in the war. Their youngest, a lieutenant in the York and Lancaster Regiment, was killed in the battle of Loos and their eldest, Bernard Henry, a major in the Indian Infantry, was reported killed in Mesopotamia.[7] Mercifully Mima and her husband, grandson of the 5th Earl of Carlisle, had been blessed with a large family, and one son and five daughters remained to them.

THE SANDS OF TIME

In March 1920, Mrs Leonora Digby, the only Wasey cousin of that generation, died. Held in affection by the family, many attended her funeral, where numerous mourners gathered at North Runcton to pay their last respects. Here, in the flat country south of Kings Lynn, so different from the lush Severn valley of her birth, Leo was buried alongside her husband.

The following year Edward Wasey of Bradley Court was on holiday with his family at Southsea, when he became ill. Having undergone an operation at a local nursing home he appeared to be making a good recovery when, a few days later, he died, aged 64 years. His shocked widow, Amy, was left with a son and daughter of 8 and 7 years, in addition to their grown family.

The funeral was attended by a vast gathering, the church path lined with members of the Berkshire Constabulary. In addition to family and friends, tenants, employees and colleagues gathered to pay their last respects: fellow Justices, representatives on the Board of Guardians, sportsmen from the Craven Hunt, clergy from several parishes, local residents and parishioners. The last few sentences from his obituary would surely have pleased him: '. . . a typical country gentleman of the old school . . . . He was not one of those to shirk the responsibilities to which he was born, but in all these things he did his duty, helping his neighbours with his advice, and in a practical manner . . . . His word was his bond, and if he said a thing, he would stand by it. The outstanding traits in his character were straight-forwardness, sincerity, and simple-mindedness. He was simple in speech and manner; he abhorred side, and his knowledge of human nature gained on the ranch enabled him to brush aside the superficialities, and quickly sum up a man for what he was worth . . .'.[8]

Edward J.S. Wasey

At Savernake, having inherited the *Family Book* from his cousin, Leonora, George Wasey became fascinated with its contents. There were references to the family connection with the Lords Cullen and, what is more, a painting, thought to be of one of their ilk, was now his to hang at Leigh Hill House.

He wrote therefore to his distant kinsman, Lord Cullen of Ashbourne, and, in the course of their correspondence, told of the letter addressed to his great grandmother, Colonel Wasey's wife, from Barbara, wife of the Hon. William Cockayne, Lord Cullen's great grandfather (quoted in a previous chapter). The two families became acquainted again, corresponding from time to time, and the interesting outcome of the friendship is a handwritten pedigree showing their mutual descent from Charles Cockayne, the 1st Viscount Cullen, executed by none other than Lord Cullen's father, the renowned George Edward Cokayne, Clarenceux King of Arms.

Meanwhile, the Revd and Mrs Howard, having spent the greater part of their married life at Brightwalton, where Mima had worked for more than forty years as a pioneer of the Mothers Union,[8] retired to Wokingham. Here, in 1938, three months after the death of her husband, Mima passed away. Great numbers attended her funeral at All Saints Church where they laid her to rest, spared the sufferings of yet another world war.

Time was running out for this generation and, in 1940, the family's maiden sister, Harriet, died at Newbury. She had lived for eleven years alone with her nurse and staff at Foscote Lodge, the home she had shared with her younger, now deceased, maiden sister, Mary. Neither of these elderly sisters, one feels, would have cared for the enormous change in lifestyle which the Second World War was to bring, and so Hattie's demise, at the age of 84 years, was, perhaps, a happy release.

George Wasey of Savernake, suffering now from a crippling illness, was to live for only another three years. Lionel, however, the youngest of the brothers, had several more years left to him. On the family's return from Chelmsford after the First World War they had settled at Southmead, adjacent to Newbury race course.

THE NEXT GENERATION

The eldest surviving son of Chieveley's squire, Tom, as he was known, was educated at Forest School, Essex, and, with a military career in mind, went on to Sandhurst. In common with other members of the family, he was fond of country pursuits and was a good shot. Having decided against the life of a country gentleman, however, he joined the Royal Corps of Signals, serving, during the years 1919 to 1921, in Iraq and in north-west Persia.[9]

Tom's elder sister Evelyn had participated in the war effort as 'Lady Supervisor, War Office', for which she received the MBE in January 1920.[10] A photograph of her reveals an attractive woman, standing on the verandah of a tennis or cricket club pavilion, holding a cigarette. At her death, her share of a farm in Sussex was bequeathed to her sister, Dolly (photographed on a donkey with brother Ben, at Priors Court, many years before). The third sister, Muriel Sophie, married Donald McLachlan Macmillan and had a family of one son and three daughters.

When Edward J.S. Wasey of Bradley Court had died in 1921, Tom, the eldest son, was already committed to a military career. As his younger brother was a

Prior's Court Farm

child of only 8 years at the time, he and the trustees decided, two years later, due
to heavy death duties, upon the sale of the Priors Court Estate with its three
farms, cottages, land and timber. All was put up for auction.[11]

Tom's birthplace, Priors Court Farm, was described as a 'gentleman farmer's
attractive farmhouse'. Priors Court itself, a desirable Queen Anne residence built
on the site of a much older one, had a history dating from the thirteenth century.
The manor of Chieveley had been attached by the priors of Poughley to their
surrounding manors and they conducted their courts at the principal messuage,
which thus became known as Priors Court. The entrance porch and a hall of the
present house is said to date from the original building.[12] Comprising fourteen
bedrooms, halls and four reception rooms, it stood in about 85 acres of grounds
and grandly timbered park with stabling and garage. With the farms and
woodlands it amounted to about 858 acres. It must have been in many respects a
sad day when this estate went under the hammer.

Four years later, Tom married Kathleen Isobel, the daughter of George Evans
of Co. Limerick, Ireland, and of Buenos Aires. He remained in the army, rising to
the rank of major, and when, in due course, he retired to Rowledge, Farnham, he
named his house 'Bradley Cottage' after his old home. He was, said a member of
the family, 'a staunch churchman and country-lover, fond of all natural creatures,
and wildlife'.

In 1956 Tom, with the consent of his brother, decided to sell the beautiful
'Wasey Candlesticks'[13] which had descended through the family from their third
great grandfather, Doctor Wasey. This, one feels, would have dismayed their
great-uncle, the Quatford parson, who, in his will, directed his daughters to
ensure that they, with other Wasey heirlooms, 'be kept . . . by my Brother
Spearman and his eldest descendants of the name of Wasey in Succession'.
Perhaps they had become too much of a liability: the cost of insuring them would
be considerable, but their leaving the family was sad.

Tom's brother, Benjamin, who was only 8 years old when their father died, had
remained with their mother and little sister at Bradley Court for some seven years
before that estate too was sold. Ben will have been away at Forest School during

Benjamin J.S. Wasey and his wife, Vera

much of that time, but the wrench at parting from his old home was great. The family removed to Hermitage, where Ben remembered his two Canadian cousins, Arthur and Edward, visited on one occasion.

In common with most of his cousins, Ben enjoyed shooting and cricket; he was also fond of classic cars and car rallying. At the outbreak of war in 1939 he joined the RAF and was evacuated from Dunkirk. Later he was transferred to the REME where he served until the end of the conflict. Subsequently, Ben became a forestry and agricultural engineer, working for a while at Thetford, in Norfolk. He married, in 1947, Vera, the daughter of Robert Leete of Cambridge, and in 1948 they returned to Berkshire, where, ten years later, Ben was appointed head forester at Lockinge Estate, Wantage.

It was in 1981 that the writer met Mr and Mrs Ben Wasey in their seventeenth-century cottage on the Berkshire Downs. A quiet, unassuming country gentleman, Ben showed little interest in his family's history, although he did recall: 'father did once say we were descended from Edward III'. He found the book brought along about hospital life in the eighteenth century, when his ancestor was a leading physician, interesting and amusing. Vera, his wife, understood the interest generated, having been fascinated, during visits to cousin Joan, with the *Family Book* and other memorabilia.

THE YOUNGEST SON'S HEIR

Lionel, or Bob, as he was known, the only son of Lionel and Edith Wasey, had as his earliest memories, Argentinian ranching and, later, mixed farming in the idyllic Berkshire countryside. Naturally, therefore, he had a proclivity for the pursuits of gentlemen farmers; as a lad he regularly went shooting, rabbits mostly, with his cousin, Tom, on his uncle's Bradley and Priors Court estates.

Tom was the only male cousin with whom he was acquainted of about the same age. Tom's younger brother Ben was not born until 1913; his uncle George's eldest son, nine years his senior, went, at the outbreak of war, to fight in France and alas was killed; while his youngest son, Geoffrey, died at school. The two sons of his uncle Arthur, nearest of all in age to himself, were unknown to him. They had spent much of their time in Canada and, although the family made their home for a while in England, when tragedy struck, they and their mother returned there.

Bob was educated, in common with several of the family, at Haileybury College and, on leaving, had decided, as had his father and uncles before him, to make his niche abroad. In about 1921 he went to Ceylon where, for nearly twenty years, he was a tea-planter in that beautiful country. He married Estelle, the daughter of tea-planter, R.J. Austin, late of Australia, and had, besides two daughters, Carol and Jennifer, a son, Timothy John, born in 1930.

The outbreak of the Second World War altered his life significantly as it did for so many. Having joined the Contingent Army in Ceylon, he completed an army course at Belgaum and Lahore, eventually being commissioned in the RAF Regiment. He then went to Calcutta, where, in time, he was posted to Delhi.

'There', he told the writer, when he was nearly 86 years of age, 'every morning I asked, "can I have a job please?"' The answer was always in the negative until, one morning, he met a neighbour from Ceylon. This, as chance would have it, was a great friend, now made wing commander. He arranged that Bob should fly with him to Ceylon: 'a matter of luck really . . . I got matey with a Squadron Leader who was about to go to Calcutta to take over a new job and he took me there as his adjutant: a Spitfire Squadron, 136, known as the Woodpecker Squadron'.

Lionel Robert Traill Wasey (Bob) in the RAF

A photograph shows him wearing forage cap and khaki drill uniform with the insignia of flight lieutenant; in another he wears officers' uniform with the wire removed from his peak-cap, as was the unofficial custom of the time. When asked for what reason he was awarded the MBE, Mr Wasey became rather reticent, telling a very funny and rather risqué story involving a pretty Burmese girl, a cow and the need to evade the Japanese, which had the company in roars of laughter. It was at this point that Tim, Bob Wasey's son, reminded him of the signals of congratulation received by the squadron in 1944, one from Winston Churchill.

Kay, Bob's second wife, joined the conversation: 'there was great excitement,' she said. 'I was working for the Navy in Colombo, and we used to get all this "dope" through. One day, 136 had an absolute ball, and shot down a great many enemy planes'. Mr Wasey went off to rummage among his papers and returned with the wording of the messages. First, the one received on 7 January, from the prime minister, Winston Churchill: 'My congratulations and compliments on your brilliant exploits.' Another, received by Air Commander Pearce, from Sir Archibald Sinclair, the Secretary of State for Air: 'the brilliant exploits of your fighters yesterday is grand news for the New Year. Congratulations to you and the Squadron that fought so well. Clearly the Spitfires find themselves in good hands. Good luck to all . . . . Please convey to all ranks of 136 Squadron . . . [and] to all concerned my own congratulations on their success.'

Mr Wasey continued to serve in Burma and Ceylon, finally completing his service at BHQ, Colombo. He returned to the UK for demobilization where, in June 1945, he was awarded the MBE. Feeling the occasion for this award should be recorded, the writer made enquiries from the Ministry of Defence enabling the wording of the citation to be quoted here:

> Flight Lieutenant Lionel Robert Traill Wasey (120368) No. 136 Squadron. This Officer joined the squadron in August 1943. As Adjutant he has carried out his duties in a very effective and highly efficient manner. Whilst serving at an advanced base in the Imphal Valley during the siege he planned and put into force an exceptionally well organised 'defensive box' against threatened attacks by Japanese troops, whereby the whole Squadron were able to sleep below ground level in comparative safety and also be immediately available in an emergency. He has shown initiative and unconquerable spirit and his work as a Squadron Adjutant has been exemplary.

By the time the war ended Bob's marriage had broken up. His second marriage was to Kathleen, the daughter of G.D. Burton Windus, and after demobilization they retired from Ceylon, settling for a while in England where Bob's father, Lionel, the last of that generation, died in 1955. Bob took employment as a Progress Chaser with the Atomic Weapons Research Establishment at Aldermaston for about two years, but, in 1969, he and Kay decided to emigrate to South Africa.

Timothy, Bob's only son, had a brief spell in the Merchant Navy before returning to Ceylon to take up tea-planting. There he married Dorothy Ann Wynd, by whom he had a son, Christopher, and a daughter, Susan. Due, however, to Ceylonese policy, it was impossible to send money out of the country to finance their education and consequently the family returned to England.

Bob Wasey (right) with his son, Timothy and grandson, Christopher

During this period Mr and Mrs Bob Wasey made periodic visits from Natal to family and friends in England but it was not until 1984 that they decided to remain, settling near Timothy and his family. There are several grandchildren, but only one grandson from this branch of the family to further the name of Wasey.

WASEY DAUGHTERS

Having married Captain Philip Wykeham Leigh Pemberton in 1930,[14] Bob's sister, Gladys (or Anne, as she was known), remained childless. She had a genuine interest in her brother's children, however, and was to evince a caring attitude to those less fortunate than herself. Having served in the WRVS during the war, she afterwards continued to help with projects such as providing 'meals on wheels' for the elderly, and prison visiting, all performed in a very down-to-earth fashion. When visited by the writer, this remarkable lady, then 81 years of age, was still taking part in many of these activities, in addition to hours spent gardening.

She recalled that as children they were imbibed with a sense of independence. When in the Argentine her mother was in the habit of 'putting me on my pony, slapping its rump, and sending me off for the day'. Later, when living in England, she sometimes visited her uncle and aunt, Mr and Mrs George Wasey, at their home in Savernake Forest. Her aunt, she said, would take her for long walks through the forest 'although wearing the most unsuitable shoes'. She remembered her Uncle George often walked from his home, along the canal, to visit her family near Newbury.

Anne's cousin, Joan, remained at home after the death of her father, George Wasey, in 1943. She recalled the disappointment she had been to her mother, refusing to participate in county events and become the 'social butterfly' expected of her. On leaving Cheltenham College she had suffered such occasions patiently until, on reaching the age of 25 years, when invitations came for the next hunt balls, she steadfastly refused to accept.

Joan had contributed to the war effort in various ways: delivering meals to the elderly and bringing refreshments to anti-aircraft batteries which, she recalled, was 'great fun'. After her mother's death she continued to live in the forest. As a girl she had taken drawing lessons, and her skill in portraying her dogs, ponies and other animals was considerable. Riding was her favourite pastime and, with stabling at Leigh Hill House, she was able to keep her own hunters. Her happiest times were those spent riding to hounds with the Tedworth Hunt in the Pewsey Vale.

THE TWO 'LOST' COUSINS

Ethel, the widow of Arthur Frodsham Wasey who, in 1914, had died so tragically in the shooting accident, decided eventually to return with her two sons to England. She died in Bognor Regis in 1934, recorded as of The Anchorage, Ryde, Isle of Wight. Letters of Administration were granted to her sons: Arthur Crawford Wasey, whose occupation was given as 'musician', and Edward Cyril Mowbray Wasey, 'bank clerk'. Both had been mentioned in the will of their aunt, Mary Caroline Wasey (or Aunt Polly, as she was known), one of the two maiden aunts of Newbury, and both had their birth details recorded in the old family bible, which had descended to their cousin, Lionel (Bob).

This 'lost' branch made no attempt to contact the rest of the family, but word did reach Mr and Mrs Ben Wasey at some stage, for they came to hear that the elder son, Arthur, had twice married, had no children and had died at Leicester in 1973. The younger son, Edward, was last heard of living in the Isle of Wight.

On attempting to contact Mr Edward C.M. Wasey it was found that he was too ill to come to the telephone, but, from information given by his wife, by her replies to pertinent questions and by other checks made, it became clear that this was the wife of the 'missing' cousin, Edward Cyril Mowbray Wasey, who died later that summer. There was one son of the marriage: Arthur Edward Wasey, now married and living in Jersey. His wife is Bea, the daughter of Kurt E.W.Van Den Broek, and they have two children.

Strangely, Arthur Wasey knew absolutely nothing of his Wasey forebears, save that his grandfather had owned a large house near Greenham Common, Newbury, and that after his death, his grandmother and her two sons had lived in Canada for some years. Neither his father nor his uncle Crawford had ever mentioned the tragedy of his grandfather's death in the shooting accident. Arthur, who possesses the same easy manner and charm of his kinsfolk, could confirm only that his father or uncle (possibly both) had attended a public school near Portsmouth or Southampton. His father, he said, had worked as a lumber-jack and in a bank in Canada before returning to the UK. He was a solitary man, fond of fishing and collecting coins and stamps.

Arthur remembered his uncle Crawford: 'He was quite a character; had three wives, and was very outspoken. He lived well, in a nice house with a good car in

Right to left: Arthur Edward Wasey, his wife Bea, Miss Joan Wasey, and Sheila and Jonathan Wasey

Worthing and was a policeman during the war.' His hobbies were photography and music. Subsequently he left Worthing to move to Southampton.

When the whereabouts of Arthur Wasey was known to other members of the family, one or two made contact and meetings were arranged. Thus this 'lost' member was brought back into the family.

Arthur and Bea Wasey have two children: Jonathan and Sheila. Jonathan, as it happens, is the senior of only two great-great-grandsons bearing the name Wasey to have descended from the Revd John Spearman Wasey, of Compton. He is also therefore the senior descendant, in the male line, of Joseph Wasey, grocer, of North Walsham, younger son of the Robert with whom this saga began.

ROBERT WASEY(1) Yeoman of Brumstead & North Walsham, Norfolk = Sarah da. of Robert & Eliz. Wilton of N. Walsham
d.11 Dec.1679 aet 76. MI N.Walsham(Rye) Norf.Archd.Will,1679 — bp.6 May 1604 N.Walsham. Adm.father's prop.1656.bur.24 Aug.1666 N.Walsham

Children of Robert Wasey(1) and Sarah Wilton:

ROBERT WASEY(2)
Legatee of Robt.
Wilton's Will,
1656. dsp 1670

RICHARD WASEY(1)
Yeoman of Tunstead &
Smallborough.
b.c.1635.Adm.to Robt.
Wilton's prop.,1656.
d.16 Oct.1678,Tunstead
N/A Will dated 1675
= Lydia (?Andrews)
m. by 1659 (Ct.Rolls)
(m.22) Wm. Linstead,
Grocer of Norwich &
latterly of Stoke Ash,
Suffolk

JOSEPH
WASEY(1)
b.c.1636

Mary
b.c.1638 (Ct.Rolls)
Legatee of R.Wilton,
her father & ROBT(2)
dsp 4 Jul.1685 MI
N.Walsham (Rye)
= Edmund
Thenylthorpe
Attorney of
Norw.& Worstead
m (1? Mary 3 Jun.
1684 Horstead.
d.1714 PCC Will

Sarah
m.1661 SS Simon
& Jude,Norwich
Leg.of fa.& of
Robt.Wilton.Adm.
to husband's
prop., 1689   Issue
= Samuel
Postle
Gent.
of
Brum-
stead

Line B (from Richard Wasey(1) = Lydia):

ROBERT WASEY(3)
Norwich Merchant
Fa's hr.Leg.of
ROBERT(1). d.13
April.1687 aet 26
MI Tuns. NCC Will
= Elizabeth
bur. St.
Etheldred,
Norwich MI
(Blomefield)

RICHARD WASEY(2)
Leg.of Fa., of
ROBT(1) & of ROBT(2)
bur.9 Jan1681 Tuns-
teed as "of Norwich"

SAMUEL WASEY
Leg. of fa.&
of ROBT(1)
d. by 1715
= Sarah
Leg.of Fa.&
Gd.father

JOHN WASEY
Gent., Grocer
of North Walsham
Leg. of Father,of
ROBT(1) & of
JOSEPH(2) of Trunch
bur.16 Oct.1727
N.Walsham. N/A Will
= Susanna
da. of Stephen &
Susannah Bunn of North
Walsham. bp.4 Nov.1681
N.W. m.3 Feb.1701/2 NW
bur.2 Jun.1717 North
Walsham

Children of Robert Wasey(3) = Elizabeth:

ROBERT WASEY
bp.& bur.
1684 St.Eth.

Elizabeth
bp.1685
bur.168(6?)

Mary
bp.4 Jan.1686
bur.1687 St.E.

Descendants (Joseph Wasey(3) line):

JOSEPH WASEY(3)
Soldier/Weaver
Leg.of Fa.& ROBT(1)
Bro.& Adm. to
RICHARD & cousin to
JOSEPH of Trunch
(Ch.Suit)
d. by 1717
= Anne
Exec.
of
Hus's
Will,
dated
1715

JOSEPH WASEY(4)
bp.20 Aug.1703
bur.15 Ap.1704
N.Walsham

JOSEPH WASEY
bp.16 May, bur.
29 May 1707 NW

Children of Joseph Wasey(4) = Mary Greene:

JOSEPH WASEY(4)
Grocer of N.Walsham &
Worstead. bp.31 Aug.1708
NW. Fa's co-hr; Leg. of
JOS(2) of Trunch. bur.17
Feb.1766 Worstead
= Mary da. of
Mary & John
Greene of NW
Adm.fa's prop.
1733 (Ct.Roll)
bu.15 Oct.1764

Lydia bp.10 Dec.
1704 bur. 2 Jul.
1705 N.Walsham

Anna bp.14 Jan.
1705/6. bur. 1
Sep.1712 NW

Susannah
bp.10 Dec.
1710. bur.
21 Sep.
1712 NW

Lydia
bp.12 Mch.
1712/13
N.Walsham
m. 25 Mch.
1734
Brampton,
Norfolk
Fa's co-hr.
1727. Surr.
NW prop.
1734/38/55
bur.9 Aug.
1784 Cley-
next-Sea
aet 72
= Daniel
son of
Rev.
Rowland
Clarke
of
Skeyton &
Brampton
bp.1712
Skeyton
bur.1776
Cley-
next-
Sea
  Issue
(NNGS Vol13)

Susannah
bp.17 Sep.
1714 NW
m. 1 Aug.
1738
Brampton
Fa's co-hr,
1727
bur.4 Apr.
1766 NW
= Joseph
Saul
of
Worstead
  Issue

JOHN WASEY
bp.25 May
bur.18 Oct.
1716 NW

JOHN WASEY
bp.28 May
bur.2 Jun.
1717 NW

Children of Joseph Wasey(4) = Mary Greene:

Alice
bp.23
Jan.
1730
Wors.
m.John
Tuck
23 May
1751
Wors.
(NNGS
Vol.6)

Mary
bp.29
Nov.1732
Wors. m.
Nimrod
Burdett
22 Oct.
1751
Horsham
St.Faith,
Norwich
Issue

Ellen
bp.31
Dec.
1734
Wors.
m.?
John
Nant
6 Nov.
1758
Wors.

Eliza-
beth
bp.30
Mch.
1737
Wors.

WILLIAM
WASEY(4)
bp.12 Aug.
1742 Wors.
(?m) Eliz.
Pardon
14 May
1764
North
Walsham

JOSEPH
WASEY(5)
bp.16
April
1749
Wors.

LEGEND
b. = born bp = bap
m/= = married d = died
bur = buried
/ between dates = old & new calendar
dsp = died without issue

JOSEPH WASEY(1) Gent., Grocer of North Walsham. = Mary da. of Robert Woorts of Trunch. Sis. & hr.of Wm. Woorts, Gent.
Adm.to fa's prop.1679,d.12 Sep.1701 aet 65 MI (Arms) NW .NCC Will   Applied for m.lic., Edingthorpe 1661/2. bur.2 Sep.1700 N.Walsham

ROBERT WASEY(4)
bp.13 Feb.1662/3
NW. bur.17 Feb.
1687/8 N.Walsham

JOSEPH WASEY(2) Gent.,Grocer of N.Walsham
& Trunch. bp.4 Feb.1663/4.Legatee of
ROBERT(2): Father's hr. bur. 5 Oct. 1718
N.Walsham. PCC Will

WILLIAM WASEY(1) Attorney of Brumstead. = Bridget da.of Wm.Durrant
bp.27 Nov.1668 NW   of Scottow. m(2) Spencer
Worstead & N.Walsham.   Chapman of Wors. 30 Jan.
m.23 Oct.1688 Scottow. d.25 Dec.1700   1701/2.bur.27 Aug.1707 NW
bur.N.Walsham(MI Rye) PCC Will

THOMAS
WASEY
bp. 7
Jul.1675

Mary
bp.20
July 1681
bur. 1687

WILLIAM WASEY(2) Physician of Westminster = Margaret da.of Gilbert Spearman of co.
bp.27 Nov.1691 Brumstead.Gr.Arms,1729. President RCP,1750-4.   Durham.bp.10 Feb.1705/6.m.24 Jun.1730
Hr.to fa.1701 & to JOS(2),1718. d. 1 Apr.1757. PCC Will   St.Antholin's,London. Predeceased hus.

JOSEPH WASEY
bp.21 Feb.1692
bu.14 Mch.1693
Brumstead

Elizabeth
bp.26 Feb.1694
Men.Fa's Will,1701 bur.
Stepfa's Will,1723 1696

Maria
bp.&

Margaret b.19 Aug.1731 Soho
d.24 Nov.1794 Bath. bur.
Bathampton. PCC Will

WILLIAM JOHN SPEARMAN WASEY Lt.Col.2nd Troop Lifeguards = Elizabeth Honoria da. of George Spearman of Bishop Middleham,
b.18 Dec.1733 bp.14 Jan.1733/4 St.Anne's,Soho.   co. Durham. b.26 Mch.1742. m.24 Aug.1758 Bishop Middleham
d. 12 Mch.1817 Marylebone. PCC Will   d. 28 Jul.1824. bur. Edgcote, Northants.

WILLIAM GEORGE WASEY
Paymaster,HEICS, Madras
b.10 May bp5 Jun.1761
St.James, Westminster.
m.18 Jan.1785.d.23 May
1785 Palamcottah,E.Ind.
= Hannah da.of
Wm.Butterworth
& wid.of James
Johnson. m(3)
N.E.Kindersley
HEICS

SPEARMAN
WASEY
b.8 Apr.
1771.Bd.
Rugby,d.
there,24
Aug.1785
MI Rugby
Church

Rev.CLEMENT
JOHN WASEY
Rec.of South
Shoebury,Essx.
& Ulcombe,Kent
b.26 Oct.1769
Bp.St.Anne's,
Soho.d.22 May
1811.bur. St.
Marylebone.
PCC Will

Anne Elizabeth
2 Feb.1763 -
30 Mch.1767

Anna Margaretta
20 Feb.1764 -
26 Feb.1770

JOHN WASEY
19 Aug.1765 -
7 Jan. 1766

Rev. GEORGE WASEY Rector
of Whitington, Glos; Wytham
Berks; Albury,Oxon.& subse-
quently of Ulcombe, Kent.
b.9 Jan.bp.8 Feb.1773 St.
Anne's,Soho.d.24 Mch.1838
Wardington,Oxon. bur.
Edgcote, Northants. MI
PCC Will
= Anne Sophia
da. of Capt.
J.Frodsham
RN.b.17 Nov.
1781 bp.
Broadwell,
Glos. m. 2
Jun.1810 St.
Marylebone
d.1 Dec.1845

WILLOUGHBY JOHN
WASEY
b.22 Jan.bp.23
Feb. 1778
d.17 Apr.1779
bur.St.Anne's,
Soho

Eliza Honoria Margaret b.29 Oct.1785
India.d.17 Dec.1847
Edgcote, MI at Wardington, Oxon.

Rev. WILLIAM GEORGE
LEIGH WASEY Vic. of
Morville & Quatford,
Salop. b.26 May 1811
Albury, Oxon. d. 9
Jun.1877 Quatford MI
= Eliza Lenora
da.of Philip
Monckton b.5 Jul.
1815 India. m. 23
Apr.1844 Brewood
d.29 Jul.1877 Quat.

WILLOUGHBY
CLEMENT WASEY
bp.12 Oct.
1812 Albury,
Bucks. d. 1
Oct.1827.
bur.Edgcote
MI

Emma
Honoria
b.5 Jul.
1816
Swanbourne,
Bucks. d. 1
Oct.1827.
bur.Edgcote
MI

Sophia =
Elizabeth
b.27 Dec.
1814 bp.
4 Oct.1815
Brighton
m. 21 Apr.
1840
Wardington
d.5 Nov.
1840 bur.
Tickencote,
Stamford MI

Rev. George
Wingfield
of Glatton,
Hunts.

Rev. JOHN
SPEARMAN
WASEY
b. 1817

Captain EDWARD FRODSHAM = (1) Maria Louisa
NOEL KINDERSLEY WASEY RN   da.of General
b.26 Dec.1819 bp.3 Apr.   Thos.Marriott of
1820 Swanbourne, Bucks.   Pershore, Worcs.
m (1) 5 Aug.1869 St.   & wid.of George
Marylebone, London.   Stewart MacKenzie
m (2) St.James,   of Seaforth
Piccadilly. dsp 5 Apr.   d.1 Oct.1890 aet
1902 Touchen End, Nr.   71,Boynes,Upton-
Maidenhead. MI   on-Severn.bur.
    Touchen End MI
    = (2) Jane Mary
    Anne, wid. of
    John Haig & da.
    of John M.Davis
    of Cardiganshire
    d. 11 Oct.1918

Sophia
Honoria
b.18 Jan.
1847.d.9
Aug.1881
Quat.MI

Leonora = Capt.Henry Almarus
Sabrina   Digby RN, JP.b.9
b.26 Oct.   Feb.1843 dsp 18 Sep.
1848.m.24   1913 bur.North
Sep.1874   Runcton, Norfolk
d.9 Mch.
1920 bur.
N.Runcton

C

Rev. JOHN SPEARMAN WASEY Vicar of Compton Parva, Berks.　　　　　＝　　Harriet Jemima da. of Edward Cockburn Kindersley of Harley Street
b.30 Sep.bp.21 Nov.1817 Swanbourne. d.21 Nov.1899 bur.Compton MI　　　　　b.1830 Middx. m.24 Nov.1853. d.20 Feb.1908 aet 78. MI Compton

| EDWARD JOHN SPEARMAN WASEY JP | = | Amy Florence da.of Wm. Ison of Yorks. & Fosote Of Nr.Newbury. b.4 Apr.1857 m. there 1 Feb. 1892 d. 3 June 1921. bur. Chieveley, Berks. MI | ARTHUR FRODSHAM WASEY of Newbury & Canada b.15 Mch. 1859 Mdx. m.20 Jun. 1899 d. 1 Aug. 1914 | = | Ethel da. of G.Crawford of Swan Lake, Manitoba, Canada. d.18 Apr. 1934 Bognor Regis | GEORGE KINDERSLEY WASEY Civil Engineer of Goa, India & Leigh Hill Hse,Savernake b.10 Jun.1861 Compton. d.25 Feb.1943 bur. Savernake MI | WILL- OUGHBY FRANK WASEY 1864- 1882 bur. Compton MI | Mary Caroline b. 3 Jan. 1863. Of Godfrey, Foscote Lodge. d.20 Jun. 1929 | = | Sidney Jane da. of Col.C.M. of Bombay Staff Corps. d.19 Dec. 1892 India d.4 Jun. 1947 MI | CYRIL LEIGH WASEY Lt.RN b.1866 d.1892 Malta MI | LIONEL TORIN WASEY Gentleman Farmer of Southmead, Newbury b.15 Jul. 1870. d.23 Apr.1955 Newbury | = | Edith Anne da.of Robt. Walter Trail of Las Palmas,Argen- tine. m.15 Nov. 1899 d.28 Jan. 1945 | LIONEL ROBERT TRAIL WASEY Tea Planter, Ceylon. b.17 Nov.1902 Newbury. m.(2) Kath- leen da.of G.D.Burton Windus. Liv. 1994 UK | = | (1)Estell da.of R.J. Austin ex. Australia m. Kandy, Ceylon div. d.12 Jul. 1961 |

Elizabeth Harriett Mima b.23 Jane Dec. 1854 Aynhoe b.6 m. 1878 Jan. Rev. Hy. 1856 Fredk. Of Howard, Foscote Rec. of Lodge Bright- New- walton bury d. 1938 d. 1940

Issue

Gladys Edith b.19 Oct. 1900 m. Capt. Philip Wykeham Leigh Pember- ton dsp 1992

| EDWARD ARTHUR WASEY b & d 1893 | WILLOUGHBY SPEARMAN WASEY Maj. RCS.b.12 Jul.1899 m. Kathleen Isobel da. of G.Evans of Limer- ick,Ire- land & of Buenos A's dsp 3 Nov. 1977 MI Chieveley | BENJAMIN JOHN SPEAR- MAN WASEY Forestry Consultant b.24 Jul. 1913.m.15 Nov. 1947 Vera Ruby Alice da. of Robert Victor Leete. dsp 6 Jan. 1987 | = | Amy Elvira b. 18 July 1914 Liv. 1994 | | | ARTHUR CRAWFORD WASEY b.20 Feb. 1900 m.(2)? dsp 10 Feb. 1973 Leics. | = | (1) Vic- toria Walker d.13 Jun. 1941 = (3)Nora Breacher d. 1967 | EDWARD CYRIL MOWBRAY WASEY b.13 Sep. 1902 d.21 Jul. 1981 IOW = Worthing | | | CYRIL WALTER CARLETON WASEY Capt.R. Warw.Rgt. b.29 Sep. 1893. M.C;Leg. of Hon. Attach. RFC.k. in action 28 Oct. 1917 France | = | Evelyn Alice Mary da. of Arth. Joseph Nash of IOW.wid. of Dr. Radford d.18 Jul. 1983 | Sydney Joan Leonora b. 15 Mch. 1903 d. 18 Aug. 1989 | GEOFFREY CHARLES MARSDEN WASEY b. 16 Dec. 1907 d. at school aet 9 | TIMOTHY JOHN WASEY b.4 Dec. 1930 Ceylon Now of Devon, UK | = | (1) Dorothy Ann Wynd m.Ceylon d. 1977 (2) Thelma Mary Hitch- cock m. UK | Jennifer Ann b.26 Jan.1933 Ceylon m. John R.M. Collins Ceylon Liv. UK 1994 Issue |

EDWARD Muriel ARTHUR Sophie WASEY b. 1 b.6 Oct. Apr. 1897 1895 d.10 m. May Evelyn 1974 Donald McLach- lan MBE b.6 Apr. 1895 Issue

| ARTHUR EDWARD WASEY b.13 Jan,1937 Seaview, IOW m.15 Nov,1975 Now of Jersey | = | Bea da.of Kurt Erich Willie Van Den Broek of Barneveld, Holland | | Carol Elizabeth b. 31 Dec. 1928 Ceylon | = | (1) Michael Clarke Ceylon. Issue = (2) John Neville Sheard, UK,.Liv, S.Africa Issue | CHRISTOPHER JOHN WASEY b.13 Sep.1959 Ceylon | = | Susan Jennifer b.5 Apr.1961 Ceylon | (1) Angela Jane b.26 Mch.1966 UK |

ARTHUR EDWARD WASEY b.13 Jan,1937

Sheila Anne Eliza b.15 May 1978

JONATHAN ARTHUR EDWARD WASEY b. 10 Jul. 1976

KING EDWARD III = Phillippa of Hainault
1312-1377   c.1309-1369

EDWARD = Joan   LIONEL Duke of = Lady Elizabeth   JOHN of Gaunt d.1399 = (3) Katherine   EDMUND 1st Duke of York = Isabella
Black Prince Holland   Clarence d.1368   da.of Wm.de Burgh   Duke of Lancaster   Swynford d.1403   d.1402   da.of King of Castile

KING RICHARD II   Phillippa = Edmund de Mortimer   John Beaufort d.1410 = Margaret da.of Thos.Holland   Joan = (2)Ralph Neville d.1425
murdered 1400   1355-1382   3rd Earl of March   1st Earl of Somerset   2nd Earl of Westmorland   yst.da   1st Earl of Westmorland

Roger Mortimer d.1398 = Lady Eleanor,da.of   John Beaufort d.1444 = (2)Margaret da.of   Joan (?Antingham) = Sir Nicholas
4th Earl of March   Thos.Holland,Earl of Kent   1st Duke of Somerset   Lord Beauchamp   Wichingham d.1453/4

Lady Anne Mortimer = Richard, Earl of Cambridge   Margaret Beaufort = Edmund Tudor d.1456   Elizabeth = Sir Thomas, Ld Hoo
ex.1415   Earl of Richmond   Wichingham   & Hastings d.c1455

Richard, 3rd Duke = Lady Cecily Neville   Ann Hoo = Sir Geoffrey
of York ex. 1460   d.1495   c1425-1501   Boleyn d.c 1463

KING EDWARD IV = Elizabeth   Lady Anne Plantagenet = (1) Henry Holland, Duke of Exeter   Elizabeth Boleyn = Sir Henry Heydon
d.1483   Woodvyle   eldest da. 1439-1476   (1) Sir Thomas St. Leger ex.1483   (Ann)   d.1503

KING EDWARD V   Princess Elizabeth = KING HENRY VII   Lady Anne St.Leger = Sir George Manners, 12th   Bridget Heydon = Sir William Paston
md.in The Tower   of York d.1503   d.1509   d.1526   Lord Roos d. 1513   c1479-1554

KING HENRY VIII   Princess Margaret = (1) KING JAMES IV   Princess Mary   Thomas Manners d.1543   Eleanor Paston
d.1547   d.1541   of Scotland d.1513   1495-1533   1st Earl of Rutland   d. 1551

KING JAMES V of = Princess Mary of   Lady Eleanor = Henry Clifford, 2nd   Lady Gertrude = George,6th Earl   Lady Elizabeth = Sir John Savage of
Scots d.1542   Lorraine d. 1560   Brandon yst.da   Earl of Cumberland   Manners 1st da.   of Shrewsbury   Manners,yst da   Rock Savage d.1597

QUEEN MARY of = (2) Henry Stuart   Lady Margaret = Henry Stanley, 4th   Hon. Henry Talbot = Elizabeth, Lady   Margaret Savage = William, 1st Lord
Scots,ex.1587   Lord Darnley   Clifford b.1540   Earl of Derby   d. 1596   Holcroft,da. of   1st da. d.1597   Brereton & Baron of
Sir Wm.Reyner   Laghlin d.1631

KING JAMES VI of = Princess Anne of   Ferdinando, 5th = Alice,da of Sr John   Gertrude Talbot = Robert, 1st Earl   Hon.Mary Brereton = Henry O'Brien, 5th
Scots, I of Eng.   Denmark d. 1619   Earl of Derby   Spencer of Althorp   1588-1649   of Kingston d.1643   1580-1640   Earl of Thomond

Princess Eliza- = Frederick V El.Palatine   Lady Frances = Sir John Egerton,1st   Hon. Francis = Elizabeth, da. of   Lady Mary O'Brien = Charles Cokayne
beth, 1st da.   & King of Bohemia d1632   Stanley, 2nd da   Earl of Bridgwater   Pierrepont, MP   Thos. Bray Esq.   d. 1686   1st Vis. Cullen

Princess Sophia = Ernest Augustus,Elector   John Egerton,2nd = Lady Eliz. Cavendish   Robt.Pierrepont = Anne, da. of   Hon. Mary Cokayne = Robert Pierson Esq
1630-1714   of Hanover d. 1698   Earl of Bridgwtr   da.Duke of Newcastle   MP for Nottingham   Henry Murray Esq.   d. 1702

KING GEORGE I = Princess Sophia Dorothea   Hon.Thos.Egerton = Hester, da.of Sir   Mary Pierrepont = Nathaniel Kinderley   Margaret Pierson = Gilbert Spearman
d. 1727   of Celle d. 1726   (3rd s.) of Tatton   John Busby. d.1724   1682-1709   of Notts. & Norfolk   1679-1731   Esq., 1675-1738

KING GEORGE II = Princess Caroline of   Elizabeth = Rev.Peter Leigh of   Rev.John Kinderley = Sarah Raining   Margaret Spearman = Dr. William Wasey
d. 1760   Brandenburgh-anspach   Egerton b.1678   West Hall,High Legh   of S. Walsham,Norf   1707-1799   b.1705/6 Durham   1691-1757

Frederick,Prince = Princess Augusta of   Rev. Egerton- = (1)Ann,da of Hamlet   Nathaniel Kinders- = Jemima Wicksted   Margaret Wm.John S.= Eliz.Hon.Spearman
of Wales d. 1751   Saxe-Gotha d. 1772   Leigh,Archd.Salop   Yates,Esq.of Crowley   ley, Lt.Col.HEICS   1741-1809   Wasey   Wasey   1742-1824

KING GEORGE III = Princess Charlotte of   Rev. Peter Leigh = Mary,da of Henry   Nathaniel Edward = Hannah Butterworth   Rev.George Wasey = Anne Sophia,da.of
d. 1820   Mecklenburg-Strelitz   Rector of Lymm   Doughty Esq.   Kinderley HEICS   wid.of Wm.Geo.Wasey   of Ulcomb.b.1773   Capt.John Prodsham
d.1838   1781-1845

Edward, Duke of = Princess Victoria of   Anne Leigh = Capt.John Prodsham   Edward Cockburn = Harriet, da. of   Rev. John Spearman Wasey
Kent 1767-1820   Saxe-Coburg-Saalfeld   d. 1830   R.N. d.1791   Kinderley d.1866   (?....) Torin   Vic.of Compton. 1817-1899

QUEEN VICTORIA = Prince Albert of Saxe-   Anne Sophia = Rev. George Wasey   Harriet Jemima Kindersley
d. 1901   Coburg. d. 1861   Prodsham d.1845   of Ulcomb.b.1773   d. 1908

Chart showing Wasey descents from royal lines and also showing, far right, the entirely female descent from Joan ?Antingham c. 1400 through to Dr Wasey's daughter, Margaret, who died in 1794

Part III A Distaff Line

The Wasey epic completed, I found myself pondering upon the female members of this family. Several of the brides brought a direct descent from royalty; through females here and males there, bearing such names as Clifford, Cavendish, Pierrepont, Talbot, Manners and Egerton, their lines descend several times over from the Plantagenets and one descent is from the Tudor king, Henry VII. From thence they can be traced, also in unbroken lines, to William the Conqueror, Alfred the Great, the Emperor Charlemagne and into the mists of legend.

Another facet of the Wasey lineage presented itself: the opportunity to trace purely female descents. This is often impossible unless, as with Lydia Wasey's progeny, the mother's patronymic is retained by succeeding generations: even so it often survived for only a few. One distaff line, however, stretching back from the children of Norfolk-born Dr Wasey, struck me as remarkable. It can be taken, mother to daughter, entirely through females for some thirteen generations or more with, of course, a change of name in each generation.

There are those rather chauvinistic persons who regard genealogy as being valid if traced only through the male line, ignoring the old adage that 'it is a wise child who knows its own father' whereas a mother's child is undeniably hers.

How many bored, lonely young wives, the victims of their own or their parents' ambition, have taken a lover and passed off the resultant offspring as their unsuspecting husband's? The peerage as well as the proletariat is probably littered with them. To pursue ancestry through the distaff side, therefore, would provide a lineage, by its very nature, of absolute integrity: an approach which should surely offer great diversity. And so indeed it did.

(13) ELIZABETH WICHINGHAM = Sir Thomas de Hoo, d. *c.* 1453

Elizabeth, the daughter of Nicholas Wichingham of Wichingham in Norfolk,[1] would have been born in about 1400, soon after Henry of Bolingbroke usurped King Richard II's throne. Her father had been married first to Alice, the daughter of Roger Flete, citizen and draper of London, by whom he had a son, William, and daughters, Alice and Margery. William married and had a family, but pre-deceased their father; Alice married Sir Roger Harsike, and Margery, Sir Robert Tuddenham of Oxburgh. Their father's second wife (possibly Elizabeth's mother) was Joan (?de Antingham). By her he also had a son, Edmund, known as 'of Woodrising' who married Alice, the daughter of the renowned Sir John Fastolf.

Elizabeth was said by Cokayne to be the first and by Burke the second wife of Sir Thomas Hoo. A man of parts, he was once esquire of the chamber to Thomas Beaufort, Duke of Exeter; Sheriff, in 1430, of Beds. and Bucks.; and was in France in 1434 (three years after the death of Joan of Arc) with a retinue of 20 men-at-arms and 60 archers. Less than two years later he took part, with the Lords Talbot and Scales, in the operations in the Pays de Caux, burning and slaying all in their path, so that 'all the contre . . . was destroyed both of men and of bestis, and of all her goodis'.[2]

As reward, Sir Thomas was granted, in 1442, £40 a year out of the issues of Norfolk for his services in the French wars. Later, he and Sir Robert de Ros were commissioned by King Henry VI to negotiate his marriage with Margaret of Anjou. In 1444 he was Chancellor in France and Normandy and in 1445 he and de Ros met the ambassadors of France and Spain at Rochester.

That year Sir Thomas was installed as Knight of the Garter and, three years later, for his good service in England, France and Normandy, was created Lord Hoo of Hoo in Bedfordshire and of Hastings in Sussex.

It seems likely therefore that Elizabeth will have spent most of her married life alone, but for her attendants, in a fortified manor house in one of Sir Thomas' lordships. It would be governed during those periods by a seneschal, unless, like her Paston contemporaries, Elizabeth was well able to command its defence herself. She cannot have lived to see her husband ennobled, for she died in the early 1440s and Sir Thomas married again, we find, to Eleanor, the daughter of Lord Welles.[3]

Sir Thomas and Elizabeth's only surviving child was their daughter, Anne, who was to marry Sir Geoffrey Boleyne.

(12) ANNE HOO = Sir Geoffrey Boleyne, b *c.* 1425 d. 1463

Anne married during her father's lifetime to Geoffrey Boleyne (or Bullen), the son of Sir Geoffrey Boleyne of Salle, Norfolk. He too was knighted in 1458, the year he became Lord Mayor of London, where he 'attained great opulence' and became a favourite of Sir John Fastolf.

Bitter battles were raging at this time between the king's party (which, under his favourite, John Beaufort, Earl of Somerset, caused widespread dissatisfaction) and the king's cousin, Richard, Duke of York. In 1453, when the king was found to be mad, York had been called upon to act as Protector. All was well until the queen, Margaret of Anjou, after nine years of childlessness, gave birth to a son, and later, the king, for a while, regained his sanity. The queen promptly persuaded Henry to dismiss York from office and recall the hated Somerset to power.

This led eventually to York's marching on London and the first battle of St Albans. Hatred between the factions prevailed, one battle leading to another, and it was in 1459, soon after Sir Geoffrey Boleyne became Lord Mayor, that the Lords Warwick and Salisbury pushed with their adherents inland from the coast to London, where they were supported by the Yorkists, who threw open the gates.

After further confrontations the Duke of York came to London again and summoned a Parliament. With a hereditary claim as eldest heir of Richard II, he was no longer willing to act as regent for Henry VI but, in view of the hatred engendered by Queen Margaret and her followers, talked of taking the crown for himself.

This was the London known to Anne and her husband. They had a large family: their eldest son, Sir Thomas, died young and so did Simon, who became a priest. Their other son, Sir William of Blickling, Norfolk, and of Hever Castle, Kent, married Margaret, daughter of the 7th Earl of Ormonde, and became the father of Sir Thomas Boleyne, constable of Norwich Castle and ambassador to the court of Spain. This grandson, having been granted the earldoms of Wiltshire and Ormonde, married Elizabeth, daughter of Thomas Howard, Duke of Norfolk, and became the father of Anne, Henry VIII's ill-fated second queen. Sir Geoffrey and Anne (née Hoo) became therefore the great great grandparents of Queen Elizabeth I.

Sir Geoffrey died in about 1463, leaving orders that his burial place should be Blickling Church if his death were in Norfolk, or St Lawrence-in-the-Jury if, as happened, he died in London. Anne took as her second husband Sir Thomas Fynes and died, according to Blomefield, before 1505 when her son William was buried in Norwich Cathedral 'next to the resting-place of his mother'.

Of Anne and Sir Geoffrey's four daughters, Cecily died young and is buried in the chancel of Blickling Church while Alice, Isabel and Elizabeth married, the last named to Sir Henry Heydon.

(11) ELIZABETH (ANNE) BOLEYN = Sir Henry Heydon, d.1503

When the marriage was arranged between Elizabeth (sometimes known as Anne) and the son of John Heydon Esq., of Baconsthorpe, on the north coast of Norfolk, she must have felt apprehensive indeed, for John Heydon, a notorious lawyer and trustee to many large estates, was a man feared and hated by many. Once of Heydon Hall, he and Sir Thomas Tuddenham were two of a kind: avaricious and unscrupulous. In 1448 the mayor and corporation of Norwich complained that they were, 'purporting for great lucre to have as well the rule of the city as they had of the shire'.

An adversary of the Paston family, Heydon is named in a letter of 1451 'false shrew' for information given to the Pastons' enemy, Lord Moleyns, and was incitor of a riot of one thousand people who broke in and despoiled their Gresham manor. Sir John Fastolf complained, in 1450, of the grievances done against him by Heydon over a long period.

In another Paston letter is an accusation that when John Heydon's wife, Eleanor (daughter of Edmund Winter of Winter Berningham), was brought to bed of a child, Heydon would have nothing to do with her or the child and threatened to 'cut off her nose and make her know what she was, and to kill the

Baconsthorpe Castle

child'.[4] It was Henry, the son and heir of this man (possibly that same child), who became Elizabeth Boleyn's husband.

Lord of various manors, he had been steward of the house to the Lady Cecily, Duchess of York. At West Wickham, Kent, he built 'a noble house', living there before the death of his father who had begun the building of Baconsthorpe Castle, erecting the tower first, a necessary precaution during that lawless period when strength, not comfort, was the first consideration.

It was probably after marrying Elizabeth that Sir Henry returned to Norfolk and continued the building of Baconsthorpe, completing it in 1486. With Henry Tudor on the throne and a much greater degree of law and order, Sir Henry now made Baconsthorpe the centre of a vast sheep run. He was also responsible for building the church at Salthouse and the causeway between Walsingham and Thursford.

Seldom are the death dates recorded of wives at this period, but Sir Henry, we know, died in 1503 and was buried in the Heydon chapel built by his father on the south side of Norwich Cathedral. Intended as burial place for the family, it was probably also Elizabeth's last resting place.

The couple had three sons. John, an eminent courtier, knighted at the coronation of Henry VIII, was said, in early life, to have been a spendthrift, 'but at length grew a great husband' when he married Catherine, the daughter of Lord Willoughby of Parham. Henry junior married Anne, who brought as dowry property in Berks., Surrey and Glos. Their other son, William, was slain by peasants in the rebellion led by the Kett brothers and was buried in St Peter's Mancroft, Norwich. Of their daughters, Amy, the eldest, married Sir Roger le Strange of Hunstanton; Dorothy wed Sir Thomas Brook, heir of Lord Cobham; Elizabeth married Walter Hobart Esquire, of Hales Hall; Anne became the wife of William Gurney Esquire; and Bridget's marriage was to Sir William Paston.

(10) BRIDGET HEYDON = Sir William Paston, *c.* 1479–1554

Sir William Paston of Paston was a member of the family with whom Bridget's grandfather had had such bitter dealings: writers and receivers of the fifteenth-century letters which make us privy to the lives, not only of this family but those, also, of the great history-makers who featured in the Wars of the Roses.

Sir William's grandfather, John, was already the possessor of much landed wealth when he became heir and executor to his wife's kinsman, Sir John Fastolf, inheriting numerous manors in Norfolk and Suffolk including the great new castle at Caister. He represented Norfolk in the Parliament of King Henry VI and, again, during the reign of Edward IV, being in such favour with that king, at one stage, that he was of his Household.

Fortune changed, however, when he and his family became the victims of covetous noblemen who besieged, and took by force, some of their properties. Three times he was incarcerated in the Fleet prison. His wife Margaret displayed great courage and ability during those long years of adversity and separation.

Caister Castle

It was their son, John (the youngest of two brothers bearing the same Christian name) and his wife, Margery, who became Bridget's parents-in-law. This John fought at Barnet in 1471, was High Sheriff of Norfolk and Suffolk and an esquire of the body to Henry VII. When he died in 1504 his son, William (Bridget's husband, who became an eminent counsellor at law), received a letter from kinsman, William Barons, lately Master of the Rolls and presently Bishop of London: 'Cousin Paston I recommend me unto you and have received your letter by the which I have understand of the death of my cousin your father . . . I will counsel . . . you to take it as well and as patiently as ye can seeing that we all be mortal and born to die. . . [he continues with some advice, concluding] . . . look that ye be of as comfortable cheer as ye can, exhorting my lady your mother-in-law [stepmother] to be in like wise. . .'.[5]

Bridget's death date is not known, but Sir William died in 1554, during the reign of Queen Mary. They had five sons: their eldest, Erasmus, married Mary, the daughter of Sir Thomas Windham of Felbrigg in Norfolk, and became the father of another Sir William who lies in an ornate tomb, with life-size armoured effigy, in North Walsham Church. Their son John wed Anne Moulton and became the father of Bridget, wife of Sir Edward Coke, Lord Chief Justice of England. Another son, Sir Thomas, was a gentleman of the king's privy chamber. And Clement, their fifth son, became a great sea captain who served with distinction under three reigns, being called by Henry VIII 'his Champion' and by the Protector, Duke of Somerset, 'his Soldier'; Queen Mary called him 'her seaman' and Queen Elizabeth used the metaphor, 'her Father'.

Bridget and Sir William also had six daughters, the eldest of whom was Eleanor, who became Countess of Rutland.

(9) ELEANOR PASTON = Thomas Manners 1st Earl of Rutland,
    d.1551   13th Baron de Ros, d.1543

Eleanor was given in marriage to Thomas Manners, the eldest son of the 12th Lord Ros and the Lady Anne St Leger, first cousin to Princess Elizabeth of York, Henry VII's queen.

Lady Anne was the only daughter of Anne Plantagenet (sister of two kings, Edward IV and Richard III), who had married first, Henry Holland, Duke of Exeter, a supporter of Henry VI. On the accession of Edward IV, Exeter was attainted and the couple divorced. Soon after, the duke was found dead on the seashore, whereupon the duchess married again to Sir Thomas St Leger.

As friend and second cousin to Henry VIII, Eleanor's husband was made Earl of Rutland during that monarch's reign and they became extremely adept at swaying with every change of wind which whistled from the royal palaces during the saga of the king's 'secret matter'. The earl was party to the declaration sent to the Pope stating that, unless he complied in the affair of Henry's divorce, his supremacy in England would be endangered.

Queen Anne Boleyn (Eleanor's second cousin) was brought from Greenwich to her coronation by the earl in his barge. He was also one of the judges at her trial. Later he was appointed Lord Chamberlain to Queen Anne of Cleves, attending her at Greenwich before her marriage. All his commissions were carried out so expertly as to bring him numerous grants of lands and manors.

Eleanor took a prominent part in Court life, enjoying the plots and intrigues of lesser mortals endeavouring to reap a share of the spoils. She kept her finger on the pulse of the court, granting favours when judicious – (Lord Lisle's secretary to Lady Lisle) 'Your ladyship may not forget to send thanks . . . to my Lady Rutland, for divers causes'[6] – and she supervised the attire of Court ladies, ensuring they were fashionably dressed.

The earl was made Warden of the Marches and, among other commissions, accompanied the Duke of Norfolk, then general of an army of 20,000 men, in the invasion of Scotland, burning twenty towns and villages on their return. He was, nevertheless, said to have been a tender father and kind master to his servants. When he died in 1543 he was buried beneath a splendid alabaster tomb in Bottesford Church. Eleanor died in 1551 and her effigy is with the earl's, dressed in gown, short cape and ermine-trimmed mantle.

Of their four sons, Henry became the 2nd Earl and married Lady Margaret Nevill. Sir John became ancestor of the 1st Duke of Rutland: it was he who is said to have eloped with Dorothy, the beautiful daughter of Sir George Vernon of Haddon Hall, eventually bringing that romantic property to the family.

Of their five daughters, the eldest, Lady Gertrude, who married the 6th Earl of Shrewsbury, and the youngest, Lady Elizabeth, both became ancestors of the Wasey family. So did the earl's second cousin, the Princess Mary, sister of King Henry VIII, when, having become the dowager queen of Louis XII of France, she married Charles Brandon, Duke of Suffolk.

(8) LADY ELIZABETH MANNERS = Sir John Savage of Rocksavage, d.1597
m. *c*. 1547

The Lady Elizabeth was given in marriage to Sir John Savage of Clifton. On rebuilding the old family seat, Sir John and his heirs became known as 'of Rocksavage', a proud and influential family descended from the great Lords Stanley.[7]

Sir John's great grandfather (another Sir John) had had the charge of the left wing at the battle of Bosworth Field, where Richard III was slain, and was there when his uncle, Thomas Lord Stanley (married to Margaret Beaufort, mother of Henry Tudor) placed the crown on his stepson's head. Being instrumental with his uncle (afterwards made Earl of Derby) in promoting Henry VII to the crown, he was made Knight of the Garter by that monarch.

Rock Savage

The grandson of this Sir John (son of another Sir John and known as 'the younger'), who became the Lady Elizabeth's father-in-law, found notoriety when indicted for the murder, with his father, of one John Pauncefote Esq. and was arraigned in the King's Bench. Sir John 'the elder' confessed to the crime but, at the mediation of Cardinal Wolsey and the king's chamberlain, Charles Somerset, Earl of Worcester, they were pardoned with a fine, on condition that they should not enter the counties of Worcester or Chester again. Later, however, the king gave permission to the younger John to 'go, ride, or dwell in any place . . .'. The Stanleys and their connections were very powerful indeed during Tudor times.

Notoriety and tragedy endured. It was when Elizabeth's future husband was aged only three years that his widowed mother, daughter of the 1st Earl of Worcester, remarried to Sir William Brereton of Malpas. He was a gentleman of the bedchamber to Henry VIII who, at that time, was looking round for damning evidence against his queen, Anne Boleyn. Cromwell and his henchmen implicated Sir William in her downfall and he was beheaded (as were the queen and her brother, George, Viscount Rochford) 'for matters touching Queen Anne'.

The period through which the Lady Elizabeth and Sir John Savage found it necessary to steer a course was equally oppressive. To retain one's position, if not one's life, the proverbial coat needed turning frequently: from the Protestant reign of Edward VI to the Catholicism of Queen Mary and on to Queen Elizabeth's reign. Sir John, who was justice of the peace from 1550 until his death in 1597, weathered the changes skilfully, being elected twice for Parliament and sheriff of Cheshire seven times.

Several of the couple's sons died young; the survivor was another John who became the father of the 1st Viscount Savage and grandfather of the 1st Earl Rivers.

Elizabeth died in 1570 at Frodsham, Cheshire, several years before her husband, their youngest daughter being aged only three. Their eldest daughter, Margaret, became the wife of William, Lord Brereton of Brereton.

(7) MARGARET SAVAGE = William, 1st Lord Brereton
    1549–1597   Baron of Laghlin, 1550–1630

Margaret probably knew William, her husband-to-be, from childhood since her father was granted his wardship when he was orphaned at 9 years of age. Descended, as he was, from the most powerful of Cheshire families, the Lords Venables of Kinderton and others, Sir John Savage saw fit, two years later, to arrange their marriage, granting a portion of one thousand marks.

The couple began their married life some years later and in 1586 Margaret's husband built the lovely Tudor Hall at Brereton, described as a striking monument of his taste and splendour. Queen Elizabeth is said to have laid the foundation stone. On the chimneypiece of one room were once the Brereton arms, and in another was a striking painting of the queen, who is believed to have made a further visit on completion: the only two occasions on which she visited Cheshire.

Margaret bore Sir William seven children, only two of whom survived, but the genes brought to them and their progeny from their Brereton forebears were those of distinguished fighting men. Sir William's great great grandfather had been married to Anne, daughter of Robert Legh of Adlington (descended from the Leghs of High Legh). Their son took part in the great rebellion in Ireland aganst Fitzgerald, being sent to secure the submission of the strongly fortified castle at Maynooth. He and his men scaled the walls and took the castle by storm. They are said to have 'skirmished so fiercely . . . as both sides were rather for the great slaughter disadvantaged, than either part by anie great victorie furthered'. He was later made Lord Justice and early in the reign of Henry VIII, after subduing further rebellions, was constituted Lord High Marshal of Ireland.

His son, another William, predeceased him and so it was his grandson, yet another Sir William, who became Margaret Savage's (by then deceased) father-in-law. He had died in 1559, leaving five daughters and his son and heir a minor, hence the granting of his wardship to Sir John Savage.

Margaret died in 1597 and was buried with her infant children at the little church next to Brereton Hall. Years later, in 1624, Sir William was raised to the peerage as Lord Brereton of Leighlin, the patent declaring him 'to be sprung from an ancient, noble, and most renowned family . . . descended through many illustrious ancestors . . .'. At Margaret's death their only surviving son was a child of six years and their daughter Mary, aged seventeen, was as yet unmarried to the future Earl of Thomond.

(6) THE HON. MARY BRERETON = Henry O'Brien,
    1580–1640   5th Earl of Thomond

In July 1608 Mary married, at Brereton Church, Henry, Lord Inchiquin (later 5th Earl of Thomond). He was the son of Donough, known as the 'Great Earl', whose ancestor in the time of Henry VIII was Conor O'Brien, the 56th of their line to be termed King of Thomond. The family, for decades, had been subject to England's policy of anglicizing the Irish, educating the heads of important families in its customs and style of government. Consequently, Donough, brought up at the Court of Queen Elizabeth, sided with the government in suppressing rebellions against its authority.

When the Irish under Tyrone invaded Clare, capturing most of the castles and taking the earl's brother Daniel prisoner, he returned from London and, joining forces with the Earl of Ormonde, marched into Clare to avenge his brother's imprisonment and recover his possessions. He restored to the loyalists their castles, besieging those which resisted: when Dornby Castle surrendered, he hanged the garrison on trees. He was rewarded by being made governor of Clare and a privy councillor. These, and other similar exploits, must have been the stories related to his son, Henry, when a boy.

Brereton Hall

Henry, who had been a student at both Oxford and Trinity College, Dublin, was summoned to Parliament by the title of Lord Ibricken and was appointed, in May 1615, of the Counsel to the President of Munster. When the 'Great Earl' died in 1624, Henry succeeded as 5th Earl. In September 1633 he was appointed a member of the Privy Council to King Charles I which will have necessitated his presence in London for much of the year. Long spells, however, were probably spent at Dromoland Castle, County Clare, seat of the Lords Inchiquin. In 1639, when trouble brewed again in Scotland and King Charles made plans to combat it, Henry died. He was buried in Limerick Cathedral where, with ornate memorial, his father too lies. Mary died a year later and her remains probably rest there also.

The couple had no sons, but there were five daughters: Margaret, who became the wife of Edward Somerset, Marquess of Worcester (her dowry was £20,000)[8]; Elizabeth, the wife of Dutton, Lord Gerard of Bromley; Anne, who married her cousin Henry, the 7th Earl of Thomond; Honoria, who wed as her second husband, Sir Robert Howard, son of the Earl of Berkshire; and Mary, the eldest, who married Charles Cokayne, 1st Viscount Cullen.

(5) LADY MARY O'BRIEN d.1686 = Charles Cokayne, 1st Viscount Cullen

Mary married Charles Cokayne in 1627 at St Giles in the Fields, Middlesex, long before he was ennobled and several years before the troubles of Charles I's reign began.

Her husband was descended from an ancient family seated at Ashbourne, Derbyshire, early in the reign of the first Plantagenets. His father, Sir William, was an extremely successful and wealthy London merchant in the time of James I. That king, it is said, often consulted him on financial and commercial matters claiming: 'He never heard any man of his breeding handle business more rationally, more pertinently, more elegantly, more persuasively'.[9] Knighted at their grand London mansion, Cokayne House, after lavishly entertaining the king there, he was made Lord Mayor of London and was first governor of the Ulster colonists, founding Londonderry.

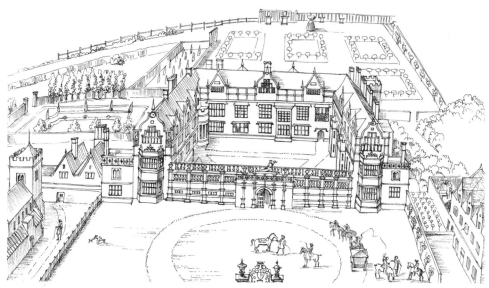

'Old' Rushton Hall

Charles, Sir William's only surviving son, had several sisters, all of whom married peers. The eldest (another Mary) was wife of the Earl of Nottingham and Baron Howard of Effingham, said to have been 'a handsome young woman . . . to bestow on a man so worn out in state, credit, years and otherwise'.[1]

In 1636 Charles Cokayne became sheriff for Northamptonshire, supporting the collection of the king's unpopular tax, ship money. That year Mary's father, the Earl of Thomond, wrote to him thus: 'Sonne The care you have had of the preferment of [?Crosse] doth cause me to render you menie thankes . . . . I take it verry thankefullie that you have affoorded yo[r] helping hand And be you assured it shall not be forgotten And I readye at all times to manifest as much . . . . Comend me to my daughter yo[r] wife . . . . With my blessing to her and yo[r] little one I shall ever rest Yo[rs] to his power Thomond Dublin 10 Novemb. 1636'.[10]

In 1642, due no doubt to his wife's ancestry, Charles Cokayne was created Baron and Viscount Cullen. That background, from the noble houses of strife-torn Ireland, must have stood Lady Cullen in good stead during the difficult years of civil war that followed. Her husband raised a troop of horse for the king, remaining loyal throughout. When the end came he is said to have lost more than £50,000 in the royal cause, compelling him to sell Coombe Nevil, and other estates in Surrey.

Other members of the family suffered greatly. The Marquess of Worcester acted for the king and was sentenced to die. He and his wife Margaret (Mary's sister) had joined the queen in Paris where they remained for some years but, on returning to England in 1652, Worcester was committed to the Tower. He lived nevertheless to see the restoration, dying in 1667. His wife, alas, became insane.

Unhappily Viscount Cokayne lived to enjoy the restoration for an even shorter period: he died in June 1661 and Mary married again, to George, the second son of Sir George Blount, Bt., of Sodington, Worcs. When Mary died in 1686, however, she was buried with her first husband in St Peter's, the ancient, now-demolished church which once stood beside the Cokayne's magnificent Northamptonshire seat, Rushton Hall.

The couple had one surviving son: Brien, the 2nd Viscount, and a daughter, Mary, who married Mr Robert Peirson.

(4) THE HON. MARY COKAYNE *c.* 1649–1682 = Mr Robert Peirson, d.1702

Born at the end of the Civil War, Mary will have known nothing of the disasters wrought by that dreadful conflict. Brien, her brother, had married during the Commonwealth to Elizabeth Trentham, a wealthy heiress, not only of the Trentham, but also of the de Vere family, Earls of Oxford. Painted twice by Lely, she was known as 'the beautiful Lady Cullen'. She was also exceedingly extravagant.

When Mary's brother succeeded as 2nd Viscount Cullen, he found managing his affairs, due to his wife's excesses, extremely difficult, a situation made more so, in 1667, when his sister Mary's portion was due, on reaching 18 years. A deed was drawn up in which Lord Cullen 'confesses himself . . . obliged to pay . . . the summe of four thousand pounds'.[11]

Mary, it seems, understanding her brother's circumstances, decided, on receipt of her portion, to surrender her right to a further £2,000, feeling no doubt that a bird in the hand was worth two in the bush. She had met the man she wished to marry, Mr Robert Peirson, a widower from Yorkshire, and by 1669 she had married him, for that year we find: 'Brian 2nd Viscount Cullen charges his estates . . . to yield annual . . . payments from 1670 to 1677 . . . to George Blount of Rushton [their stepfather, and others] . . . the Trustees of his sister Mary wife of Robert Peirson, in satisfaction of the portion of £4,000 . . . bequeathed to the said Mary by his father'.[12]

These funds were to secure to Mr Peirson land yielding him £60 a year and the balance was to be invested by Mary for her own use. None too soon. Among the documents is a schedule showing 'ye Debts of Robert Peirson and Mary his wife' amounting to more than £700.[13] In 1670 an agreement was made in which Mr and Mrs Peirson purchased from Lord Cullen for £1,200, '(being parte of the

The Hall, Bishop Middleham

porcon of the said Mary) . . . All that . . . Rectory and Church impropriate of . . . Bishops Midleham . . . and all Gleabe Lands . . . with their . . . appurtenances . . .'.[14]

It would seem therefore that the Bishop Middleham estate was never, as claimed in the text beneath a sketch of the hall in the Wasey *Family Book*, '. . . for many years the Seat of the Pearson Family; of Gerard, Roger, and Robert Pearson Esquires . . .' (none was buried there), but a myth to provide this untitled country gentleman with a background befitting matrimony to the daughter of a viscount. The couple appear to have lived at Mr Peirson's home, Startforth, Yorkshire, initially, and they probably saw little of Mary's brother and his wife, who became lady of the bedchamber to Charles II's queen.

At her death in 1682 Mary, whose heart and circumstances took her almost into obscurity, was buried at Bishop Middleham in an ordinary shroud of wool. The couple are thought to have had a son (who died a baby) and a daughter, Mary, besides Margaret, who later married Gilbert Spearman Esquire.

(3) MARGARET PEIRSON 1679–1731 = Gilbert Spearman 1675–1738

Born in 1679, Margaret was only three when her mother died. How much she and her sister afterwards saw of their father and stepbrother, James, is not known. In 1701 Margaret married, as his second wife, Gilbert Spearman, a barrister, at Durham Cathedral. His first wife had been Mary, daughter of Robert Bromley gent., of Nesbett by whom he had four children, Robert of Thornley being the only one to survive. Despite having an older sister, Margaret brought all the Bishop Middleham estate to the Spearman family at her marriage. In the notes made by G.E. Cokayne for the Wasey family, years later, he says:

> As to other issue of Robert Peirson by the Hon[ble] Mary Cokayne, [a letter of] 1858 to the . . . Rector of Wath w York [reads] 'Mr. Pierson seems to have [had] another daughter by Mary Cockayne married to (. . .) Burbeck, who also took under the settlement of Middleham, for I have in my 'Surtees' a marginal note viz 29 Aug. 1701 Marr. articles between Gilbert Spearman of Durham, Gent and Margaret Pearson, spinster, jointure £100 per annum. She had then half the Rectory and was to have the other half on the death of her nephew & niece, Burbeck. The nephew & niece must have died as hoped [!] for the Spearmans conveyed the Rectory in 1769 in its entirety.

A claim must have been made by the nephew's trustees, because the *Mickleton Manuscripts* contain a paper dated 1704 which appears relevant. The sister is named as Mary with the information that she had a son 'yet alive'. The question was posed: 'Whether Margaret shall take ye whole Estate during her lifetime and exclude ye son and heir of her eldest sister. Or if he shall take any and what Estate by this Limitacon during ye lifetime of his Aunt.'[15] The nephew's death must have resolved the matter.

Gilbert seems to have been a reckless young man in his youth. When not yet 18, he is said to have drunk a toast to the exiled king: 'Here is King James his prosperitie; Here is the confusion of King William' – and was tried for his rash behaviour at the Assizes[16]. By the time he married Margaret, however, at 26 years of age, he was not only wiser, but had become as keenly interested in antiquities and the history of Durham as his father had been.

On marrying, Margaret acquired a host of relatives. Gilbert's elder brother John, a JP of Hetton-le-Hole, married Anne, the sister of Gilbert's first wife. A sister, Dorothy, was married to John Cuthbert, Recorder of Newcastle-on-Tyne; another sister, Elizabeth, married Michael Mickleton of Crook Hall (the dedicated antiquarian responsible for the collection bearing his name). And for two years, until he died, Margaret knew her father-in-law, John Spearman, for many years under-sheriff of Durham.

Three years before Margaret died, in 1731, her husband published *An Enquiry into the Ancient . . . County Palatine of Durham*, the joint production of himself and his father. Their large collection of archives descended to the Wasey family who, in 1817, presented them to 'the Right Revd. Shute Lord Bishop of Durham'.

The couple had five sons, only one of whom, George, married and had children. They also had two daughters, the eldest being Margaret, who married Dr William Wasey.

(2) MARGARET SPEARMAN 1705/6 – *c*. 1750 = Dr William Wasey 1691–1757

Although Margaret and most of her siblings were baptised at St Mary-le-Bow, in Durham city, where their father had lived for some years, the children probably spent much of their time at the Hall, Bishop Middleham, half way between Bishop Auckland and West Hartlepool. It was described as 'a spacious old building with two regular wings' closely adjoining the churchyard, near to the old fosse. Its northern walls were said to overhang the vicarage ominously and the garden, shaded by decaying walnut trees, lay across the road up the church hill. The children will have played in the adjoining close called the Croft, which was 'filled with blackhearts, walnuts and redstreaks, rising over a close mass of hazels . . . in a warm orchardly situation on the southern slope of the hill across the Mainsforth lane'.[17]

Margaret must have grieved at the loss of her closest brother, Charles, less than a year her junior. Sent to Westminster School and to Cambridge, he appears to have been teaching at White's School, Westham, when he became ill and died. Their father erected to him a tablet of white marble, with the arms and crest of Spearman, near the porch in Westham Church.[18]

When Margaret married William Wasey she was aged 24 and brought a dowry of £5,000. William was 37 and probably set in his ways; but, successful in his career, he was able to provide a pleasant household over which she could preside. Discord arose between her husband and her brother, George, after her father's death in 1738 when no attempt was made to pay, from their father's estate, the still-outstanding sums of her marriage portion. The outcome was a lawsuit, which cannot have helped the relationship. Consequently when George married in 1741 to Anne Sneyd (said to be 'a very agreeable woman'[18]) there may have been little contact. Anne was to die eleven years later and little can the two women have guessed there would eventually be a union between their offspring.

Perhaps Margaret was an invalid for the last years of her life; her date of death and her burial-place are unknown but, by 1753, when her husband made his will, he had been left a widower.

The couple had two children: a son, William John Spearman, and a daughter, Margaret.

(1) MARGARET WASEY 1731–1794

At her father's death in 1757 Margaret's share of his estate was £10,000 which included the £2,000 portion from her parents' marriage settlement. She chose sixty books from her father's library and with his 'two best Bureaus to put or keep her things in', plus the silver, china and household linen, set up home nearby, still in the district of Leicester Fields.

As her father's executrix, Margaret set about administering his affairs; huge debts were still owed by the Herne family of Norfolk[19] and the property held there by their father against these loans was considerable. She and her brother sued[20] and were evidently successful, since Margaret is known to have been in receipt of several 'court annuities' and was in a position to reinvest, making large loans to her brother and others.

Eleven years later we find Margaret living in Barbourn, Worcestershire, from whence she institutes another chancery suit: this time against William Heath Esq. of Hawkwell, Northumberland, for failing to repay a loan of £6,000.[21] Margaret's brother and their kinsman, John Cuthbert of the Inner Temple, assisted in bringing the case and again the court appears to have found for them. Margaret continued to help financially her extravagant brother who, soon after their father's death, had married their first cousin, Honoria, co-heir of the family's northern estates.

Eventually Margaret removed to Bath, as did so many gentlewomen in her position. One can picture her seated in her tall Georgian house, looking across towards the abbey, while working at the delicate patchwork curtains and chair covers later bequeathed to her nephew, Clement Wasey.

Towards the end, Margaret suffered a long illness and will no doubt have visited the Cross or the Queens Bath to 'take the waters'. All to no avail: on 24 November 1794 she passed away aged 63 years and was buried nine days later at Bathampton.

Although Margaret failed to marry and further this particular female pedigree with a daughter, the progeny of her brother William John bear the genes, too, of course, from these remarkable families.

Among their other maternal ancestors are those bearing the celebrated names of history such as Beaufort, Neville and Mortimer. These, in turn, lead back through royalty to the great European houses and the ancient rulers of the Irish, Scots, Welsh and Saxons. It is interesting to note, on studying some of these ancestral lines, the number of Norfolk and northern families which occur: Waseys descend several times over from names like Leigh, Brereton, Stanley and Egerton; and both my Wasey history and the distaff line featured begin in Norfolk.

This repeated sharing of ancestors applies to us all, of course, but is less discernible in most families, hence the fascination I have found in threading my way through the ramifications of these, the forebears of the Wasey family. Their descents from Edward III were shared, at the time the Massue de

Ruvigny compiled his *Plantagenet Roll* early in the twentieth century, with some 60,000 known persons and although it can be said with truth that we all have ancestors leading back to the time of Edward III, the Conqueror, or indeed, to Adam, I join with Ruvigny when he observed 'it is quite a different thing to be able to *trace* the line'.

We are largely what our ancestors have made us. To know who one's ancestors were and what they contributed to history, is the goal. The Wasey family, in this respect, are the possessors of a rich heritage.

Notes and References

(NB Most references are in the narrative (Pts II & III) to avoid duplication)

Part I THE SEARCH

1 NRO, Pollard MSS 16601 and others in the series. If the hypothesis regarding Lydia's 2nd marriage is correct, then the Lydia Wasey of the city of Norwich bur. Tunstead in 1681 is not Richard's wid. (poss. a grandchild)
2 NRO, NCC Will, 1687 OW5; Norfolk Archd. Will, 1727, 516
3 *Eynsford Families, Norfolk Genealogy*, NNGS Annual Publications
4 *Norfolk Pedigrees* Pt.III (*Norfolk Genealogy*, vol.13) NNGS
5 Listed in G.R.C. Davis, *Oxford Medieval Cartularies*
6 *Return of Owners of Land* (of 1 acre or more) 1873
7 Manorial Documents Register, Quality House, Quality Court, Chancery Lane, WC2A 1HP
8 Berks. RO, C/DE 4; D/EBMT7
9 Berks. RO, D/E Z11 F4
10 PRO, PCC PROB. 11. 1412 Fol.513 p.140
11 Northampton RO, YZ 9583
12 Northampton RO, C 2550
13 Sir George Arthur, *The Story of the Household Cavalry*, 1909
14 The Bernau Index at the SOG can reveal defendants' names in some instances; published and unpublished Finding Aids are listed in PRO Leaflet No. 30 on Chancery Proceedings
15 Now at Oxford RO
16 The *FB* contains correspondence in 1857 from Mrs Fanny Holden, sister of Wasey Sterry. She tells of friends who 'met a clergyman, a Mr Wasey, so extremely like my brother that they supposed he must have been of our family'. Her father, Wasey Sterry of Romford, was of the 4th generation to bear the name. He had, she said, a friend, Col. Wasey, and once met a clergyman who said he was related to him. Burke's *Family Records* shows the first Sterry on this pedigree to be Thomas of Southwark who married Elizabeth, dau. of Joseph Wasey. She does not fit on to 'my' chart but the will of Norwich Quaker, Samuel Wasey (Norwich Archd. 1707/8 f.333) shows her to be the dau. of his brother, Joseph. See also Thomas Sterry's Surrey Archd. Will (MFx/32/16, 1726). In view of the physical resemblance, six generations later, one wonders whether the three brothers named in Samuel's will were the nephews of Robert Wasey, the first on my Wasey pedigree

Part II THE HOUSE OF WASEY

Chapter One: Norfolk Roots
1 NRO, Norwich Archd. Will, 277, p. 271 (1656)
2 NRO, North Walsham Ct. Roll (Norwich Bishopric Estates) 164355
3 North Walsham Poor Rate Books, Church Chest, St Nicholas' Church
4 PRO, E.179 154/656
5 PRO, E.179 154/700 (payable on houses worth more than 20s p.a., whose owners paid church and poor rates)
6 NNGS, *Norfolk Genealogy*, vol. XV
7 NRO, MS 16613 Pollard

8   Rye, *Norfolk Families; Norf. Archaeology*, vol. 37 Pt. 3. p. 319: M.J. Sayer; Vol. 38 Pt. 2.p. 193: Una Long

9   NRO, Norfolk Archd. Will, 515 (1670)

10   PRO, C11 226/55 *Ann Wasey* v. *Themylthorpe*

11   NRO, Norfolk Archd. Will, 422 (1675)

12   NRO, Norfolk Archd. Will, 67 (1679)

13   His application for lic. to marry (Edingthorpe) 1661, gave him as 23 yrs; but his MI gives his yr. of birth, 1636

14   E.A. Tillet, *The Tokens of Norfolk*, Goose & Co., 1882

15   NRO, MSS 16601, 16610, and others in the series

16   NRO, PD4/1 St Etheldred; Blomefield, *Norfolk*, vol. IV

17   PRO, C11 2336/20, C33/336 *Wm Wasey & Eliz. Postle* v. *Themylthorpe*

18   Blomefield, *Norfolk* (North Walsham)

19   NRO, NCC Will, OW5 (1687)

20   Until the change from the Julian to the Gregorian Calendar in 1752, Jan., Feb., & part of March were at the end of the year, the New Year beginning on 25 March, with the difference indicated by an oblique, e.g. 8 Feb. 1721/2

21   NRO, PD 145

22   Wm Durrant is recorded in NNGS, *Norfolk Genealogy: Norfolk Pedigrees*, Pt. III, as marrying Sarah Wasey. She is not thought to be Sarah, dau. of Richard Wasey of Tunstead. She can only have been a child in 1675, and her grandfather, Robt. Wasey, would have referred to her as Sarah Durrant not Sarah Wasey in his will of 1679 had this been so

23   PRO, C10 506/118 *Wasey* v. *Baispoole*

24   NRO, MS 826, 3E3 p. 9

25   PRO, C10 532/58 *Jos. Wasey & Jos. Wasey* (jun) v. *Ward*

26   PRO, C10 263/83, C33/296, C33/304 *Jos. Wasey* v. *Preston*

27   This was to promote the wool trade

28   PRO PCC Will, PROB.11. 459 Fol. 30 (1701)

29   Bridget's father bequeathed her (NRO 1692, ref. MS 11682 29E 2) 'the Messuage in Scottow wherein I now live'

30   NRO NCC Will, OW 128 (1701)

31   d. 1694 (PCC Will); NRO Trunch Rectory Ct. Rolls PD 242, 1713

32   Venn, *Alumni;* NNGS, *Norfolk Genealogy: Norfolk Pedigrees*, Pt. IV Wo(o)rts of Trunch

33   Sir Edmund D'Oyly bur. 24 Oct. 1700: Burke's PB

34   Benj. Wrentmore, rec. of Swafield, vic. of Tunstead, Norfolk; rec. of Ackworth, Yorks.; Foster, *Alumni*

35   Rate Books, North Walsham (Church Chest)

36   Poll Books, Local Studies Library, Norwich; *The Commons, 1715–1754; Parliaments of England*, ed. F.W.S. Craig

37   PRO, C11 2336/20, C33/336 *Wasey* v. *Themylthorpe*

38   PRO, C33 328 pp 232, 361 *Wasey* v *Themylthorpe*

39   PRO, C11 35/22, re-hearing of C11 2336/20; C33/338. Three of the legatees of Robert Wasey(2)'s will were minors at his death and did not reach 21 years until Mary Wasey, his sister and executrix, married Edmund Themylthorpe

40   PRO, PCC Will, PROB.11. 568 Fol. 118 Jun. (1719)

41   Poor Rate Bks (Church Chest); *North Walsham in the Eighteenth Century*

42   Ransome Pedigree Chart in possession of D.D.A. Bantock, Bristol

43   Guildhall Library, Corporation of London, Ms 11, 936/13 (1721)

44   NRO, Norf. Archd. Will, 516 (1727)

45   *Three Mariners* renamed *The Nelson* NRO NRS 5597, 18.B.1. Since converted again: Nelson Lane now pinpoints it

46   'Sister in law', a term used then for 'stepsister'

47   Guildhall Library, Corporation of London, Ms 11, 936/26

48   NRO, Nch. Bish. Estates 164361 p. 349

49   NRO, PRs Skeyton & Brampton; Rae P. Collins, *A Journey in Ancestry*, Gloucester, Alan Sutton, 1984

50   NRO, Nch. Bish. Estates 164361 pp 380, 381

51   NRO, Nch. Bish. Estates 164362 pp 15, 16
52   A cousin, W.J.S. Wasey, however, held property here until the end of the century

Chapter Two: The Physician
1   Information from the archivist, Caius College, Cambridge
2   PRO, PCC Will, PROB.11.568 Fol. 118 (1719)
3   NRO, MS 16355, 59x1
4   PRO, C11 35/22, C33/338 *Wasey* v. *Themylthorpe* (a re-hearing of the case below)
5   PRO, C11 2336/20, C33/336 *Wasey* v. *Themylthorpe*
6   NRO, WAL. 60 268x6
7   Caius College Records; Munk's *Roll of Physicians*, etc.
8   NRO, NCC Will, 164, 1723
9   Ruvigny; LG 1886 Edit., Spearman of Thornley & Eachwick; GEC
10   Family papers
11   Burke, *General Armory*; Grant in the possession of the family
12   Westminster RO & Library, *The London Survey* (Soho); Rate Books, Leicester Fields Ward, A121
13   St George's Hospital, Board of Governors' Minutes, 1733–1745
14   NRO, PD 402/96, 1739
15   Norwich Local Studies Library, Norfolk Poll, 1734; *The Commons 1715–1754*
16   Hester Lynch Piozzi, *Anecdotes of Samuel Johnson*
17   Westminster RO, *The London Survey* (Soho), (36 now numbered 37); Rate Books
18   PRO, C11 868/99, C33/374 p. 400 *Wasey* v. *Spearman*
19   Sir George Clark, *A History of the Royal College of Physicians of London*, Vol. II, Clarendon Press, 1966
20   PRO, PCC Will, PROB.11. 830 (1757)

Chapter Three: The Soldier
1   *Family Book*
2   Venn, *Alumni*; Clare College Records (Safe D: 5c/3)
3   Records of Household Cavalry Museum, Windsor; Sir George Arthur, *The Story of the Household Cavalry*, Vol. 11, 1909
4   NRO, Nch. Bish Ests. 164363
5   LG 1952, Scott-Moncrieff (formerly Sneyd of Keele Hall)
6   Surtees Scty. Journal Vol. 118; C.R. Spearman, *The Northern Spearmans*
7   Sir George Arthur, *The Story of the Household Cavalry*
8   PRO, C12 21/40; Westminster RO, Rate Books
9   *Annual Register*, 1761
10   PRO, C12 21/40, (1762); C33/418, C33/424 *Wasey* v. *Howard*
11   A.L. Reade, *Johnsonian Gleanings*
12   John Cuthbert: *Family Book* gives him as Recorder of Durham
13   PRO, C12 348/101, C33/416 *Wasey* v. *Herne*
14   Margaretta Maria, d. 3 April 1763 (bur. West Ham, Essex, FB)
15   PRO, Kew WO 12/4 (Musters)
16   Information from the curator, Household Cavalry Museum; Sir George Arthur, *The Story of the Household Cavalry*
17   FB; *The London Survey* (Soho)
18   Westminster RO, Rate Books
19   Besant, *London Survey; Survey of London*
20   Robert Surtees, *History of Durham*, Vol. III, p. 9.
21   Wright, *England Under the House of Hanover*, i.438
22   PRO, C12 870/30, C33/436 *Wasey* v. *Heath*
23   Became General Richard Vyse, Col. of the 3rd or Prince of Wales' Dragoon Guards. His 2nd marriage was to Anna, dau. of Field Marshal General Howard KB; Anna Susanna, née Spearman, his 1st w. bur. St Chad's, Stow-on-the-Wold (FB)
24   FB; *The Regimental Register*, Household Cavalry Museum, Windsor, Berks
25   FB; HEICS Records
26   *The Regimental Diary*, Household Cavalry Museum, Windsor, Berks. SL4 3DN

27   Sir Chas Oman, *A History of England*, Edw. Arnold, 1921
28   FB, 'Fortified' should read 'Fortitude', see DNB, Sir Richard Bickerton
29   PRO, Kew ADM 51.472
30   DNB, Sir Edw. Hughes
31   DNB, Montagu
32   Information from Marylebone librarian; Potter's Map c.1832 shows 12 Queen Anne St., corresponding to what was No. 4 in 1832
33   NRO, Land Tax Returns (Norf. County Council)
34   NRO, Petre Archive: 899/1/6/7/8/9; 903/4/10/17; 1061–16
35   NRO, Pet.1095
36   House of Lords RO, Private Bill, 26 Geo. III c.39
37   FB; Rugby School Register (published); MI Rugby Church
38   PRO, C12 2012/61, C33/468 *Wasey* v. *Brograve*
39   FB; HEICS Records, IOR:N/2/2/f 18
40   PRO, C33 641 from p. 1741
41   NRO, NRS.22193; Petre Archive (various refs)
42   There is a discrepancy over the date for Hannah's 3rd marriage: HEICS, IOR:N/2/2/f 188
43   A daughter married Wm. Adams LLD., and became the mother of George Edward (who, in compliance with his mother's will, assumed, by Royal Licence, the surname of Cokayne)
44   Eric Partridge, *The Routledge Dictionary of Historical Slang*, 'tabbies' i.e. 'old maids'
45   Beresford, *A Country Parson, James Woodforde's Diary, 1759–1802*; Custance of Elton Hall, LG 1972
46   G.H. Tucker, *A Goodly Heritage – Jane Austen*, Manchester, Carcanet; Bath RO; the City Rate Books show a 'Mr Wasey' at No.1 in 1793 & in 1794, a 'Mr Vasey'. In the Church Rate Books (Taunton RO) 'Mrs Wasey' is recorded at No. 1 in 1788 (only two Church Rate Books survive for the period: 1772 & 1788)
47   PRO, PCC Will, PROB.11/1253
48   Bodleian & British libraries
49   PRO, PCC Will, PROB.11.1525
50   PRO, PCC Will, PROB.11.1590, fol. 166

Chapter Four: The Georgian Parson
1   *Family Book*
2   PRO Kew, ADM.51/82; ADM.51/472
3   British Record Scty., *Act Books of the Archbishop of Canterbury*
4   Royal Archives, Windsor RA 21851; Court & City Reg. 1802–1820
5   Common descent from William Cockayne (d.1626): Burke PB 1970
6   Jacob's *Law Dictionary* (1728)
7   PRO, C13 2399 *Wasey* v. *Bradley & Bishop of Bath & Wells*
8   PRO, C33 522; C33 530
9   Ruvigny, *Tudor Vol.*, Tables: XCI, LXXXVIII, LXXXIII, LXXXII, XIV, I.
10   Anne & Henry Doughty Esq., of Broadwell, Glos.
11   G. Ormerod, *A History of Cheshire*; LG 1952, pp 1503-; FB (Capt. John Frodsham was the 3rd child (b. 1736) of Revd Robt. Frodsham, vic. of Rostherne (d. 1758) & Catherine, dau. of Wm. Leigh (d.1741) & his 2nd wife, Sarah Hanmer)
12   William Cobbett, quoted in O. Sitwell and M. Barton, *Brighton*, Faber & Faber, 1948
13   Information from the archivist, Royal Archives, Windsor
14   Sussex RO, PR (transcripts), Brighton (Old?) Church
15   Anne Fremantle, *The Wynne Diaries*, OUP, 1940
16   *Who's Who*. He was to be nominated KCB, GCB, & made a baron of the Austrian States
17   PRO, C33 641 pp 1741–43
18   Ruvigny, *Exeter Vol.*, pp 315–318; LG 1921
19   Lord Sudeley, *The Montgomeryshire Collections*, vol. 62 Pt. 2, 1971 (issued June 1973); Lord Hanbury Tracy, *The Tracys of Toddington* (Domesday – 900 Years of England's Norman Heritage, Domesday 600 Exhibition)
20   J.T. Wasey Esq., of Priors Court, was the son of John Wasey, attorney, of Newbury, who may have been the son of John Wasey, victualler, of Stowe, Bucks. & Mary Pead of Buckingham
21   Rugby School Registers (published)

22   Oxfordshire Cty. RO, QSD.L.293. (The Manor House, as it happens, was built in 1665 by George Chamberlayne, MP for Bucks., but there appears to be no connection)
23   Burke's *Commoners* Vol. II; C.R. Spearman, *The Northern Spearmans*
24   FB; Alexander Young Spearman jun., made baronet in 1840
25   FB; MI, Broadwell Church
26   FB; Bath RO, Walcot Rate Books
27   Buckinghamshire Record Office, D/FR 130/12
28   Probably quarter-acre allotments
29   MP for Bucks., 1827–46; made Secretary to the Treasury that year
30   PRO, C33 696
31   PRO, PCC Will, PROB.11.1896 Fol. 364
32   LG 1952 pp 2762, 3; Burke's PB, Vis. Powerscourt
33   Revd F.E. Witts, *The Diary of a Cotswold Parson 1783–1854*, ed. David Verey, Gloucester, Alan Sutton, 1979

Chapter Five: Two Clergymen and a Sailor
1   *Family Book*
2   Their mutual kinship was with the Hamond-Graeme & Doughty families of Broadwell, Glos., FB; Burke's PB 1970
3   FB; Burke's PB 1970; DNB, Sir Graham Eden Hamond
4   *The Times*
5   *London Gazette*, November 1848
6   Letter published in the press at his death, FB
7   Probably *The Times* (from a book of press cuttings)
8   LG 8th edit., etc.
9   MI (behind organ) Wardington Church
10   Letter published in the *Bridgnorth Journal* with his obituary
11   Revd G.L. Wasey, *Our Ancient Parishes*
12   Maternal relations (Sheppard) are believed to have lived in the locality, (Firgrove, Shropshire)
13   FB; Burke's PB
14   Ruvigńy, *Exeter Vol.*, p. 315; Burke's LG 1921
15   A news item dated 5 March 1787 from *The Mercury* quoted in the local press years later (no date, FB)
16   *Macclesfield Courier & Herald*
17   FB; LG 8th edit.
18   LG 1871, 5th edit.
19   Burke's PB
20   The annual income from the Compton Living was £370
21   The church has now been converted into residences

Chapter Six: The Twentieth-century Families
1   FB. Probably the family recorded in Burke's *Irish Family Records*, pp. 1125, 26, 27
2   Gaskill Jones & Co. Ltd (1905), C.A. Manning Press, *Berkshire Leaders: Social & Political*; John Grant (ed.), *Berkshire: Historical, Biographical & Pictorial*. London & Provincial Publishing Co. 1912, Berkshire Library & Information Service
3   Victoria County History, Glos.Vol. VI
4   Not named on invitation list pub. by Georgiana, Lady de Ros (dau.of the Duchess of Richmond) in her memoirs
5   News cutting, FB
6   *The Times* 3.11.1917
7   FB, probably *The Times*; see Burke's PB
8   *Newbury Weekly News*
9   *Who's Who in Berkshire*
10   *London Gazette*
11   Estate Catalogue, Reading Central Library, Berkshire Library & Information Service
12   Now a school
13   Date of sale supplied from the Royal College of Physicians
14   LG 1952

Part III: A DISTAFF LINE

1   G.E.C's *Peerage*
2   G.E.C's *Peerage*, Hoo p. 562 note c
3   Burke's *Dormant & Extinct Peerage*
4   Rye, W. (Heydon): a Paston Letter dated 1461
5   Norman Davis, *The Paston Letters*, OUP, 1983 (No.142)
6   Muriel St Clare Byrne, *The Lisle Letters*, Penguin, 1985 (180)
7   Another descent from Henry Stanley, 4th Earl of Derby, came to Anne Sophia Frodsham, wife of Revd George Wasey
8   G.E.C., *Peerage*: Marquessate of Worcester
9   Nichols, *The History & Antiquities of Leicestershire*
10 Northants RO, Ref. 33 C 2769
11 Northants RO, Ref. YZ 9583
12 Northants RO, Ref. C.3007
13 Northants RO, Ref. C 3223
14 Northants RO, Ref. C 2550
15 Durham University Library, Mickleton MSS 37 p. 452
16 John Sykes, *Local Records, Northumberland & Durham*, vol. 2, 1833
17 Robert Surtees, *The History & Antiquities of the County Palatine of Durham*, vol. III
18 C.R. Spearman, *The Northern Spearmans*, 1984
19 NR0, NRS MSS 7754, 7676 (& others in the series)
20 PRO, C12 348/101 *Wasey* v. *Herne*
21 PRO, C12 870/30 *Wasey* v. *Heath*

GENEALOGICAL SOURCES AND THEIR WHEREABOUTS

CIVIL REGISTRATION 1837 TO THE PRESENT, St Catherine's House, The Aldwych, London.

CENSUS RETURNS, PRO, Chancery Lane, London.

LOCAL CENSUS RETURNS, LARGE SECTIONS OF CIVIL REGISTRATION INDEXES, IGI, etc., CROs & Libraries; Mormon Libraries.

DIRECTORIES, PUBLISHED PARISH REGISTERS (& SOME UNPUBLISHED TRANSCRIPTS); PEDIGREES, e.g. *Heralds' Visitations*; SCHOOL & UNIVERSITY REGISTERS, e.g. VENN'S *Alumni Cantabrigienses*, FOSTER'S *Alumni Oxonienses*; COUNTY, TOWN, VILLAGE, HOSPITAL & FAMILY HISTORIES; MIs; DNB; MUNK'S *Roll of Physicians*; Burke's (LG etc.); Massue de Ruvigny's *Plantagenet Roll; 1873 Return of Owners of Land*, etc., County, Archaeological Scty., Genealogical Scty., University, Local Studies Libraries.

WILLS & ADMINISTRATIONS FROM 1858 TO THE PRESENT, Somerset House, Strand, London.

PRE-1858 WILLS, ADMONS, INVENTORIES; DEPOSITED PRs, BT/ATs; TITHE MAPS; LAND TAX ASSESSMENTS; POLL BOOKS; MANOR COURT RECORDS; DEPOSITED FAMILY/ ESTATE/COMPANY/PRIVATE COLLECTIONS; DEEDS; RATE BOOKS, etc., CROs, County, Local Study & other Libraries.

PCC WILLS & ADMONS; CHANCERY PROCEEDINGS, etc, PRO, Chancery Lane, London.

MILITARY RECORDS, etc, PRO, Kew, Surrey.

EAST INDIA COMPANY RECORDS, India Office Library, 197 Blackfriars Rd., London SEI 8NG.

NEWSPAPERS, JOURNALS etc., Libraries, ROs, Colindale Newspaper Library, London.

Bibliography

Angus, L.M. *Old Cheshire Families & Their Seats*, Butterworth

Arthur, Sir George. *The Story of the Household Cavalry*, 1909

Astley, H. *Memorials of Old Norfolk*

Besant, *Survey of London*

Blomefield, F. *The History of Norfolk* (11 vols)

Blomfield, J. *St George's Hospital 1733–1933*, Medici Society

Burke, *A History of the Commoners; Landed Gentry of Gt Britain; Peerage & Baronetage; Dormant & Extinct Peerages*

Byrne, M. St Clare. *The Lisle Letters*, Penguin, 1985

Clark, Sir George. *A History of The Royal College of Physicians of London*, Clarendon Press, 1966

Cokayne, G.E. *Peerage; Baronetage*

Collins, A. *Peerage*

Davies Langdon, J. *Westminster Hospital 1719–1949*, Wyman & Sons, Ltd., 1952

Davis, Norman. *The Paston Letters*, OUP, 1983

Fremantle, Anne (ed.) *The Wynne Diaries*, OUP, 1940

Hanbury Tracy, Lord. *The Tracys of Toddington* (Domesday 600)

Hervey, Lord. *Memoirs*, ed. Romney Sedgwick, Batsford

Hughes, G.T., Morgan, P. and Thomas, J.G. *Gregynog*, University of Wales Press, 1977

Humble, J.G. and Hansell, P. *Westminster Hospital, 1716–1966*, Pitman Medical Publishing, 1966

Jones, Gasgill, C.A., *Berkshire Leaders: Social & Political*, Manning Press, 1905

Loraine, H. *Paston, Some Notes On The Church of St Margaret and The Paston Family*

Mackenzie, Gordon. *Marylebone*

Masters, Brian. *The Dukes*, Anchor Press

Mee, Arthur. *Norfolk*

Munk, *Roll of Physicians*

Nichols, *The History & Antiquities of Leicestershire*

North Walsham WEA, *North Walsham in the 18th Century*, ed. Christopher Barringer, 1983

O'Brien, The Hon. Donough. *The History of the O'Briens*, Batsford, 1949

O'Hart, J., *Irish Pedigrees*, vol. 1; *Irish & Anglo-Irish Pedigrees*

Ormerod, G. *History of Cheshire* (3 vols)

Owen, W. Scott. *Parochial History of Tregynon*

Peachey, George C. *The History of St George's Hospital*, 1913

Pearce, David, *London Mansions*, Batsford

Ruvigny, Massue de. *Plantagenet Roll*, Exeter & Tudor Vols.

Rye, Walter. *Norfolk Families; Monumental Inscriptions of the Hundred of Tunstead; Three Norfolk Armories.*

Sanders, Margaret. *Letters of England's Kings*

Shipman, E.A. *Bottesford Church Guide*, Bottesford PCC

Sitwell, Osbert and Barton, Margaret. *Brighton*, Faber & Faber, 1948

Spearman C.R. *The Northern Spearmans – Index To One Spearman Family of Durham & Northumberland, 1519–1980*

Spencer, Walter G. *Westminster Hospital – An Outline of Its History*, H.J. Glaisher, 1924

Sudeley, Lord. *Montgomeryshire Collections*

Surtees, Robert. *The History & Antiquities of the County Palatine of Durham*, vol III

Verey, D. (ed.) *The Diary of A Cotswold Parson* (Revd F.E. Witts), Gloucester, Alan Sutton, 1979

Wasey, C.J. *Corsica, A Poem*, printed for Fletcher & Hanwell, 1795

Wasey, Revd G.L. *Our Ancient Parishes*, Bridgnorth, Clement Edkins, 1859

Heralds' Visitations; Victoria County Histories; London Survey

Index

Abercromby, Lord 106
Abingdon, Earl of 76
Adlestrop 79, 88
Albourne 105
Albury 9, 10, 12, 76, 79
Aldermaston 121
Alexandria 109
Allen, Revd William 90
Altamont Wash Common 115
Amyand, Mr/Sgt Surgeon 44, 46–8, 50, 51
Andrews, John 2, 3, 24
  Lydia 2, 24
Anjou, Margaret of 130
Antingham, Joan de 130
Argentine 109, 111, 122
Arnold, Dr 90
Artiss, William 67
Ashbourne 137
Ashmul, John 69
Astley, Sir Jacob 35
Aston Eyre 95, 96, 102
Aston, Sir Willoughby 63
Austen, Jane 73, 78, 79
Austin, Estelle 120
  R. J. 120
Ayers, Mary 74
Aylesbury, Lord 113
Aylsham 72
Aynhoe 104

Baconsthorpe 132
Bacton 23, 25, 26
Baispoole, Miles 29, 30
Ballard, Revd J. 82
Ballycastle 105
Barbourn 142
Barons, Wm, Bishop of
  London 133
Barwis, Dr 61
Bates, Thos, the elder 86
Bath 51, 73, 77, 84–7, 142
Bathampton 73, 142
Batt, Mr John Thomas 70
Beaufort, Margaret 135
  John, Earl of Somerset 130
Beeston St Lawrence 24, 26

Belgaum 120
Bellet, Revd Geo. 120
Belloc, Hilaire 46
Berney, Thomas 36
Bertie, Lord Robert 63
Bickerton, Sir Richard 64, 65, 67
Bigg, Lovelace 105
Bird, Edward 14
Bishop Middleham 57–9, 140, 141
Blackhead, Elizabeth 27, 42
Blake, Mary 74
  Mary the younger 74
  Robert 28
  Thomas 54, 57, 67, 70, 72, 74
Blickling 131
Blount, George 138
  Sir George 139
  Mary 139
Boddington, Miss Rosa 101
Bognor Regis 123
Boleyn, Alice 131
  (Queen) Anne 131, 134, 135
  Cecily 131
  Elizabeth 131, 132
  Sir Geoffrey 130, 131
  Isobel 131
  Sir Thomas 131
  Simon 131
  Sir William of Blickling 131
Boleyne, Anne 130
Bolton 90
Bombay 65, 67
Bosanquet, Commander 91
Boswell, James 50, 61, 73
Bottesford 134
Bowdler, Mrs Harriet 84, 86
Box 86
Bradley, Revd Warre Squire 77
Bradley Ct. 107, 109, 112, 114, 118, 119
Brampton 38
Brandon, Chas, Duke of
  Suffolk 134
Brereton 136

Brereton, Margaret 135
  Mary 136
  Wm, 1st Bn of Laghlin 136
  Sir Wm, of Malpas 135
Brewood 94
Bridgnorth 95–7
Bridport, Lord 90
Brighton 10, 79
Brightwalton 107, 114, 117
Britiffe, Robert 18
Broadwell 78, 82, 84, 88, 107, 114
Broek, Bea 123
  Kurt Erich Willie Van Den 123
Brograve, Mr Berney 67, 69, 70
Bromfield, Mr 61
Bromley, Ann 141
  Robert 140
Brook, Sir Thomas 132
Brooke 30
Broxholme, Dr 48, 50, 51
Brun(m)stead 6, 24, 25, 29–31, 39
Brussels 84
Buckingham 15
Buenos Aires 118
Bunn, Stephen; Susannah 32
Burbage 113
Burbeck, Mary 140
Burke, Edmund 56, 61
Burkitt, Mr 84, 85
Burlington, Lord 48
Burma 121
Burney, Fanny 62
Burton, Dr Simon 48, 50
Butterworth, Hannah 11

Cabenda 91
Caister 133
Calcutta 120
Calver, Mr 42
Cam, Mrs 44
Cambridge 44, 119
Cannes 98
Cape Tres Forcas 92
Carey, Mr 48

Caroline, Princess 51
   Queen 48, 50–2
   of Ansbach 41
Carter, Mr 83, 84
Castro Sarmento, Jacob de 53
Ceylon 120, 121
Chamberlain, Mr 82
   Revd T.C. Hughes 82
Chapman, Bridget 39
   Mr Spencer 4, 18, 36, 39, 44
Chapuset, Miss 88
Chelmarsh 97
Chelmsford 115
Cheselden, Mr 45
Chester 101
Chesterfield, Lord 48, 51
Chesterton, G.K. 46
Chetwynd, Hon. John
   Whitmore 64
Chieveley 81, 111, 118
Churchill, Winston 121
Clarence, Duke of 106
Clarke, Daniel 1, 38
   Lydia 1, 38
   Revd Rowland 1, 38
Cley-next-the-Sea 38
Clive, Mr 35
Cokayne, see Cullen, Lords
   Barbara 71, 117
   G.E. 72, 117, 140
   Hon. Mary 16, 17, 137–40
   Hon. William 70–2, 117
   Sir William 138
Coke, Sir Edward 133
Collier, Sir George 64
Colombo 121
Coltishall 26
Compton Parva 7, 9, 11, 12,
   104, 105, 109, 110, 124
Condover 90
Conisford 43
Cooke, Mr Edward 29, 30, 43
Corfu 89
Cork 94
Cornelis, Mrs 61, 62
Corsica 73
Cotton, Capt. Rowland 64, 75
Coulson, Elizabeth/Mrs 19,
   29, 40, 43
Cove 94
Cranston, Capt. 64
Crawford, Ethel 112
   G. 112
Cuddalore 66
Cullen, Brien, 2nd Vis. 16, 17,
   139
   Charles, 1st Vis. 16, 117,
      137, 138

Charles, 5th Vis. 71, 72
   Lady 16, 71, 72
   Lord 71
   Lord, of Ashbourne 117
Custance, Squire 72
Cuthbert, Mr John 60, 61, 67,
   141, 142
   Dorothy (née Spearman) 141

Day, Mr 85
Delhi 120
Dickens, Sgt Surgeon 44, 48, 50
Digby, Henry Almarus 99,
   100, 107, 114
   Hon. and Revd Kenelm 100
   Leonora 102, 104, 106, 107,
      110, 113, 114, 116
Dilham 57
Donnington 111
Doyly, Sir Edmund 33
Dublin 94, 95
Dunfermline, Lord 106
Durham 141
Durrant, Bridget 4, 28, 72
   Margaret 28
   Sir Thomas 72
   William 4, 28, 40

Eardington 96, 97, 101, 103
Earle, Erasmus 35
East Ruston 31, 39, 57
Easton, Reginald 97
Ecchinswell 111
Edgcote 84, 87
Edward IV 134
Elizabeth I 131
Ellingham 4
Englefield, Miss 71
Erwin, Mr 70
Evans, George 118
   Kathleen Isobel 118
Exeter 100

Fairfax, Mrs 71
Farnham 118
Farquhar, Sir Walter 81
Fastolf, Sir John 131, 133
   Alice 130
Felmingham 4, 18, 57
Felthorpe 4
Ferrers, Lord 58
Fleetwood 105–7
Flete, Alice 130
   Margery 130
   Roger 130
   William 130
Forcett 17
Forster, Capt. 92

Fort St George 67, 68
Fowey 100
Fox, John 106
Foxleys 106
Francis, Henry 37
Frederick, Prince of Wales 48,
   50, 51, 59
Fremantle, Admiral 80
   Capt. 80
   Lady Elizabeth 80, 85
   Sir Thomas 80
   Sir T. F. 85
Frettenham 43
Frodsham 135
Frodsham, Anne Sophia 11,
   74, 78
   Capt. 74, 78, 84
   Emma (Miss 82) 84, 86
Fuller, Edward 35
Fynes, Sir Thomas 131

Galway, 1st Vis., see Monckton
   94
Gardner, Lieut. 93
Garrick, David 48
Gay, John 45
George I 45, 50
George II 17, 45, 50, 53
George III 59, 63, 72
Gerard, Dutton Lord 137
   Elizabeth Lady (née
      O'Brien) 137
Gerard Street 46, 50, 52
Gibraltar 92, 94
Gimingham 39
Glasgow 92
Glatton 10, 87
Gloucester 102
Goa 112
Godfrey, Col. C. W. 112
   Sidney Jane 112
Goldsmith, Oliver 56
Gordon, Lord George 63
Great Hautbois 4
Green, Catherine 52
   Mr 47
Greenaway, Elizabeth 39
   Joseph 39
   William 39, 54
Greene, John 37
   Mary 37
Gregynog 10, 80
Grey, Thomas de 34
Gurney Wm 132
   Ann (née Heydon) 132

Haig, John 110
Hall, Sir Benjamin 83

Hamilton, Lady 80
Hamond, Andrew 91
    Sir Graham 91, 100
    Lady 100
Happisburgh 39
Hare, Sir Ralph 35
Harrogate 71
Harsike, Sir Roger 130
    Alice (née Wichingham)
        130
Haversham 15
Hawkwell 62, 142
Heath, William 62, 142
Helsdon, Henrietta 34
Henry VI 133, 134
Henry VII 129, 135
Henry VIII 134, 135
Hermitage 119
Herne, Paston family 60, 142
    Paston 19, 43
Herstmonceux 90
Hertingfordbury 104
Hetton-le-Hole 141
Heverland 43, 60
Heydon, Amy 132
    Bridget 132
    Eleanor 131
    Elizabeth 131
    Sir Henry 131, 132
    John 131, 132
High Legh 16, 78, 82, 136
Highley 97
Hoadley, Dr Benjamin 50, 51
Hoare, Mr Henry 40, 45
Hobart, Elizabeth (née
        Heydon) 132
    Walter 132
Holbeck, Misses 88
Holland, Henry, Duke of
        Exeter 134
Hoo, Anne 130
    Elizabeth (née
        Wichingham) 130
    Sir Thos de 130
Hood, Viscountess 104
Hopper, Ralph 61
Horning 4
Horstead 26
Howard, Bernard Henry 116
    Baron of Effingham 138
    Charles 59
    The Lady Elizabeth 131
    Hon. Revd Hy Edward Jn,
        DD 107
    Revd Hy Fdk 107, 117
    Honoria (née O'Brien) 137
    Mary (née Cokayne) 138
    Mima 107, 110, 116

Sir Robert 137
Thomas, Duke of Norfolk
    131
    Mr 60; Mrs 114, 117
Hughes, Sir Edward 66
    Thomas 90
Hulse, Sir Edward 44, 50, 51,
    56
Hutton, Dr Addison 50
Hyeres 99

Ibbotson, James 74
Imhoff, Sir Chas and Lady 88
Ingham 30, 41
Isle of Wight 123
Ison, Amy Florence 111
    James T. 69
    Mary 111
    William 111

Jefferey, Revd Mr Thomas 36
Jeffery, Revd Mr John 36
Jersey 123
Johanna 65; Prince of 65
Johnson, Hannah 67
    James 11
    Dr Samuel 20, 50, 56, 59
Jones, Thomas 13
Jones, Cdre William 91
Jurin, Dr 53

Keen, Richard 74
Kelly, John 41
Kettering 71
Kindersley, family 82
    Caroline 88
    Edward 80
    Edward Cockburn 104
    Francis 110
    Hannah 82, 104
    Harriet Jemima 7, 9, 104
    Nathaniel Edw. 10, 11, 70,
        74, 80, 104
    Sir Richard Torin 80, 82
    Mr 70, 80; Mrs 80
King, Anne 30
    William 30
Kings Lynn 114, 116
Kipping Fair 34
Knapton 4, 23, 39
Knoll/Knowle Sands 12, 94,
    95, 97
Knutsford 82, 107

Lahore 120
Lamb (Lord Melbourne) 106
Lane, Mr 47
Lanesborough, Lady 48

Leete, Robert Victor 119
    Vera 119
Legh, Piers 16
    Robert of Adlington 136
Leicester Square 58
    Fields 142
Leigh family of Adlestrop 79
    Anne 16
    Egerton, Mr 88, 100, 106,
        107
    Elizabeth 82
    Adm. Jodrell 114
    Revd Peter 16, 82
    the Misses 88
Lessingham 31
Leydon 39, 40, 42, 54
Lichfield 59, 107
Linstead, Lydia 3, 26, 37
    William 3, 26; sister 27
Lisle, Lord; Lady 134
Little Massingham 34
Liverpool 91
Lock, Edmund 36
Lodington, Mrs 7
London 8, 9, 15, 23, 26, 29, 32,
    35, 37, 40, 41, 45, 46, 50,
    54, 58, 60–4, 71, 79, 83,
    100, 113, 131, 136, 137
Londonderry 137
Loring, Fanny 88
    Henry Lloyd, DD 80
Lovick, William 43
Lymm 16

Macartney, Lord 69
MacCleverty, Mr 92; Capt. 93;
    Commander 92
Mackenzie, George Stewart
    107
Macmillan, Donald
    McLachlan 117
Madras 63, 66, 67
Maidenhead 106, 107
Maitland, Wm 48
Malta 109
Manners, Eleanor, Countess of
    Rutland 133
    Lady Elizabeth 134
    Lady Gertrude 134
    Henry, 2nd Earl of Rutland
        134
    Sir John 134
    Thomas, 1st Earl of Rutland
        134
Maranham, Brazil 91
Margaret of Anjou 131
Maria Charlotte, Princess 59
Marlborough 105

Marriott, Maria Louisa 107
    General 107
Marylebone 107
Mead, Dr Richard 50
Merriman, Harry Mowbray
    115
Mickleton, Michael 141
    Elizabeth 141
Moleyns, Lord 131
Mollington 82, 90
Monckton, Alice 101
    Charlotte 114
    Edward, of Somerford 94,
    95
    Elizabeth (Eliza) Lenora 94
    Philip 94
Montgomery 14
Moore, Samuel 44
Mordaunt, Lt. Gen. Charles
    52
Morville 9, 90, 95, 96, 102
Mosley, Mrs 100
Mundesley 39

Nalder, Thomas 14
Nash, Richard (Beau) 48
Natal 122
Neatishead 4
Needwood 104
Nelson, Lord 80
Nesbett 140
Neville, Lady Margaret 134
Newbury 13, 105, 109–12, 114,
    117, 122, 123
Norgate, Mr 43
North Runcton 114, 116
North Walsham 1–7, 18, 23,
    25, 27, 28, 31–9, 43, 46,
    57, 67, 69, 114, 124, 133
Norwich 3, 5, 19, 26–8, 32, 41,
    132

O'Brien, Lady Anne 137
    Conor 136
    Donough 136
    Henry, 5th Earl of
        Thomond 136–8
    Henry, 7th Earl 137
    Mary, Countess of
        Thomond 136
Oldbury 97, 100
Oxford 72, 78, 90, 104

Painter, Mr 75
Palamcote/Palamcottah 10, 20,
    67, 68, 70
Paris 7
Paston family 131, 132

Bridget 133
Clement 133
Eleanor, Countess of
    Rutland, 133, 134
Erasmus 133
John 133
Margaret 133
Margery 133
Sir Thomas 133
Sir William 132, 133
Pead, Alexander 14
    Mary 15
Pearce, Air Commander 121
Pearson/Peirson family 62,
    140
    Gerard 140
    James 140
    Margaret 10, 140
    Hon. Mary 139, 140
    Robert 16, 17, 139, 140
    Roger 140
Peartree, Anne 43
Pell, Mr 34
Pemberton, Philip Wykeham
    Leigh 122
Perrot, Mr; Mrs 73
Peters, Dr Charles 50
Petre family 70
Piccadilly 58
Plantagenet, Anne 134
Pole, W. B; Mundy 88
Pope, Alexander 50
Portsmouth 64, 106, 123
Postle, Elizabeth 21, 40, 41
    Robert 32, 41
    Samuel 24, 25
    Sarah 24, 25
Preston family 33
    Revd Charles 4, 32–4
    Sir Isaac 4, 32
    Jacob 33, 43
    Mary 33
Primrose, Roger 37
Prior's Court 9, 12–15, 81,
    107–9, 112, 118, 119
    Farm 111, 118

Quatford 9, 12, 90, 94–6,
    98–103, 105, 109
Queenstown 94

Radcliffe, Dr 90
Ramsay, Capt. George 91
Ranby, Dr 51
Ransome, Micah 37
Raylton, Thomas 43
Raynor, Capt. 75
Redstone, Alan 5

Rendall, John 38
Reynolds, Sir Joshua 56
Richard III 134
Rio de Janeiro 65, 91
Rome 99
Ros, 12th Lord de 133
    Sir Robert de 130
Rosario de Santa Fe 111
Ross, Dr 48, 53
Rostherne 106
Rugby 69, 90, 104
Rushton Hall 71, 72, 139
Rutland, Earls of, see Manners
Rysbrack, Michael 48

St George's Hospital 48, 51,
    53, 56, 58
St Leger, Lady Anne 133
    Sir Thomas 134
Salisbury 90
Sandwich, Lord 43
Sarmento, Jacob de Castro 53,
    54
Saul, Joseph 38, 72; Susanna
    38
Savage, Lady Elizabeth 134, 135
    Sir John of Rocksavage 134,
        135, 136
    Margaret 135
Savernake 105, 113, 114, 117,
    122
Scarborough 71; Lord 46
Schomberg, Isaac 54
    Dr Meyer 53
Sco Ruston 39
Scottow 4, 28, 31, 35, 40, 54,
    57
Sewell, Mr 99
Shaftesbury, Earl of 53
Shepherd, Gen. 101
Sheridan, Richard 56
Shipton, a surgeon 51
Shrewsbury, 6th Earl and
    Countess of 134
Shute, Rt Revd (Lord Bishop
    of Durham) 141
Sierra Leone 91
Simpson, a butcher 42
Sinclair, Sir Archibald 121
Skeyton 38
Sloane, Sir Hans 51
Sloley 31, 57
Smallburgh 31, 39, 57, 69
Sneyd, Anne 57, 58, 141; Mr
    70
Soho 7, 8, 11, 46, 48, 56, 61, 81
Somerset, Chas (Earl of
    Worcs) 135

Edward, Marquess of Worcs. 137
Margt, Marchioness of Worcs. 138
South Shoebury 9, 74
South Walsham 4
Southampton 75, 123, 124
Southrepps 4
Southsea 15, 81, 104, 107, 116
Spearman family 46, 82, 140
  Major Alexander Young 82
  Alexander Young, jun. 82
  Anna Susanna 60, 61
  Mrs Anne, 58, 141
  Charles 141
  Elizabeth Honoria 7, 57
  George 7, 46, 53, 57, Mr 58, 59, 141
  George Wasey 82
  Gilbert 7, 10, 53, 140
  John 88, 141
  Margaret 7, 8, 45, 53, 140, 141
  Margaretta 60
  Robert of Thornley 140
Stac(k)pool(e) Hugh 14
  Jane 12, 15
  Mrs 104, 105
Stalham 30
Stanley, Thomas, Lord 135
Startforth 140
Sterry, Wasey family 22
Stevens, Thomas 45
Stoke Ash 3
Stow 15, 88
Strange, Sir Roger le 132,
Stratton, George 107
  Wilhelmina 107
Stuart, Dr Alexander 40, 44, 45, 47–51
Suffield, Harbord Lord 18
Suffren, Bailli de 66
Swafield 33
Swan Lake, Manitoba 112
Swanbourne 9, 10, 80
Swanton Abbot 23, 31, 39, 57, 67

Taylor, Mr 93
Teissier, Dr George Lewis 41, 48, 50–2
Tewkesbury 102
Themylthorpe, Charles 35, 36, 40, 41
  Mr Edmund 35, 42, 43
  Mary (néeWasey) 26, 27, 42
  Mr 27, 35; Mrs 35, 41
Thetford 119

Thomond, Earls of, see O'Brien
Thornley 140
Thorpe-next-Norwich 29
Tickencote 88
Tittleshall 100
Tompson, Mr 34
Topcliffe's (property) 29, 30
Torin, Mr 70
Touchen End 107, 110
Tracy, Chas. Hanbury 76, 77, 80; Mrs 76, 77
  (later) Lord Sudeley 90, 96
Traill, Edith Ann 111
  Robert Walter 111
Trentham, Elizabeth 139
Trimingham 4
Trunch 4, 5, 8, 26, 32, 36, 39
Tuddenham, Margery (née Wichingham) 130
  Sir Robert of Oxburgh 130
  Sir Thomas 131
Tudor, Henry 132, 135
  Princess Mary 134
Tunstead 2, 3, 5, 15, 20, 24–6, 28, 30, 32, 33
Twisleton Mr; Mrs 88
Tyburn 58

Ulcombe 9, 10, 74, 79, 84, 85
Upper Slaughter 88

Vavasour, Mr, Mrs 88
Vernon, Dorothy 134
  Sir George, of Haddon Hall 134
Vyse, Anna (née Spearman) 62
  General Richard 62

Wade, Robert 35
Wales, Prince of 18, 76, 79, 81, 106
  Princess of 79
Walpole, Horace 60
  Sir Robert 18, 20, 43, 48, 51, 63
Wantage 119
Ward, George 30; Joshua 51
Wardington 9, 10, 82–4, 88, 95, 107
Waring, Ven. Archdeacon 96, 98
Wasey family 101, 134, 141, 143
  Alice 37
  Amy 4 (Dolly) 112, 116
  Anna 34, 62

Anna Margaretta 11
Anne 13–15, 20, 21, 35, 36, 40, 42, 81
Anne Sophia 10, 11, 16, 87, 96
Arthur 112, 115, 119, 120
Arthur Crawford 123
Arthur Edward 123, 124
Arthur Frodsham 103, 112, 123
Bea 123, 124
Benjamin John Spearman 112, 118, 120, 123
Bridget 4, 8, 29–31
Captain 60, 61, 106
Capt. E. 108
Carol 120
Christopher 121
Clement John 8, 9, 11, 12, 62, 67, 73, 142
Cyril 112, 115
Cyril Leigh 109
Dorothy Ann (née Wynd) 121
Edith Ann 111, 119
Edward Cyril Mowbray 123
Edward Frodsham Noel Kindersley (Ned) 13, 81, 91, 105, 107, 110, 112, 119
Edward John Spearman 12, 13, 105, 111, 116, 117
Eliza 87, 100 (Miss 101)
Eliza Honoria Margaret 8, 11, 70, 95
Elizabeth 5, 8, 18, 26, 29, 31, 36, 37, 39, 42, 44
Elizabeth Honoria 11, 57, 58, 60, 62, 73, 74, 142
Eliza(beth) Lenora 12, 94, 103
Elizabeth Mima 104, 107, 109
Ellen 37
Estelle 120
Ethel 112, 115, 123
Evelyn 117
Geoffrey 113, 116, 120
George 8–11, 13, 15, 16, 72, 75, 80, 85, 87, 107
George, see Wm. (George) Leigh
George Kindersley 112–17, 122
Gladys 111 (Ann 122)
Hannah, formerly Johnson (née Butterworth) 10, 11, 67

Harriet Jane 13, 109, 110, 117
Harriet Jemima 12, 109, 110
Honoria, *see* Elizabeth Honoria
James Frederick 13
Jane 14
Jane Mary Anne (née Davis) 110
Jemima, *see* Harriet Jemima
Jennifer 120
Joan, *see* Sydney Joan
John 2–3, 5, 6, 8, 11, 13–15, 20, 31, 32, 34–7, 39 (John, *see* William John Spearman)
John Spearman (Spearman) 7, 9, 11, 12, 13, 81, 90, 107, l01, 103–5, 107–11, 124
John Thomas 11–15, 81, 104
Jonathan 124
Joseph 2–5, 7, 8, 14, 20, 21, 25, 26, 28–38, 40, 42, 124
Kathleen (Kay) 121
Lenora, *see* Eliza(beth) Lenora
Leonora Sabrina 12, 95, 99, 107
Lionel Robert Traill (Bob) 111, 119, 120–3
Lionel Torin 117, 119
Lydia 1, 3, 5, 25, 26, 34, 38, 129
Margaret 8, 10, 11, 19, 47, 55, 56 (Mrs 73, 142)
Maria Louisa (née Marriott) 107, 110
Mary 2, 4, 7, 12–15, 25, 26, 28, 30, 31, 37, 101, 104, 105, 107–9 (Polly 110)
Mary Caroline 123
Muriel Sophie 117
Richard 2–5, 15, 21, 24–6, 32, 35, 36
Robert 2–6, 20, 21, 23, 25–8, 32, 35, 40, 42, 124
Samuel 21
Sarah 3, 24
Sheila 124
Sidney Jane 112, 116

Sophia Elizabeth 10, 79, 87, 88, 89
Sophia Honoria 12, 95, 98
Spearman 9, 11, 62, 69
Susan 121
Susanna(h) 5, 8, 34, 35, 38
Sydney Joan 113, 122, 123
Timothy John 120–2
Tom, *see* Willoughby Spearman
Vera Ruby Alice (née Leete) 119
William (1) 2, 4, 6, 8, 19, (Capt. 10, 11) (Dr 6–8, 10, 14, 16–21) 28–32, 36, 37, 39–44, 46, 52, 54, 55, 129, 141
William George 8, 10, 11, 59, 63, 67, 69
William (George) Leigh 9–13, 79, 81, 90, 94–8, 100, 102, 103, 104
William John Spearman 6–12, 14, 15, 18–20, 47, 56, 59, 63, 64, 69, 70, 71, 74, 80, 93, 103, 142
Willoughby Clement 10, 81, 89
Willoughby Frank 109
Willoughby John 62
Willoughby Spearman 12 (Tom) 112, 117, 118, 120
Mr 37, 73, 83, 85, 99
Mr John 105, 111, 119, 121
Mrs 7, 47, 59, 61, 63, 69–74, 89, 95, 99, 105, 107, 108, 113, 119, 122
Webb, Miss 58
Welles, Eleanor, da. of Ld 130
Wellington, Duke of 114
Wenn, Mr 36
Westminster 8, 39, 40, 44, 59, 60
Weston Longville 72
Westwick 31, 57, 69
Whichcote, Charlotte Sophia 95, 114
Gen. George 114
Whitington 9, 10, 76, 77
Wichingham, Norfolk 130
Wichingham, Alice (née Fastolf) 130

Edmund of Woodrising 130
Elizabeth 130
Margery 130
William 130
Wilberforce 107
Wilkes, John 62
Willoughby, Catherine, da. of Lord W. of Parham 132
Wilton, Robert; Sarah 3, 23
Windham, Ash 43
Mary, da. of Sir Thos of Felbrigg 133
Windsor 106
Windus, Gordon Dennis Burton 121
Kathleen 121
Wingfield, Hon. Emily 88
J. 88
Revd George J. 10, 87, 88
Sophia 10, 87, 88
Winslow 80
Winter, Eleanor, da. of Edm. 131
Witton 23
Witts, Revd F. E. 88
Wokingham 117
Wolfhall 113
Wolsey, Cardinal 135
Wood, Dr 44
Woodforde, Parson 72
Woodhouse, John 34
Wo(o)rts, Elizabeth 32
Mary 4, 26
Robert 4, 26
Susan 26
William 32
Worstead 27, 29–31, 35–7, 39, 41, 44, 48, 57, 61, 19, 72
Worthing 124
Wrentmore, Revd Benjamin 32, 33
Wynd, Dorothy Ann 121
Wyndham, George 72
Wynne, Elizabeth (Betsey) 80
Wytham 10, 76

Yarmouth 26, 37
York 71, 72
Lady Cecily, Duchess of 132
Princess Elizabeth of 133
Richard, Duke of 130, 131